REFUGEES OF THE FRENCH REVOLUTION

Refugees of the French Revolution

Émigrés in London, 1789–1802

Kirsty Carpenter

First published in Great Britain 1999 by
MACMILLAN PRESS LTD
Houndmills, Basingstoke, Hampshire RG21 6XS and London
Companies and representatives throughout the world

A catalogue record for this book is available from the British Library.

ISBN 0–333–71833–X

First published in the United States of America 1999 by
ST. MARTIN'S PRESS, INC.,
Scholarly and Reference Division,
175 Fifth Avenue, New York, N.Y. 10010

ISBN 0–312–22170–3

Library of Congress Cataloging-in-Publication Data
Carpenter, Kirsty, 1962–
Refugees of the French Revolution : émigrés in London, 1789–1802 /
Kirsty Carpenter.
p. cm.
Includes bibliographical references (p.   ) and index.
ISBN 0–312–22170–3
1. French—England—London—History—18th century. 2. France–
–History—Revolution, 1789–1799—Refugees. 3. French—England–
–London—History—19th century. 4. Political refugees—England–
–London—History. I. Title.
DA676.9.F74C37   1999
942'.00441—dc21   99–13682
                                                                              CIP

© Kirsty Carpenter 1999

All rights reserved. No reproduction, copy or transmission of this publication may be made without written permission.

No paragraph of this publication may be reproduced, copied or transmitted save with written permission or in accordance with the provisions of the Copyright, Designs and Patents Act 1988, or under the terms of any licence permitting limited copying issued by the Copyright Licensing Agency, 90 Tottenham Court Road, London W1P 0LP.

Any person who does any unauthorised act in relation to this publication may be liable to criminal prosecution and civil claims for damages.

The author has asserted her right to be identified as the author of this work in accordance with the Copyright, Designs and Patents Act 1988.

This book is printed on paper suitable for recycling and made from fully managed and sustained forest sources.

10 9 8 7 6 5 4 3 2 1
08 07 06 05 04 03 02 01 00 99

Printed and bound in Great Britain by
Antony Rowe Ltd, Chippenham, Wiltshire

à mon mari

Contents

Lists of Figures and Tables	viii
List of Illustrations	ix
Acknowledgements	xiii
Introduction	xiv
1 First Impressions	1
2 1789–92: a Prolonged Vacation	17
3 1792: the Influx	29
4 Soho	49
5 Marylebone, Richmond, Hampstead – the High Life	62
6 St Pancras, Somerstown, Saint George's Fields – the Low Life	87
7 Educational Pursuits	100
8 Politics: Their Own Worst Enemies?	116
9 Émigré Writers and Writing about Émigrés	133
10 Franco-British Culture and Society	155
Conclusion	175
Appendix 1: Chronology	185
Appendix 2: Figures and Tables	189
Notes	206
Bibliography	243
Index	256

Lists of Figures and Tables

Figures in Appendix 2

1.	Towns listed as lay émigré centres in the British Relief Lists	191
2.	Lay émigrés receiving relief from the British government, 1794–97	192
3.	Place of origin given by the refugees in London	193
4.	Money-flow into the voluntary relief fund in its first year	194
5.	Date of emigration from France	195
6.	Émigrés in and outside London in 1797	196
7.	Refugee addresses in London	197
8.	British subscribers to the voluntary relief fund	198
9.	Servants receiving relief, 1794–97	199
10.	Gender analysis of servants receiving relief after 1796	200
11.	Lay émigrés receiving relief in 1797	201
12.	Lay émigrés receiving relief in 1799	202
13.	All émigrés receiving relief in October 1801	203
14.	All émigrés receiving relief in March 1802	204

Tables

4.1	Illnesses among émigrés, 1796	59
A.1	Statistical analysis of lay émigrés receiving relief, 1794–97	205

List of Illustrations

1. *A French Family* by Thomas Rowlandson, 1792 (British Library, Prints and Drawings No. 9686, published by Fores, Piccadilly in 1792) © British Museum xxvi

2. *Salus in fuga: La France se purge petit à petit* by George Cruickshank (BL Prints and Drawings No. 7663, 29 July 1790) © British Museum xxvii

3. Map of London and Westminster, John Fairburn, 1796 © British Library (Maps C 27. b. 73) xxviii

L'exil est quelquefois, pour les caractères vifs et sensibles, un supplice beaucoup plus cruel que la mort.

Mme de Staël, *Corinne*

Acknowledgements

There have been many people whose help, patience and wise counsel have contributed to this book. It is based on a thesis directed by Michel Vovelle (Paris I, 1993) and, for me like many, his great example as a researcher has been an inspiration. I have many French friends whose enthusiasm, support for my work and generous hospitality have made the experience of writing a thesis then a book so very enjoyable. I would particularly like to mention the Rolland family in Angers who were wonderfully supportive in the first year of my time in France and the Domenech family who are very dear to me, especially Claire and Didier Marillet. The tolerant scrutineers who gave invaluable comments on the manuscript include Maurice Hutt, Philip Mansel, and Dominic Bellenger. I would also particularly like to thank Pamela Pilbeam and the members of the Modern French History Research Seminar at the Institute of Historical Research and the Institut Français for their support and constructive criticism.

I have had help and support from the staff of many institutions: the British Library, the Public Records Office, the Bibliothèque Nationale, the Archives Nationales, the Ministère des Affaires Etrangères, and from my university colleagues in France, the UK and now New Zealand where I have taught since 1994. Special thanks must go to a dear friend and mentor, Robert Neale, who edited the manuscript with meticulous care.

To all these people I am extremely indebted and profoundly grateful but none more so than to Andrew who has lived with the French Revolution and émigrés for many years now and shared the happy times and the heartaches with tolerance and love.

Introduction

Since the time of the Revolution the Emigration has received a very bad press. The émigrés have been accused of many crimes in the intervening years, against humanity (which the Revolution claimed to defend), against the French people and against the French state. Yet what was their crime? We find the most comprehensive reply in the mouth of one of Balzac's characters:

> Quitter la France est, pour un Français, une situation funèbre.
>
> For a Frenchman, leaving France is a sorry business.[1]

The fact that they left the country, isolated themselves from political developments and alienated themselves from individuals with similar political sympathies inside France, was an important factor. When communications broke down and emigration was made punishable by death, this indeed became a 'situation funèbre'.

The émigrés have been refused a place in the history of the French Revolution and refused a voice in the crowd because they deserted their country and some took arms against it. By revolutionary legislation they were stripped of their rights as French citizens and condemned to death if caught on French soil. These laws left little possibility for them to make their case before their fellow-citizens.

Popular images of emigration, like *Salus in fuga*, portray the émigrés as deluded aristocrats who left France in dribs and drabs hastening to the frontier to join the forces being raised by the princes near Coblenz or slipping across the British channel under the cover of darkness in stormy seas. They took the only option left to them, their political views surpassed and defeated by the euphoria of the National Assembly in its glory days.

These are myths, powerful myths it is true, which, throughout the nineteenth century, Republican tradition has had no interest in toppling. Many Frenchmen thought that the émigrés received their compensation in the Indemnity Bill of 1825 – much too much, in the eyes of many nineteenth-century liberals.

In French political tradition the émigrés have become inextricably linked with a movement of staunch inflexibility which characterised the ultra-royalist or 'ultra' faction at the time of the Revolution.

Ex-émigrés who dominated politics during the Restoration saw to it that the emigration was entirely associated with support for the Bourbon cause. *Constitutionnels* or those who supported a compromise between absolute monarchy and republic were objects of ridicule from both sides for reasons treated fully in Chapter 8.

In Britain, the destination of many émigrés, the scene was set for the ideas of Revolution to come into conflict with reason and the good sense of the Glorious Revolution, particularly in regard to issues of taxation and equity before the law. Moreover, the British response was important. Britain did not join the war against France until February 1793 and it did not want to be involved in a European war with the economic wounds of the recent colonial conflict still painful. The British reception of the refugees was therefore somewhat involuntary but prompted by a sense of duty, honour and obligation to support those whose position was in sympathy with their own.

The diplomatic history of the eighteenth century had been a series of defeats for France inflicted primarily by Britain.[2] In 1789 France was still smarting from the humiliation of the Seven Years War but, at great expense, it had won the latest round when the American colonies gained their independence from the British throne and a parliament in which they had never been represented.

For the British it was national pastime to to dislike the French. They were a shady lot who lived on onions and could not be trusted.

'Ah,' says one man to his companion, 'one had need to go to France to know how to like old England when one gets back again.' 'For my part,' rejoined another, 'I've never been able to get drunk once the whole time I was in France – not a drop of porter to be had – and as for their victuals, they call a bit of meat of a pound and a half, a fine piece of roast beef.'[3]

Politically, relations between the two states were tense and suspicious. Culturally, they were as cordial as ever with the British consuming just as much French wine, coveting the latest French fashions and reading as much French literature.

My liking for Mme de Sévigné is, I suppose, owing to my very ignoble love of gossip, which, if it be but honest and natural, I always like, whether on paper or de vive voix. And French, being the very language of chit-chat and prittle-prattle, is one reason why I like so much the mémoires and letters of that gossiping nation.[4]

By the end of the eighteenth century, French was the time-honoured language of chit-chat and prittle-prattle on the social and political scene. Prominent members of both communities engaged in lengthy discourse *par écrit*; Horace Walpole and Madame du Deffand are an extreme case but many others were in regular contact like Jules de Polignac and the Duke of Devonshire.[5] It was in the best of taste to cultivate things French not only in London but also in the provinces.[6]

Ah! les Anglais, les Anglais ont bien des singularités![7]

Ah! The English, the English have many peculiarities!

Yet by 1793 attitudes towards the British inside revolutionary France were far from neutral. The British, and the émigrés with them, were held responsible by the revolutionaries for all the problems which France was facing. In Paris Barère and other prominent Jacobins were advocating national hatred for the British as an integral part of French republicanism.[8] Barère was among those who incited the French to believe that, without the British, Europe would be free from its shackles.

que les esclaves anglais périssent et l'Europe sera libre.[9]

At a time when political propaganda was discovering its potential among a rapidly expanding readership, information, or lack of it, was central: central to the effectiveness of revolutionary propaganda and central to the case made against the Revolution by the émigrés. By portraying them as one group, united by the political aim of destroying the Revolution and restoring the absolute monarchy, the revolutionary government controlled opinion. Censorship legislation saw to it that the royalist press had no outlet in the capital and therefore had no access to the public. From 10 August 1792 until the death of Robespierre, the royalist press inside France was silenced. On 29 March 1793 the death penalty was voted in for anyone seeking the re-establishment of the monarchy. Many political journalists were victims of the guillotine, like the two poets Roucher and André Chénier, who died two days before Robespierre condemned 'writers hired by the tyrant to mislead and corrupt public opinion'.[10] The Law of Suspects (17 September 1793) left writers with royalist sympathies few options: they emigrated, they transferred their talents to the Republic or they disappeared in the provinces in order to avoid arrest and certain death.

Royalist newspapers did re-emerge cautiously during the Thermidorean period because the revolutionary laws were not policed with the same vigour, and this continued during the First Directory. However, the Fructidor coup of September 1797 put an end to any leniency and during 1798 and 1799 journalists, editors and owners of newspapers were deported in significant numbers.[11] Effectively by the time Napoleon came to power in December 1799 the royalist press in France had virtually ceased to exist. Then, during the Empire, well-policed censorship completely eradicated the royalist voice inside France and left the field clear for the émigré press based in London.[12]

Therefore, in a revolution where political communication was, more than ever before, central to the spread of ideas and the popularity of revolutionary propaganda, it is very important that punitive laws suppressed the voice of those who challenged revolutionary government. Many émigrés were the authors of reasoned polemics like the early political writings of André Chénier advocating nothing more, initially, than moderate constitutional monarchy. Yet André Chénier, who paid for his reason with his head, like many émigrés, underwent a political evolution from reasoned moderation to fanatical anti-Jacobinism. Chateaubriand is a parallel example who underwent a similar transition from moderate constitutional monarchist to ultra-royalist between his two works *The Historical Essay on Ancient and Modern Revolutions* (1797) and the *Genius of Christianity* (1802).[13]

Polarisation in the case of individual opinions was a characteristic of the emigration, just as it was a characteristic of the Revolution. No individuals returned from exile unchanged. All émigrés endured long periods of relative inactivity due to a host of constraints, geographic, financial, political and social, which left them nothing else but their political positions to re-examine. This alone was a new experience for many used to constant society and a very different lifestyle. Many of the émigrés describe the soul-searching which went on day after day among both women and men trying to come to terms with the Revolution and the options which remained open to them.

It is imperative to underline the fact that there was no one political philosophy represented in emigration but that there were a number of political positions which co-habited, sometimes uncomfortably, outside France. A dominant faction has been identified in retrospect, and in the knowledge of the Restoration but, at the time when a Restoration was far from certain, the politics of emigration were as diverse and unpredictable as the politics of the Constituent Assembly. Studies which have detailed the shifts in voting patterns during the two initial phases of the Revolution, the Constituent Assembly (1789–91) and the Legislative Assembly (1791–92) emphasise the haphazard nature of votes and the unpredictability of the outcomes due to the multitude of political views and the assertion of individuality on the part of the deputies.[14] Many of the émigrés of late 1791 to 1792 shared the diverse visions and the social background of the members of the Constituent Assembly, which make these studies illustrative of a broader phenomenon: that of the diversity of political opinions in general in France before the radical phase of the Revolution which began on 10 August 1792, and the lack of any model for political behaviour. This diversity, or lack of agreement in regard to political solutions, was responsible for many defections into emigration.

There are many correspondences too between émigrés and Frenchmen who did not leave France. The period directly after the fall of Robespierre is particularly illustrative of the similarities between the moderate elements of both sides. The members of the government which had survived the Terror and shed the radical Jacobin deputies (i.e. Robespierre, Saint Just, etc.) were preoccupied with the preservation of the Revolution and the Republic while ensuring that the Terror could not legally be reinstated and that the monarchy could not be restored. Throughout this period, moderate Republicans and moderate Royalists are almost indistinguishable in their political desires and objectives except on the question of head of state, and even this is ambiguous.

What that illustrates is the lack of any clean-cut divisions between a significant proportion of émigrés and the vast majority of republicans. By the late 1790s France was manifesting the essential characteristics of French politics in the nineteenth century. Even in regard to 1830, tales of an old aristocratic monarchist France at war with a new bourgeois country are dismissed as ultra-royalist anachronisms.

> While the vast majority preferred to maintain a constitutional monarchy because they knew they could not agree amongst themselves on an alternative and were fearful of popular upheaval, their monarchism was entirely pragmatic.[15]

This is primarily the reason that royalists in France accepted the Constitution of Year III[16] because, although a monarchy could not legally be restored during the life of that Constitution, it provided the effective basis of a constitutional monarchy with five Directors sharing the responsibilities of a King. It is significant that this Constitution contained clauses which reaffirmed the position of the French state in regard to émigrés. Under no circumstances were they to be allowed to return and the Constitution prohibited the Legislature to make new exceptions to existing émigré legislation. It also reaffirmed that émigré property was the property of the Republic and that purchasers of this property, providing that they had acquired it through the legal channels, could not be dispossessed.[17] Yet, significantly, nowhere in the Year III Constitution was a definition of the term 'émigré' attempted.

Political pragmatism perpetrated by a property-owning liberal elite was therefore beginning to assert itself as early as 1795 when the stranglehold represented by the Maximum on the economy was lifted (December 1794) and the Constitution of Year III simultaneously institutionalised the commitment of the government to 1792 and the rejection of the Terror.[18] The resultant weakness and instability of the Directory governments were not a product of the Constitution *per se* but, rather, a product of the political situation in which it was introduced. It was written not for a wartime economy but for a peacetime environment and that quickly became apparent.

The turning-points for departure from France are the Great Fear (July 1789), Varennes (June 1791), from 10 August 1792 to the September Massacres, and the 1793 legislation. This was passed on 28 March–5 April and tidied up all the loose ends in relation to émigrés and enemies of the state. The 1793 legislation which made emigration punishable by death and decreed all émigrés forfeit of their French citizenship, is treated more fully in Chapter 3.

The turning-points for returns are less numerous. The first opportunity came at the end of 1791 when an amnesty period of two months was declared in order to allow émigrés to return or face prosecution for conspiracy.[19] This decree of 9 November 1791 was vetoed by the King and could not be put into effect yet, in practice, the amnesty applied. On 8 April 1792 another law declared the property of all émigrés absent since 1 July 1789 forfeit to the state if they had not returned within a month. The King consistently vetoed legislation relating to émigrés and refractory priests until his deposition in August 1792.[20] Once the Convention met in September 1792 the position on the émigrés became law. On 23 October they were banished in perpetuity from French soil and those caught on French soil were condemned to death. A short amnesty (of 15 days) was accorded to allow those who wished to re-enter the country to do so. The next opportunity to return after the passing of the 1793 legislation did not come until after the death of Robespierre and the end of the Terror. The laws against émigrés were still in force and émigrés were still inscribed on the police lists but there were few deaths during the Thermidor period and only the most extreme cases were deported. This had more to do with a revulsion for blood shed in the aftermath of the Terror than any revision of policy on émigrés.[21] Under the First Directory, which came into existence in October 1795 with the completion of the Constitution of Year III and subsequent elections, moderate royalists within France began to re-establish their influence in the Assembly, which had changed its name from the Convention (too closely associated with the Terror) to the Council of Five Hundred. Fears of election victories for deputies with either royalist or radical Jacobin sympathies led to the contravention of this Constitution before it was even implemented. The parting gesture of the old Convention was to pass the Decree of Two Thirds on the same day that it accepted the Constitution (22 August 1795) which ruled that two-thirds of the existing deputies had to be re-elected to the new legislature and thereby ensured republican dominance.

This provoked the uprising of 13 Vendémiaire which became a milestone in the French Revolution because, for the first time since 1792, the Paris mob did not get what they wanted from government by threatening lack of support and in turn found themselves brutally repressed. This revolt was supported by many different strains of counter-revolutionaries who did not want to see the former members of the Convention retain their seats and, in its wake, several deputies with known royalist sympathies were arrested. The law of 3 Brumaire an IV (25 October 1795) was the legal reaction to the Vendémiaire uprising. It prohibited from holding elective public office any member of the primary or electoral assemblies who had been in any way associated with protest against the Law of Two Thirds and it also excluded from public office anyone who had been listed as an émigré without obtaining full radiation or any relative of a listed émigré. Women related to émigrés were required by the same law to return to their domicile of 1792 and remain under the surveillance of the municipal authorities and the laws against priests, which had effectively been suspended, were reimposed with a vengeance.

The passage of the 3 Brumaire law ensured that issues regarding émigrés and their relatives, *bien nationaux* and refractory priests were high on the agenda of the First Directory. There were many inconsistencies in the sale of *bien nationaux* and many sales and potential sales were being contested. Catholic issues too were of central importance for a variety of political and private reasons. What this highlights is that the political ramifications of any repeal of the émigré laws rendered revision impossible. The cost of investigating the issues which would have had to be faced were any revision to take place was far too high for any fragile Directory Government to give it serious consideration. But the issue here was larger and more dangerous than it appears at first reading. It was not the émigrés but the legality of the regime which had condemned them that was in question and therefore throughout the Directory any suggestion of injustice towards émigrés directly implicated the foundations of the Republic itself. While the Republic remained at war with Europe, the émigré question could not be resolved.

The course of 1796 was crucial for the royalist cause in France. The strong anti-Jacobin reaction which produced the White Terror in the provinces gave the moderate royalists some room to manoeuvre. This was a particularly important year for the destiny of the Revolution and a point at which it threatened to change course. It is also one of the best illustrations of the lack of coherence and trust between the royalists within France and the royalists without. Many royalists inside France felt that cooperation with the émigrés undermined their support and their constitutional position. Furthermore, Louis XVIII in the Declaration of Verona had alluded to a backlash against constitutional royalists should an absolute monarchy be re-established. This left a great many people with royalist sympathies stranded. They were bound to monarchy by their tradition and culture but the monarch Louis XVIII refused to consider a constitution, which left them looking for a monarch who would.[22]

It was this group of royalists who were in a strong position going into the elections of Year V (1797). They drew support from their moderation and the fact that their constitutional royalism linked them to the period of the Revolution which had preceded the radical events of the Terror. This royalism also appealed to many provincials for whom the more radical aspects of Revolution, and in particular the dechristianisation, made little sense. This, allied to the re-emergence of a radical Jacobin political element in French society, all contributed to the disadvantage of the republicans, many of whom were still former regicides, and to the favour of the moderate royalists.

Many émigrés returned in the period directly preceding the elections of 1797 in anticipation of a royalist victory and the imminent relaxation of the émigré laws. Many were waiting, not only for a relaxation of the laws which put them under threat of death, but also of the laws which deprived them of their properties and their children of their inheritance. There was even question of letting returned émigrés vote and in fact those who had managed to obtain provisional radiation in the provinces were allowed to do so, which showed how much ground had been gained by the royalists. The events surrounding the Year V elections were complicated by a host of issues related to the provincial administration and the waning of popular support for the Directory but the outcome was a resounding victory for the royalists and the prospect of an imminent relaxation of the émigré laws.

Between April and September 1797 (Floréal and Fructidor Year V), some major changes were made to the situation of the émigrés. On 27 April Boissy d'Anglas gave a speech in the Council of Five Hundred where he referred to the 'barbarous justice' by which the émigrés could be condemned to death on the strength of a simple identification if caught on French soil, and pleaded for trial in the ordinary courts. On 4 May the law of 3 Brumaire was amended to allow relatives of émigrés to hold office and on 27 June it was withdrawn altogether. There were other events in this period which indicated the strength of the royalist faction such as the election of Pichegru to the office of President of the Council of Five Hundred and the election of Barthélemy as a Director. It was also at this same time that polemics like Lally Tolendal's 'Defence of the Émigrés' appeared in print in exile.

The election result reached through legal channels left the executive of the Republic only one option: an unconstitutional one. In September 1797, therefore, the Fructidor coup purged the Assembly of the newly elected royalists and appointed candidates of known republican pedigree to the vacant seats or left them unfilled. The fact that a two-week amnesty was again declared before the émigré laws were reinforced to the letter suggests just how many émigrés had attempted to return. The government also introduced an oath of hatred to royalty which all ecclesiastics had to take.

The outcome was known as the Directorial Terror. The revolutionary regime's first action was to reinstate the law of 3 Brumaire and it quickly rendered the émigré position that which it had been in 1792–93. Unlike the Terror of 1794 the Directorial Terror shed little blood and used instead the 'guillotine sèche' or deportation to Guiana as its method of execution but it did establish the law of 9 Frimaire an VI (29 November 1797) whereby ex-nobles were excluded from public office and regarded as foreigners if they could not prove that they had served the Revolution. This law was the subject of much debate in 1798 because no test for proving service to the Revolution was included in the legislation. In practice it was implemented very sparingly because it threatened people in very high places like Barras and Bonaparte.

The events of Year VI offered little hope of change to the émigré situation. The war, the economy and the renaissance of Catholicism in France all contributed to keep government policy rigid. Elections were always contentious: those of Year VI produced the Foréal Coup, which purged the Assembly of legally elected radical Jacobin deputies in order to prevent a shift to the far left, and those of Year VII, preceding the Brumaire coup by a few months, were characterised by an even more unsatisfactory result. The government, known as the Second Directory once it had contravened the Constitution of Year III, had to go on doing so. The deterioration of the economy and the desperate need of conscripts for the army resulted in the Law of Hostages (24 Messidor an VII, 12 July 1799) which outlawed any resistance to new measures. By this law local authorities were empowered to arrest relatives of émigrés, imprison them at their own expense and impound their property to pay for damages. It was a new Law of Suspects with wider and more frightening consequences than that of 1793 for families of émigrés resident in France.

Effectively after the Fructidor coup the next return opportunity for the émigrés did not come until the Peace of Amiens was signed on 25 March 1802. From the arrival of Bonaparte as First Consul the signs of a pending reconciliation between the royalists and the Jacobins emerged. In November 1799 the Law of Hostages was repealed and the government also lifted the legal penalties on the relatives of émigrés and commuted the oath of hatred to royalty to one of loyalty to the Constitution. Relatives of émigrés and nobles were restored to full voting citizenship and the Revolution was declared to be at an end (15 December 1799).

On 3 March 1800 a further decree closed the émigré list and a commission was appointed to speed up the radiation process. Although émigrés began to return, encouraged by the positive signs, it was still dangerous. However, after Bonaparte's dazzling victory at Marengo, Pope Pius VII, despite the views of the émigré bishops in Britain, was persuaded of the desirability of reconciliation and the Concordat, signed on 15 July 1801, achieved it. Catholicism was named the religion of the majority of Frenchmen.

This was the point at which the vast majority of émigrés, including the ecclesiastics, returned to France. Those who remained in exile after 1802 were those who refused to give up plotting to restore the monarchy. It is this *'noyau dur'* of emigration whose social make-up and political actions have been attributed to the entire émigré population.

It is therefore the legislation which provides the clue to the real level of émigré commitment to the Bourbon cause. The revolutionary legislation reveals how few alternatives the émigrés had after 1792 and that same legislation holds the clue to the multitude of related issues which prevented any revision of the émigré laws before 1802.

The fact that the last returns of 1814 represented the smallest number of émigrés (with far greater numbers returning in 1802) certainly suggests that the link between the émigrés and the Bourbon monarchy was more tenuous than it has been portrayed both by Revolutionary and Counter-Revolutionary historians.[23] Moreover the fact that the Charter, which was the basis of Louis XVIII's restored government, represented a concession to moderate constitutional monarchy illustrates not only the pragmatism of the architects of the Restoration but the minimum requirement of the French nation in the wake of Revolution and Empire in order to avoid civil war.

In 1814 Europe was exhausted and peace was the overriding objective. For many it would not become clear until after the failure of the Second Republic and the creation of the Empire in 1851 that the French wanted strong government worthy of historical precedents like François I, Henry IV, Louis XIV and Napoleon but, at the same time, worthy of the collective intellectual tradition of the Enlightenment and the Revolution. One hundred years after the Revolution they achieved it in the Third Republic, the longest, most stable and most internally contradictory regime France has ever known.

This study of the émigré population in London will I hope bring out some of the diversity present in the exile community and overturn the notion that the émigrés represented one united voice. I have particularly focused on the social intercourse between the émigrés and the British during the 1790s which, while it develops these themes, also explores the antecedents of the complex love–hate relationship which characterises the two nations to this day.

Like Zeldin, I believe that historical study is a personal experience.[24] My own fascination for the Revolution years comes from my love of eighteenth- and nineteenth-century French literature. I have always found myself especially drawn to literature which does not fit neatly into any established category: the political pamphlets, the memoirs and the poetry which was written not to dazzle the reader with its literary quality but to contribute to a political debate. It is from this literature that many of the quotes in this book are chosen. They are passages which would otherwise be ignored or discarded but, in their own social and historical context, are often humorous and enlightening.

K. CARPENTER

1 *A French Family* by Thomas Rowlandson, 1792

2 *Salus in fuga: La France se purge petit à petit* by George Cruickshank, 1790

3 Map of London and Westminster by John Fairburn, 1796

1 First Impressions

> Rien ne sauroit égaler la commodité de ses trottoirs, où l'on marche avec aussi peu de fatigue que sur un plancher; ni la richesse de ses magasins et de ses boutiques; où l'on voit les productions de toutes les parties du monde étalées avec le soin le plus ingénieux. Il n'est pas de ville dont on puisse dire avec plus de vérité qu'elle est l'abrégée de l'univers.[1]

> Nothing compares to the convenience of the pavements where one walks with as little fatigue as on rugs, nor to the richness of the shops and boutiques where one sees items from all corners of the world displayed with meticulous care. There is not a town of which one can say with more truthfulness that it is a miniature of the universe.

Throughout the eighteenth century London and Paris rivalled each other to be the most important capital city in Europe. By the 1790s, the one had become the undisputed commercial centre, and the other the cultural mecca, of the civilised world.[2] But the rivalry was only skin-deep; a knowledge of English was an asset to the cultured French and fluency in the French language was a matter of social survival for the British upper class. Traffic between the two countries flowed freely and enterprising artisans made comfortable livings out of copying the fashions of the one for the other.[3] Among the elite, the young and fashionable were happy to be mistaken for their sophisticated neighbours:

> Il fallait que tout fût copié sur nos voisins, depuis la Constitution jusqu'aux chevaux et aux voitures. Certains jeunes gens même, tels que Charles de Noailles et autres affectaient l'accent anglais en parlant français et étudiaient, pour les adopter, les façons gauches, la manière de marcher, toutes les apparences extérieures d'un Anglais. Ils m'enviaient comme un bonheur de provoquer souvent, dans les lieux publics, cette exclamation: 'Voilà une Anglaise.'[4]

> Everything had to be copied from our neighbours, from the Constitution to horses and to carriages. Some people, such as Charles de Noailles and others, affected an English accent in French and studied, with the intent of adopting them, the awkward

ways, the style of walking, all the exterior appearances of an Englishman. They envied me the exclamation, 'There goes an Englishwoman' which I had the good fortune to hear often in public places.

This love–hate relationship between the two cities, their courts and their inhabitants, which existed long before the Revolution, was perpetuated and subtly modified by the émigrés. The French learned to love London, which was partly as a projection of the gratitude they felt towards the British but also as a surprisingly heartfelt attachment subsequently transferred to future generations. The son of Madame de Staël described Britain as:

> le pays des contrastes, c'est une tragédie de Shakespeare, c'est un roman de Walter Scott, tout s'y trouve réuni, et tout y est plein de vie et d'originalité.[5]
>
> the country of contrasts, it's a Shakespearian tragedy, it's a Walter Scott novel, it has everything and everything is full of life and originality.

British culture, although so often represented as the antithesis of the French, had a powerful appeal for many reasons. Never were these two nations to enjoy a closer knowledge of each other, or a better understanding of the differences between them, than during the years 1789–1814.

London was not the first choice for many émigrés leaving France in 1789. It only became the favourite destination after the creation of the Republic when any émigrés caught by the invading republican armies were killed in accordance with revolutionary legislation. Initially, many émigrés took up residence in the German city of Coblenz or in the southern Netherlands. Northern Italy was also a popular choice because it offered not only the clemency of the weather but also the hospitality of the house of Savoy in Turin.[6] As time went on, the military success of the Revolution forced these émigrés to relocate. After Bonaparte's Italian campaign in 1796–97 émigrés were forced to flee from this area and they were likewise expelled from Berne in 1796, and from Geneva and Hamburg in 1798. These places had significant émigré settlements.

Yet émigrés, by settling in London, avoided having to move out of range of the Republican armies and were also better prepared when

First Impressions

the emigration turned long-term. In the panic to get away from Brussels in 1794, Madame de la Tour du Pin describes how,

> Les plus sages, en même temps que les mieux pourvus d'argent, résolurent de passer en Angleterre.[7]
>
> The wisest, and those most plentifully supplied with funds, decided to cross to England.

They were initially very loath to admit the reality of the political situation in France and to acknowledge just how long it was likely to be before they could return home. Burke, one of the most staunch émigré supporters, couldn't help being floored by their naivety. When asked by an émigré in August 1791 when they would return to France his reply was an emphatic 'never' which he followed with,

> Messieurs, les fausses espérances ne sont pas une monnoie, que j'ai dans mon tiroir, dans la France vous ne retournerez jamais.[8]
>
> Gentlemen, false hopes are not a currency I hold, you will never return to France.

For the lucky few who had established contacts in London society the transition from aristocrat to émigré was relatively painless. The generosity of English families, particularly English Catholic families who sympathised with the plight of their friends, was spontaneous. More importantly still, the sense of relief the émigrés felt in escaping from France was heightened by a sense of adventure and anticipation of better times in London. This was vividly captured by the marquise de Falaiseau who wrote,

> Nous voilà lancés dans notre char à travers les rues de Londres, larges et brillantes de lumières.[9]
>
> There we were, riding our chariot through the wide and well-lit London streets.

She went on to say that her arrival in London was one of the highlights of her life because it had aroused such a mixture of feelings: exhaustion, isolation, trepidation, astonishment and hope.[10]

The duchesse de Gontaut remembered it in similar terms.

En arrivant à Harwick [sic], le premier mot d'anglais que j'entendis et pus comprendre me fit battre le coeur par l'espérance d'un meilleur avenir. C'était un heureux pressentiment, car, dès cet instant nous éprouvâmes la bonne et loyale hospitalité anglaise.[11]

Arriving at Harwick the first word of English that I caught and was able to understand made my heart beat faster in the hope of a better future. It was a happy premonition because from that moment we experienced the good and loyal hospitality of the English.

From the French point of view London was, next to Paris, the most exciting city in Europe. Abbé Tardy described it as

une des villes les plus imposantes par l'immensité de son étendue et de sa population; la richesse, l'activité et l'industrie de ses habitans; la distribution générale de ses rues et de ses trottoirs; le nombre, la beauté, et la variété de ses places![12]

One of the most imposing cities in terms of its size, its population, the wealth, activity and industry of its inhabitants, as well as the general layout of its streets and pavements, and the number, beauty and variety of its public places.

Contrast this with a British woman's reaction to Paris in 1790:

We have been driving at a furious rate for several days past through the city of Paris which I think bears the same resemblance to London (if you will allow me the indulgence of a simile) that the grand natural objects in a rude and barren country bear to the tame but regular beauties of a scene rich with cultivation. The streets of Paris are narrow, dark and dirty; but we are repaid for this by noble edifices which powerfully interest the attention. The streets of London are broad – airy, light, and elegant; but I need not tell you that they lead scarcely to any edifices at which foreigners do not look with contempt. London has therefore most of the beautiful, and Paris of the sublime according to Mr. Burke's definition of these qualities; for I assure you a sensation of terror is not wanting to the sublimity of Paris while the coachman drives through the streets with the impetuosity of a Frenchman. ...[13]

With a population of not quite a million inhabitants, London was the most densely populated city in western Europe. It seethed with activity and those who braved the pavements could expect to be spattered with mud. The Abbé Baston hated it. He described venturing out in London without a carriage (which he could not afford) as a dreadful ordeal.

Si l'on voulait savoir pourquoi Londres, avec toutes ses richesses, n'était point de mon goût, je le déclarerai sans aucun détour. C'est d'abord que les grandes villes, même en France, ont toujours été pour moi un objet d'aversion, et Londres est une ville immense, monstreuse pour les dimensions: un gouffre où se sont déjà perdus une autre ville et quarante villages dont elle s'est agrandie; un chancre terrestre qui, de tous les points de son vaste contour, pousse de longues ramifications dans les plus belles prairies du monde et les dévore, menace d'atteindre et d'envahir les colonies dont elle est environnée et de s'approprier les habitations qui les couvrent; après quoi elle les dépassera. Dans une ville de cette espèce, une visite est un voyage, et ce voyage, est à pied, souverainement incommode; en voiture, très dispendieux. C'est le vacarme épouvantable et continuel des carrosses, des charrois, des cris mercantiles qui vous offrent, en fredonnant, pain, lapins, cresson, pommes de terre, tous les comestibles. C'est tous les désagréments inséparables d'une population qu'on porte à plus d'un million d'hommes. C'est l'adresse et l'imprudence des filous, l'imprudence plus grande encore des demoiselles qui vous arrêtent en plein jour et devant tout le monde. C'est la grossièreté, la malveillance, la méchanceté même de ce qui est artisan, peuple, à l'égard de ce qui est étranger et surtout français.[14]

If one must know why London with all its riches was not to my taste, I will quite willingly explain. Firstly, it is because large cities even in France have always been for me an object of aversion, and London is an immense city of monstrous dimensions, a void where another town and forty odd villages have already disappeared, a terrestrial canker which from all the points along its vast periphery pushes ever further into beautiful fields and devours them. It threatens to reach and invade the colonies around its edge and to appropriate the dwellings that are found there before it moves on. In a city of this sort, a visit is a voyage, and that voyage is, on foot, royally inconvenient; by cab very expensive. It's the awful and constant racket of vehicles, carriages, of merchants' cries offering you bread, rabbits, greens, potatoes, and all sorts of foodstuffs. It's all the disagreeable aspects which come with a city of more than a million inhabitants. It's the backchat and cheek of rogues, the impudence of young women who stop you in full daylight and in front of everybody. It's the vulgarity, the malevolence, the wickedness, of the artisans or working people toward anyone foreign and especially French.

Fortunately, the Abbé did not stay long in Britain.

The very different reactions of the marquise de Falaiseau and the Abbé Baston are polar opposites. Some of the French were adventurous and keen to enjoy their enforced stay while others were more conservative and reluctant to find anything pleasurable about London or the British. Some, like Montlosier, who had no love for the British, put it down to the climate which he held responsible for the all the shortcomings of the country.

> Un peuple est toujours, à quelques égards, le produit de sa constitution atmosphérique. ... Il trouvera que par la nature et la constitution de son climat, le peuple anglais, en général, est un peuple privé d'esprit.[15]

> A nation is always, in many respects, the product of its atmospheric constitution. ... You will find that by the nature and constitution of their climate, the English are, in general, a nation devoid of flair.

He even reports Mme de Staël, when asked what messages he could take to France from Britain for her, laughingly to have said, 'when you see the sun give her my regards'.[16] The comtesse de Boigne was inclined to agree.

> On conçoit, que le nuage orange, strié de noir, de brun, de gris, saturé de suie, qui semble un vaste éteignoir placé sur la ville, influe sur la morale de la population et agisse sur ses dispositions.[17]

> It is quite understandable that this orange cloud struck through with black, with brown, with grey, saturated in sweat and which seems like a huge weight placed over the city has an influence on the morale of the population and determines its moods.

As time went on, these attitudes softened a little but, apart from some like Montlosier who had political reasons for finding fault with the British, it is clear that those émigrés who refused to make any effort to get to know the people or the country found life dull and uninteresting. The comtesse de Boigne, who left copious memoirs, is a good example. She wrote of London;

> Cette grande cité composée de petites maisons pareilles et de larges rues tirées au cordeau, toutes semblables les uns aux autres, cette frappée de monotonie et d'ennui. [...] Quand on s'est promené cinq minutes, on peut se promener cinq jours dans des quartiers toujours différents et toujours pareils.[18]

> This huge city made up of identical little houses and wide regimented streets all exactly the same, a cocktail of monotony and boredom. [...] When you have wandered for five minutes you may as well have wandered for five days through suburbs which are always different and always the same.

Among the younger émigrés few could resist the excitement of a new city the size of London which offered so much variety within its boundaries. Peltier described it as 'la plus riche métropole de l'univers'.[19] Chateaubriand declared it an appropriate metaphor for the entire British nation.

> Toute l'Angleterre peut être vue dans l'espace de quatre lieues, depuis Richmond, au-dessus de Londres, jusqu'à Greenwich et au-dessous. Au-dessous de Londres c'est l'Angleterre industrielle et commerçante avec ses docks, ses magasins, ses douanes, ses arsenaux, ses brasseries, ses manufactures, ses fonderies, ses navires; ceux-ci, à chaque marée, remontent la Tamise en trois divisions: les plus petits d'abords, les moyens ensuite, enfin les grands vaisseaux qui rasent de leurs voiles les colonnes de l'hôpital des vieux marins et les fenêtres de la taverne où festoyent les étrangers. Au-dessus de Londres, c'est l'Angleterre agricole et pastorale avec ses prairies, ses troupeaux, ses maisons de campagne, ses parcs, dont l'eau de la Tamise, refoulée par le flux, baigne deux fois le jour les arbustes et les gazons. Au milieu de ces deux points opposés, Richmond et Greenwich, Londres confond toutes les choses de cette double Angleterre: à l'ouest l'aristocratie, à l'est la démocratie, la Tour de Londres et Westminster, bornes entre lesquelles l'histoire entière de la Grande Bretagne se vient placer.[20]

> The whole of Britain can be seen in the space of four leagues from Richmond above London to Greenwich below. Below London, it's

commercial and industrial England with its docks, its ships, its customs, its arsenals, its eating houses, its manufactures, its foundries, its ship-yards. With each incoming tide the Thames brings three classes of vessel, the little ones first, the middle sized ones next, then the huge ships that shave with their sails the columns of the hospital for the old sailors and the windows of the taverns where the foreigners drink. Above London, it's pastoral and agricultural England with its fields and its flocks, its country houses, its parks where twice a day tidal waters from the Thames bathe the shrubs and the lawns. In the middle of these two extremes, Richmond and Greenwich, London combines all the elements of this double England, in the West aristocracy, in the East democracy, the Tower of London and Westminster, limits between which the entire History of Britain can be situated.

It was to this city of enormous contrasts that the émigrés came to add their colour to the existing mêlée.

For many the transition from Paris to London society presented few unknowns. The etiquette of the elites of Europe was as universal in the late eighteenth century as it would ever become. French, the language of well-educated society, made communication easy with the help of a sense of humour and a tolerant ear. Fanny Burney, writing of a dinner party including Arthur Young and the duc de Liancourt, wrote:

> The French of Mr. Young, at table was very comic; he never hesitates for a word, but puts an English one wherever he is at a loss, with a mock French pronunciation. Monsieur Duc, as he calls him [the duc de Liancourt], laughed once or twice, but clapped him on the back, called him un brave homme, and gave him instruction as well as encouragement in all his blunders.[21]

This amused tolerance was evident on both sides. The duchesse de Gontaut recounting a visit to the Bentinck's house in Surrey noted that

> Lady Edouard parlait mal le français, mais avec une originalité d'esprit très amusante.[22]

> Lady Edward spoke appalling French but she did it with such originality that it was most amusing.

Émigrés tackled the English language with differing amounts of success. It is significant that Abbé Baston, who had a good knowledge of literary English, declared it impossible to master on a day-to-day basis.[23] Others who, like Madame de la Tour du Pin, had relations in Britain spoke fluently. Fanny Burney left a detailed portrait of two French women who took tea with her and her travelling companion Mrs Ord at Winchester:

> The elder lady was so truly French – so vive and so triste in turn – that she seemed formed from the written character of a Frenchwoman, such, at least, as we English write them. She was very forlorn in her air, and very sorrowful in her countenance; yet all action and gesture, and of an animation when speaking nearly fiery in its vivacity: neither pretty nor young, but neither ugly nor old; and her smile, which was rare, had a finesse very engaging; while her whole deportment announced a person of consequence, and all her discourse told that she was well-informed, well-educated, and well-bred.
>
> The other lady, whom they called Mademoiselle, as the first Madame, was young, dark, but clear and bright in her eyes and complexion, though without good features, or a manner of equal interest with the lady she accompanied. Sensible she proved, however, and seemed happy in the general novelty around her. She spoke English pretty well, and was admired without mercy by the rest of the party, as a perfect mistress of the language. The Madame spoke it very ill indeed, but pleasingly.[24]

Although it is easy to refute the erroneous claim made often through the nineteenth and indeed twentieth centuries that the emigration was made up entirely of aristocrats, it is true that we are to a considerable extent dependent on the diaries of the educated émigrés for much of our knowledge of their society. These diaries are eloquent, voluminous and written by émigrés who enjoyed writing.[25] They are an important source of information because, while it is true that the emigration included a cross-section of people far more varied than merely the upper classes, it is also true that many of those who left France in this period and settled in Britain had a direct relationship with that socio-economic group. For instance, many domestic servants emigrated, and many craftsmen, whose work would have found little application in Republican France, also quitted the country.[26] Many artisans, makers of watches, fashion accessories and other fine goods by virtue of working for and among the aristocracy, also shared royalist or counter-revolutionary sympathies which made them suspect. A couple of the most striking examples are Elizabeth Vigée Le Brun and Rose Bertin, the first an acclaimed painter, the second the *modiste* or fashion designer of Marie Antoinette, who made her fortune among the émigré elite. For these reasons, the social predominance of the nobility in London is difficult to ignore.

Sources of information concerning the Emigration in London range from the émigrés' diaries to the records of the British relief fund held in the Public Records Office at Kew. They are a mixture of English and French documents where numerous variations in the English spelling of French names create endless confusion. In actual fact, little survives of the official records, passports and travel documents because the émigrés came under the jurisdiction of the Aliens Office which, when reintegrated into the Home Office in 1836, preserved only ten years of records. Surviving records of the Relief committee include monthly accounts of funds distributed to non-ecclesiastic émigrés by name for the years 1794–96[27] and annual lists for the years 1797[28] and 1799.[29] For the ecclesiastics the lists are more complete.[30] From these lists it has been possible to reconstruct a picture of French life in London but, as always, many questions remain unanswered.

The historiography of the Emigration is not voluminous. There are several general histories produced approximately at the time of the centennial of the Revolution which contain sections on Britain. A limited number of general works in French, some dating from the emigration itself, have concentrated on Britain but the overriding focus of these studies is the clergy. There is a very limited number of general histories dating from the twentieth century and only one comprehensive account of the émigré clergy in Britain.[31]

Yet despite this relative paucity of studies, which have focused solely on the Emigration, there remains an enormous amount of relevant material, including great quantities of archival material in Britain and France relevant to the Counter-Revolution. Examples include the archives of the Armée de Condé kept at the Chateau of Chantilly, the repatriated records of the French embassies kept at the foreign affairs archival centre at Nantes, the lists of émigrés and the radiation records from the lists of émigrés in the F7 series at the French Archives Nationales. Many studies of the Counter-Revolution also contain references to émigrés and their activities in Britain and elsewhere.[32]

First Impressions

Until now, the lack of academic focus on the emigration and on the émigrés can be attributed to two things. Firstly, there is the difficulty of using sources which are spread out across Europe because the émigrés moved around a great deal. This makes it extremely difficult to ascertain the period of time any given émigré spent in any one place. As the Emigration became prolonged there was generally less movement but, even so, tracing an individual émigré can take the researcher from the Archives in Paris, to the provinces, St Petersburg, Portugal or London, or all of these places, without necessarily giving satisfaction. The existing general studies of emigration have tended to rely very heavily on French sources or selective use of foreign archives, for obvious reasons. Only now are studies of émigré communities in localised areas being attempted.[33]

The second and more serious intellectual obstacle to the study of the emigration has to do with the nature and orientation of French History and the enormous sway of republican historians who have successfully managed to sideline the subject. From the republican point of view émigrés are non-people because the Revolution stripped them of their French citizenship and thereby their legal existence. This highly tenuous legal position has been given added weight over the years by the fact that many Counter-Revolution historians are dismissive of émigrés because their military contribution was unsuccessful.

The émigrés therefore find themselves at the centre of a bizarre identity crisis. They had no doubts about their French nationality. The inhabitants of the countries who took them in had no doubt that they were French. Yet the Revolutionaries blotted them out of existence, sequestered their property and denied them the very human rights it prided itself upon. Article XVII of the Declaration of the Rights of Man and the Citizen stated:

> Since property is a sacred and inviolable right, no one may be deprived thereof unless a legally established public necessity obviously requires it and upon condition of a just and previous indemnity.[34]

An entire thesis has been devoted to the laws which concerned the émigrés and their complexities.[35] The main body of laws was codified and drawn together between 28 March and 5 April 1793. These laws defined as an émigré: anyone who had left France since 1 July 1789 without justifying his return by 9 May 1792; anyone absent from his normal domicile who could not justify his uninterrupted presence in France since 9 May 1792 by a certificate of residence; anyone who had left France during this time (since 9 May 1792); anyone who left without fulfiling the appropriate formalities; any government agent who had not returned to France within three months of his recall; anyone who defected during an invasion to reside on enemy territory, and any girl or woman who had married a foreigner, left the country or sold her personal effects.[36]

These laws devastated the émigrés and particularly those who had envisaged an imminent end to the Revolution. The penalty specified by the Decree was decisive and final.

1. The émigrés are banished in perpetuity from French territory; they are civilly dead; their property is acquired by the Republic.
2. Infraction of the banishment pronounced by article 1 shall be punished with death.[37]

Madame de la Chartre, a resident at Juniper Hall in Surrey, shared her dismay with Fanny Burney:

> with great franchise entered into details of her situation and embarrassment. [...] She told me that she was a little recovered from the first shock – that she should gather together a small débris of her fortune, but never enough to settle in England – that, in short, her parti était pris – that she must go to America.[38]

Living in London or in the south of England was expensive and required funds. Even the rent of a modest cottage in Richmond, Twickenham or Surrey proved beyond the purse of many. Madame de la Chartre was not the only émigré to settle on America as an alternative but it was very much a last resort which partially explains why some of the French émigrés treated America and the Americans with such distaste.[39]

From the fortune and foresight (or lack of it), which meant that émigrés had more or less money when they arrived in Britain, evolved a whole geography of French settlement in London. The pattern started to emerge in 1791 with émigrés already settled in the more prestigious locations and it gradually consolidated itself into a complete socio-economic picture by 1800. These geographic divisions reflect many deeper currents within the Emigration.

The spread of émigré settlement in London offers few surprises because, in the 1790s, the social hierarchy of districts in London was well-established. However, the city to which the émigrés came was very different from the London of the late twentieth century. For instance, the village of Marylebone, which became a favourite French address and indeed today retains a little of its once French flavour, was on the very edge of the city and to the North looked out on to fields where children could play. Knightsbridge was still removed from the main part of the capital and Chelsea was more easily accessed by river than by road.

One of the most popular features of the London landscape was its parks and tea gardens – Ranelagh and Vauxhall. The French loved to dance and mingle and these places provided a relatively affordable entertainment on summer evenings after the day's work. Detailed descriptions of Ranelagh and Vauxhall containing opening times and prices appear in the Manual of the Abbé Tardy[40] while Jacques Delille, the poet of the emigration, celebrated the delicious mixture of fashion and fantasy which the French found in the English playgrounds.

> Il est des lieux publics où le peuple s'assemble,
> Charmé de voir, d'errer, et de jouir ensemble;
> Tant l'instinct social dans ses nobles désirs
> Veut, comme ses travaux, partager ses plaisirs!
> Là, nos libres regards ne souffrent point d'obstacle
> Ils veulent embrasser tout ce riche spectacle;
> Ces panaches flottants, ces perles, ces rubis,
> L'orgueil de la coiffure et l'éclat des habits;
> Ces voiles, ces tissues, ces étoffes brillantes,
> Et leurs reflets changeants, et leurs pompes mouvantes.
> Tels, si dans ces jardins où la fable autrefois
> A caché des héros, des belles et des rois,
> Dans la tige des lis, des oeillets et des roses,
> Les dieux mettoient un terme à leurs métamorphoses
> Tout-à-coup nous verrions, par un contraire effet,
> S'animer, se mouvoir l'hyacinthe et l'oeillet,
> Le lis en blancs atours, la jonquille doré,
> Et la tulipe errante en robe bigarrée.
> Tels nous plaisent ces lieux: aux champs élysiens
> Tel Paris réunit ses nombreux citoyens;
> Au retour du printemps, tels viennent se confondre
> Au parc de Kensington les fiers enfants de Londres;
> Vaste et brillante scène, où chacun est acteur,
> Amusant, amusé, spectacle et spectateur.[41]

Others were not so enchanted, Danloux described his first visit to Vauxhall on a moonlit summer's night:

> Je n'avais jamais vu cet endroit-là. On voit qu'on y a fait d'excessives dépenses, mais l'effet n'y répond pas. La décoration y est comique; les illuminations sont belles mais tristes et monotones; la musique de mauvais goût.[42]

> I had never seen this place [Vauxhall]. It was obvious that an excessive amount of money had been spent but the effect was disappointing. The decoration was comical, the lighting effects were beautiful but gloomy and all the same; the music was in bad taste.

Perhaps the fact that he and his party walked the three miles there and back on foot from Soho had dimmed their enjoyment!

The French actively sought ways to lighten the gloom of the political storm which loomed over them and this drew such a mixed reaction from the British that Madame de la Tour du Pin felt it necessary to explain:

> Les Français sont naturellement gais. Aussi, malgré que nous fussions tous désolés, ruinés, furieux, nous ne trouvâmes pas moins le moyen d'être de bonne humeur et de rire.[43]

> The French are naturally cheerful. So in spite of the fact that we were all destitute, ruined, furious, we were none the less disposed to good humour and laughter.

The marquise de Falaiseau also noted that the British

> ne concevaient pas comment on pouvait supporter tout cela et conserver de la gaieté.[44]

> couldn't imagine how we could go through all that and still retain a sense of humour.

Which, if nothing else, illustrates the irony of the words of Tom in Hannah More's *Village Politics*: 'These poor French fellows used to be the merriest dogs in the world; but since equality come in, I don't believe a Frenchman has ever laughed.'[45] Not all the British were critical: Mary Russell Mitford marvelled in retrospect:

Something wonderful and admirable it was to see how these Dukes and Duchesses, Marshals and Marquises, Chevaliers and Bishops, bore up under their unparalleled reverses! How they laughed and talked, and squabbled and flirted, – constant to their high heels, their rouge, and their furbelows, to their old liaisons, their polished sarcasms, their cherished rivalries![46]

And Helen Maria Williams, an ardent francophile, maintained that the quality of wit was inherent in the French language.

Happy are a people, so fond of talking as the French, in possessing a language modelled to all the charming purposes of conversation. Their turn of expression is a dress that hangs so gracefully on gay ideas, that you are apt to suppose that wit, a quality parsimoniously distributed in other countries is in France as common as the gift of speech. Perhaps that brilliant phraseology, which dazzles a foreigner, may be familiar and common to a French ear: but how much ingenuity must we allow to a people, who have formed a language, of which the common-place phrases give you an idea of wit.[47]

The French use of humour as a strategy for dealing with the disappointments of exile and the reaction this produced in the host population has not entirely escaped the historians' notice:

The émigrés kept, as we say in France, their smile; they never ceased to believe in their right to fight back even at the worst of times and in the name of this point of honour, that most of their foreign hosts did not understand, they persevered. This was a logical approach and in some cases it was accompanied by complete intelligence and an untiring curiosity, a will to dominate their circumstance by force of mind.[48]

And particularly, as time went on, there was a great deal to be gloomy about; so it was as well that the émigrés conserved their sense of humour.[49] Budgets became pinched, friends and relatives perished on the guillotine and the emigration seemed to become more permanent with every republican victory.

Between 1793 and 1814 the British government, albeit somewhat reluctantly, provided the most comprehensive financial backing for the overthrow of the Republic of any European power, and was the only country to offer financial aid to the refugees. News of anti-republican activity, like news of political developments in Paris, reached and circulated in London quicker than it reached any other European centre. Quite logically therefore, London, which was home to the largest population of refugees, became and remained, from 1793 until 1814, the capital of the Emigration.

2 1789–92: a Prolonged Vacation

Only in the casual chat of letters or diaries has this first year (1789) of the emigration in England left any trace. It was politically insignificant, it was generally believed to be temporary, and the only problems it posed were such as might arise in the ordinary intercourse of society.[1]

The Emigration, like the Revolution, began in July 1789.[2] And, like the Revolution, it began slowly and steadily gained momentum. The constant trickle in the latter months of 1789 became a flow toward the end of 1790 but did not burst the banks until late 1792. Moreover the Revolution took place during the summer months when a month or two in the country or in Italy or at one of the fashionable bath towns of Europe presented no great hardship.[3] Europeans and the French in particular were accustomed to spending periods of time abroad, sometimes quite lengthy, visiting friends and relatives or simply enjoying the fresh air away from the city.

The motivation of those who decided to emigrate prior to 1792 can only be speculated at. It is clear that many nobles were subjected to a certain amount of pressure to leave or to follow the lead of their friends. In one of the comtesse de Flahaut's novels the heroine's husband was subject to this sort of coercion.

> Les lettres des amis qu'Edmond avait hors de France se succédaient rapidement. Les uns touchés d'un véritable intérêt l'invitaient à ne plus différer de les rejoindre; d'autres moins indulgens blâmaient sa faiblesse; tous le rappelaient à sa bannière.[4]

> Letters from Edmund's friends outside France came in rapid succession. Some, who were genuinely concerned, urged him not to procrastinate any longer about joining them, others, who were more brutal, accused him of weakness. All of them reminded him of his duty.

It is often put forward that those who emigrated were those who had the most to fear. This is often juxtaposed with the fact that a significant proportion of the *ancien régime* elite survived the

Revolution by living quietly on their country estates and worrying no one.[5] Yet while this hypothesis has been applied to a limited number of émigrés there is no evidence to suggest that a generalisation can be drawn from it.[6]

It is more likely that the early-comers to Britain who invariably managed to extract their fortunes from France were the few whose reason told them that, whatever the outcome of the Revolution, the France of the future was not going to resemble the France of the *ancien régime*. The duc de Luxembourg and his family were reported in London on 17 July 1789.[7] Villedeuil, Louis XVI's minister of State, arrived with his family, bringing sufficient funds in 'jewels, valuables and funded property' to assure him an income of £156 per annum in 1802.[8]

> Mme de Cambis is also come; *il en fourmille*, but all of them almost beggars; some few, I hear, have letters of credit. Poor Mme de Boufflers as Lady Lucan writes me word is *dans un état pitoyable*.[9]

The famous session of the National Assembly on the nights of 4–5 August 1789 ushered in the first serious wave of emigration. Although this was nothing near the scale of the exodus in 1792, it was brought to the attention of the French National Assembly on 9 October that there had been 300 requests for passports in the preceding two days.[10] On the night of 4 August many provincial nobles found themselves stripped of their main source of income, which was made up of the feudal dues and payments in kind levied on the peasants who worked their land. Although many dues were commuted into compensatory payments, in effect, income was suspended because the payments were rarely made. This was a decisive blow for those nobles who were struggling to survive.[11]

In the initial months of the Revolution there was more traffic across the Belgian and Swiss borders than across the Channel, but by September there were increasing numbers of aristocrats in London, which remarks like this confirm:

> I came to town with a great curiosity to see some of their illustrious exiles and as I began with the president de la noblesse, M. de Luxembourg, I found that Madame had manifested no concern or solicitude when she came to England about anything she had left in her native country but that all her anxiety was expressed in her inquiries to know if there was any mass [catholic services] in London.[12]

George Selwyn, one of the best-informed social gossips of the period, confessed to having no idea who they all were.[13] At the end of September, Madame de Boufflers arrived with a group of women who included her step-daughter the duchesse de Biron, her daughter-in-law the comtesse Emilie, her little grandson and Madame de Cambis. Selwyn described Madame de Boufflers as 'la reine des aristocrates réfugiés en Angleterre'; she was no stranger to London and she cultivated British society.[14] Madame du Deffand wrote of her with undisguised dislike:

> Comme elle a beaucoup recherché les Anglais, qui de leur côté, la recherchent et la louent, elle ne rêve plus qu'Angleterre, elle est entourée d'Anglais comme une colonie à sucre, ne parle que du voyage qu'elle compte faire à Londres, et elle est déjà dans l'enivrement de la grande reputation qu'elle compte y trouver et de la reputation beaucoup plus grande encore qu'elle se flatte bien d'y laisser.[15]

> Because she has actively sought the company of the English, who for their part cultivate and praise her, she dreams of nothing but England. She is surrounded by the English like bees to honey and talks only of the trips she plans to make to London and she is already in a fever of excitement about the grand reputation she will find there and of the still greater reputation she flatters herself that she will leave behind.

Madame de Boufflers opened an account with Coutts Bank and she and her party took a house in Richmond, which became a fashionable place for the émigrés to live from the moment of her arrival until the end of the emigration.[16] Selwyn's witty correspondence with Lady Carlisle highlights the contrasts of her circumstances;

> When I left St James I went in search of Mme de Boufflers and found her at Grenier's Hotel which looks to me more like an hospital than anything else. Such rooms, such a crowd of miserable wretches, escaped from plunder and massacre and Mme de Boufflers among them, with I do not know how many beggars in her suite, her belle fille (qui n'est pas belle, par parenthèse) the Comtesse Émilie, a maid with the little child in her arms, a boy her grandson, called the Chevalier de Cinque Minutes, I cannot explain to you why; a pretty fair child, just inoculated, who does not as yet

know so much French as I do, but understood me, and was much pleased with my caresses. It was really altogether a piteous sight. When I saw her last, she was in a handsome hôtel dans le quartier du Temple – a splendid supper – Pharaon; I was placed between M. Fayette and his wife. This Fayette is her nephew and has been the chief instrument of her misfortunes and I hope, par la suite of his own. I said tout ce qui m'est venu en tête de plus consolant.[17]

The young Madame d'Osmond arrived in London in October with her husband and small daughter, the future Madame de Boigne. She had been a lady-in-waiting to Madame Adelaide, Louis XVI's aunt, and had been in the palace during the October Days.[18]

Quite apart from the émigrés known to be in London, odd comments in contemporary correspondence attest to the visibility of the French in the latter months of 1789. Mention of exiles 'gabbling about in every street' and George Selwyn's remark 'that if this next winter does not make a perfect Frenchman of me, I shall give it up' leave no doubt about the number of émigrés in London.[19]

In principle, they were free to leave France throughout 1790 and, until the attempted escape of the King and the royal family in June 1791, emigrating was relatively straightforward. The National Assembly was aware of the problem but was reluctant and unable to do anything to prevent their departure. A law was passed on 4 January 1790 obliging anyone holding a government appointment to return to France or lose it. A similar law was passed at the end of 1790 obliging anyone holding state pensions or grants to return to France within two months. But it was February 1791 before the question of the émigrés and what to do about them got a proper airing in the Assembly. The departure of the King's aunts prompted a motion by Barnave that a committee draw up a proposal on the obligations and duties of the members of the royal family. This suggestion led to a discussion of how to treat citizens who wished to leave the country in a moment of crisis. A committee was set up and Chapelier presented its findings at the sitting of 28 February 1791. This committee suggested that in times of crisis a council of three appointed by the National Assembly should alone exercise the right to issue passports and this council should have sufficient dictatorial powers to oblige citizens to return. It could then declare any dissidents absent and punish them by withdrawing their rights of citizenship and confiscating their incomes and properties. The skilful intervention of Mirabeau prevented this becoming law. His death two months later left the émigré cause vulnerable. Action on this issue was slow, however, because of the administrative effort involved.

Notable additions to the society in London in 1791 included Madame de Balbi,[20] the comte d'Esterhazy and his family, the comte de Boisgelin and the comte d'Avaray.[21] It also saw the first arrivals of members of the Parlements, the cream of the older generation of the legal profession whose loyalties were fiercely royalist when confronted with the attacks on privilege and the prospect of a revolutionary France. Monsieur d'Aligre, premier président of the Parlement of Paris, took a house on the Green in Richmond: he was immensely wealthy and managed to bring most of his fortune with him.[22] Monsieur de Poincarré, premier président of the Parlement de Rouen, was also noticed in London in August. He had not been so lucky and arrived almost penniless.[23] This pattern continued: for example, the Marquis de Brézé, the former grand-master of ceremonies at the French Court, arrived in London 1792 with letters of credit to the value of a few hundred louis, which was all he had saved from a fortune of millions.[24]

In this initial phase of the Emigration, which lasted from the fall of the Bastille until the escape to Varennes, émigrés moved in British circles but made little impact outside the social rounds of the elite. They added colour and novelty to the season through their presence, conversation and hospitality. There were occasional embarassing moments when political discussions touched on sensitive issues and brought out differences of opinion between ultra-royalists and constitutional monarchists.[25] But, in general, there was an infectious gaiety which appealed to a number of British francophiles. The Duke of Queensberry, Horace Walpole, who lived close to Richmond at Strawberry Hill, and George Selwyn all took pleasure in entertaining the exiled French.

Following the escape to Varennes, laws were passed which obliged any French citizen residing outside the kingdom to return within a month or pay a triple tax on their assets. Local authorities were to draw up lists of absentee persons and estimate their possessions.[26] These laws hit hard and many émigrés returned to avoid paying the penalty.

It is interesting that the French Constitution promulgated on 3 September 1791 guaranteed 'comme un droit naturel et civil la liberté à tout homme d'aller, de rester et de partir' (as a natural and civil right of every man, the freedom to move about, to stay or to leave the country.) Evidently, this natural right was designed to apply to patriotic citizens in an ideal world and there was no real thought for its meaning in relation to the émigrés.

Varennes marked a turning-point in the history of the emigration because the failed escape and the humiliation of the return to Paris sent a new wave of émigrés across the border.[27] In London it had further significance because it provoked a change in attitude towards the Revolution. This can only be understood in the context of the political climate in Britain, which from the outset of the Revolution was one of intense interest in the affairs of France, inspiring either ardent support for the National Asembly or fierce opposition.[28]

Many of the gains of the early days of the Revolution involved political problems which had been identified long before the Revolution and many of which had counterparts in Britain. Political representation of the sort which the French achieved in the National Assembly was an important issue for the British, whose electoral boundaries had been set long before towns like Manchester and Birmingham became heavily populated. The French feudal system had to be dismantled before a radical overhaul of taxation could take place and without that there was no hope of any individual tax equity. In Britain, voting involved a complex myriad of local issues, social and personal relationships, traditional and hereditary loyalties, most of which were dependent on power relationships between the propertied and the propertyless.[29] Few of these issues were in any way resolved until the Reform Bill was passed in 1832 and therefore issues of liability to taxation and equity before the law were extremely important in Britain.[30]

The Revolution rekindled the radical element in British politics which had lain dormant since the 1780s; and throughout the 1790s, when Burke published his *Reflections on the Revolution in France* and Paine replied with his *Rights of Man,* issues of human rights, of social justice, of consitutional monarchy and its merits, preoccupied Londoners.

The first phase of the Emigration therefore coincided with the honeymoon period of the Revolution in Britain when there was a general admiration for the deputies of the National Assembly and what they were trying to achieve. Varennes and the massacre on the Champ de Mars put a dampener on this enthusiasm. The fact that the French government continued to function during the absence of the King was far from lost on the radical faction within the National Assembly who were already beginning to use a republican rhetoric full of metaphorical references to ancient Rome.

The warning signals that this sent out in Britain were heeded and, well before the Seditious Meetings Act prevented debating societies from holding public debates on sensitive political issues, the reception of the Revolution became much cooler.[31] It is generally acknowledged by historians of British radicalism that one of the most significant impacts of the French Revolution on British politics was the enormous boost it gave to popular conservatism.[32] The presence of the émigrés in ever-increasing numbers from July 1791 onward significantly reinforced this conservatism. Coleridge gives one of best examples of the reformation of a young radical in a lecture given in Bristol at a time when there was a significant émigré population closeby in Bath.

> The Patriots of France either hastened into the dangerous and gigantic Error of making certain Evil the mean of contingent Good or were sacrificed by the Mob, with whose prejudices and ferocity their unbending Virtue forbade them to assimilate. Like Sampson the People were strong – like Sampson the people were blind.[33]

The second phase of the Emigration is the period from July 1791 after the escape to Varennes until the creation of the Republic on 10 August 1792. During this period émigrés were usually self-sufficient or managed to become so with the help of their friends both British and French. They were not yet refugees.

If one of the general characteristics of this period is self-sufficiency, the other is self-delusion. For whatever the reason, the émigrés seemed very unaware of the crisis they were living through. The duchesse de Duras captured the mood when she wrote:

> Ma vie présente est si éloignée de ma vie passée, qu'il me semble que je lis des mémoires, ou je regarde un spectacle.[34]

> My present life is so far away from my past that it seems as if I am reading memoirs or watching a play.

Perhaps they were too close to the Revolution to conceive that it could last into the next year, let alone into the next century, but they certainly refused to take the political reality seriously.

This was of course in stark contrast to the way the Revolution was treated by the British who devoured every newspaper report from Paris and were fully conversant with the arguments of Burke whether they were for or against. Burke's *Reflections* understandably appealed to the émigrés and several, including Mme de Cambis, are among his correspondents congratulating him on his pamphlet.[35] This extract from a letter from the duchesse de Biron to Mme de Cambis shows how wholeheartedly his pamphlet was received.

> J'ai lu Mr Burke avec une admiration inexprimable; vous avez bien raison de dire que c'est un *génie immense*. Cette lecture fait exprimer toutes sortes d'émotions différentes. On n'a jamais vu tant de pensées, tant d'âme, tant d'esprit; ces excellens principes, les combinaisons sublimes de tout ce qui doit composer un bon gouvernement, ressemblent à la profonde sagesse de la providence dans la formation du monde.[36]

> I read Mr. Burke with an inexpressible admiration, you are right to say he is a great genius. Reading his pamphlet inspired all sorts of different emotions. I have never seen so many thoughts, such soul, such spirit. These excellent principles, sublime combinations of all that make up good government, can only be compared to the infinite wisdom of providence in the creation of the earth.

There are many examples of this level of enthusiasm, particularly among the ultra-royalist émigrés who were of course completely in agreement with Burke.[37]

One is tempted to wonder whether the émigrés were not demonstrating a typically French apathy in their refusal to be preoccupied with the Revolution which by 1791 had monopolised more than its share of conversation. Yet political apathy was not confined to the French. In a letter to Lord Auckland closely following the declaration of war, Storer wrote:

> London is now alive everywhere. Casino fills up the intervals of politics. [...] More fear generally prevails lest the Opera-house should fall than that the constitution should. The report of the architects appointed to examine the house has not been deemed satisfactory, and the public says that Sheridan had better think of repairing his theatre than reforming the state.[38]

There is no evidence to suggest that the émigrés in Britain behaved as frivolously towards their situation as the group who surrounded the French royal princes in Germany whose 'levity, vanity and presumption' was reported in the society press.[39] But they were not greatly concerned about politics. The British, on the other hand, were obsessed with politics and did not understand how the French could not be.

On 9 November 1791, the National Assembly decreed that émigrés who were not prepared to return to France by 1 January 1792 were suspect and would be accused of conspiracy, prosecuted and punished with death. Failure to comply would involve prosecution for contempt of court and this would result in any income being appropriated by the State for the benefit of the nation (i.e. denied to any dependants). All payments to the absent princes were to be sequestered and, as émigrés, they were also subject to the order to re-enter the country or stand accused of conspiracy.[40] This decree was vetoed by the King and remained suspended and a source of great contention until the deposition of the monarch on 10 August 1792. But on 18 January 1792, the comte de Provence was stripped of his right to the Regency because of his refusal to return to France and on 1 February 1792, a further law introduced the requirement of passports for all travellers.

In April 1792, when rumours of plots to overthrow the Revolution were at their peak, France went to war. Émigrés and non-juring priests (those who had refused to take an oath to the Civil Constitution of the Clergy which effectively made clerics paid bureaucrats of the state and down-scaled the relationship with Rome) bore the brunt of suspicions generated by the inflammatory rhetoric of Brissot.[41]

> Will anyone deny that the émigrés had succeeded in assembling forces at Worms, at Coblentz, in arming them, in provisioning them? Will anyone deny that they threatened us with an imminent invasion? Will anyone deny that the electors granted them not only asylum but considerable material aid, which they collected from the various princes who had an interest in maintaining the fires of discord in the interior of France?[42]

In the face of the danger threatening him, the Elector of Trier disbanded the army which the French princes had assembled on his territory and this created its own wave of émigrés, some of whom reached Britain. Soldiers and their families sought refuge in Britain in the hope that the British would soon enter the war and the Counter-Revolution would have a powerful new ally.

Arrivals were steady throughout the early months of 1792 and the émigrés were more impoverished because travel was exorbitantly expensive and it was harder to get money out of France. There was another noticeable change. The first signs started to appear that early supporters of the Revolution were defecting into emigration. Many former deputies of the Constituent Assembly emigrated to Britain including Malouet, the comte d'Antraigues, Adrien Duport, the brothers Charles and Alexandre Lameth.[43] In late July 1792 a correspondent of Lord Auckland wrote: 'The town swarms with these ex-members of the Assemblée Nationale'.[44] These were men whose moderation in their approach to Revolution and to monarchy was overtaken by events which labelled them counter-revolutionary. The same year brought the journalist Jean Gabriel Peltier, who busied himself providing information to the government about various émigrés in the hope of some influence on British policy.[45]

From the middle of 1792 onward there was a certain apprehension about the whole émigré issue in Britain. This was due to the number and make-up of the émigré society which was rumoured to include many undesirable dissidents willing to make trouble and spread the Revolution. It was also a product of the international political scene which was evolving at pace with the Revolution. France superseded Poland at the top of the European political agenda and the end of the Eastern conflict meant that the powers were free to concentrate on the situation in France.[46] The evolution of the international situation and the escalation of the French war was of extreme importance to the British.

In the heavy atmosphere of the impending political storm the émigrés quietly consolidated their presence in London. Advertisements like the following which had started to appear intermittently in the society press in 1791 became more frequent:

> A YOUNG WOMAN, a Native of France, who has received a very liberal Education, and is perfectly Mistress of the French Language would be happy to find a situation as FRENCH TEACHER in a GENTEEL SCHOOL. Letters addressed to H. O. No. 25 Duke Street, St James will be carefully attended to.[47]
>
> To The Ladies
> A Young Person, who received her education in a French school, and speaks the language with fluency, wishes to attend on one or more young ladies as governess, or to be as Teacher in a school where French is the principal requisite. Her character and capacity for which she professes to undertake will bear the strictest investigation. Letters addressed to B. Y. at Mr. Bliss's No. 26 Tottenham Court Road will meet with immediate attention.[48]

> A FRENCH LADY about 30 years of age, good family, and who has received a very liberal education, but whose fortune has been injured by the Revolution of France, wishes to engage herself as companion to a Lady either in her own country, or in any other. She would willingly superintend Young Ladies as Governess to teach them her own language, geography, history, etc. Applications may be made M. le Vasseur à Paris homme de lui, rue Vivienne, vis à vis celle de Colbert, who will answer all enquiries in the most satisfactory manner.[49]

These pleas for jobs were made by women unaccustomed to working for their living. It is impossible to tell whether individual applicants found jobs but they must have met with a certain sympathy from the British because very few advertisements appear twice.

The émigrés practised self-help. None were better examples of this than the clergy, who by 1792 had become a noticeable group in London. Many of the noble faction within the clergy started to arrive almost as soon as the Civil Constitution of the Clergy was voted and, by the institution of the oath in November 1791, there was a significant community in London. In all some 30 French bishops resided in London during the emigration.[50]

The earliest comers to London were able to dress according to their rank and the appearance of clerical dress in the London streets created something of a sensation. On 6 April 1792 the National Assembly passed a law forbidding the clergy to wear religious dress and as a result, most of the priests who came to London were shabbily dressed in ill-fitting clothes which were visibly second-hand.

> The French Fugitive Priests, last Sunday, made a droll motley appearance at some of the Catholic places of devotion.
> A Bishop entered in one of these holy places in a pair of dirty trousers and hung up a straw hat!
> A grand Dean was habited in a carter's frock.
> An abbé was in a red jacket and postillon's boots, and a vicar was a complete Merry Andrew being in a grotesque scenic habit from the Faubourg. Others, regular and secular, were whimsically attired.[51]

It was in the period between the escape to Varennes and the September Massacres that the groundwork was done for the reception of the French clergy in Britain. In March 1791 the Bishop of Saint Pol de Léon, Jean-François de la Marche, arrived from Brittany where he had been forced to flee from his diocese after repeated defiance of the Civil Constitution.[52] He was the most important French ecclesiastic in the early years of the emigration in London. His organisational skills and his dedication to the task of helping the clergy in exile, allied to his impeccable social credentials, made him an ideal person to coordinate the relief operation. Over time, he not only helped the clergy but a significant number of the lay French population also found him a tireless champion. He was over 60 when he emigrated and his health was not good but until his death in London in 1806 he devoted himself to the Catholic royalist cause and served his cause and his faith as well as any soldier.

This one man stands out among the émigrés for his personal qualities and his leadership in a difficult political climate. He mounted the earliest relief operation in London. This was mostly relief in kind, clothing, bedding and medicine which he procured with the help of his English landlady, Mrs Dorothy Silburn. Before any monetary relief was available, he provided an information-point, and what other help he could, to get the priests settled comfortably after their tiring and stressful journeys.

By September 1792, he was dispensing significant amounts of material and financial aid to the French priests from his lodgings at 10 Queen Street, Bloomsbury. When the charitable relief and mass subscription got under way, he had the necessary networks in place to ensure that aid reached those who needed it most. The fact that his distribution system was adopted by the British government when they took over the relief payments in 1794 was testimony to the effectiveness of his management. Although others emerged later, like the Abbé Carron who came from Jersey in 1796, and showed a similar flair for organisation and management, the Bishop of Léon was the inspiration behind the Relief operation.

News of the welcoming committee that the Bishop had created in London leaked out to the non-juring priests in France. Many priests chose Britain as their destination on the strength of these rumours and it is not surprising to learn that the home of Mrs Dorothy Silburn, which remained the relief office throughout the Emigration, became known among the clergy as '*La providence*'.

3 1792: The Influx

> Even while I speak, the sacred roofs of France
> Are shattered into dust; and self-exiled
> From altars threatened, levelled, or defiled,
> Wander the Ministers of God, as chance
> Opens a way for life, or consonance
> Of faith invites. More welcome to no land
> The fugitives than to the British strand,
> Where priest and layman with the vigilance
> Of true compassion greet them. Creed and test
> Vanish before the unreserved embrace
> Of Catholic humanity: – distrest
> They came; – and, while the moral tempest roars
> Throughout the Country they have left, our shores
> Give to their Faith a fearless resting-place.[1]

In the wake of the September Massacres, it was the clergy who first brought home to the British public the plight of the victims of the Revolution. Those who escaped from the persecution in Paris and reached Britain were the first group of émigrés to whom the term 'refugee' truly applied. Athough earlier émigrés may have been destitute, they did not come to the public notice in the same way. There was a very keen distinction in the public image of emigration before and after September 1792 to which the formation of the charitable committees bear witness. This was owing primarily to the large number of refugees both lay and ecclesiastical who needed some form of basic assistance to ensure their survival. In fact, it was the nearest that the eighteenth century came to producing 'boat people'.

Many of the clergy arrived on the English coast with almost nothing. Often, any possessions they may have had, and sometimes even their clothes, had been lost in the storms at sea which were particularly bad in the autumn of 1792.[2] *The London Chronicle* described them as 'bruised, wet and fatigued'; the *Public Advertiser* reported:

> the whole of this day the refugee French were flocking in from every quarter of their unhappy shores, many in open boats and by all kinds of conveyances they could obtain, some even without hats

or other clothes than what they had on their backs and the women and children exhibiting the most afflicting scenes of distress.[3]

It was the quickened pace of emigration through the closing months of 1792 that marked the transition from a situation where Britain was host to a group of independent émigrés to a situation where Britain found herself offering political asylum to refugees of the French Revolution.[4]

By the end of September hundreds of refugees were arriving daily along a stretch of coast from Dover to Southampton, occasionally landing even further southwest.

> This place (Dover) daily exhibits the most melancholy proofs of the present struggle in a neighbouring kingdom; not a day or night passes without the arrival of hundreds of all ages, either driven forcibly from their home or voluntarily flying from those scenes of horror, to which they were obliged to be the unavailing witness.[5]

Even if the reports were exaggerated, there were still a great many French men, women and children arriving each day during the months of September and October. The initial trend slowed a little but it continued in a sustained manner for the rest of 1792. Lord Sheffield wrote from Lewes:

> I have been particularly occupied in favour of the French Clergy about 1200 have landed in this country. There is little prejudice in respect of the popish priests but abundance of nonsense even among better informed people in regard to the effect so many additional mouths will have on the price of provisions. Unfortunately the crop was not good and in consequence of extreme bad weather it will be half lost in the West and in the North. This will be much against the poor French, but altho' many wish them at the Devil rather than here yet upon the whole they have had a very good reception such as does credit to the Country.[6]

The number of refugees caused delays and strains on accommodation. Locals did what they could to help. Hot food and dry clothing were provided in many cases and when inns were full the refugees depended on local hospitality. Émigrés who did manage to get a room at an inn often had to share beds and there was an occasion in

Hastings where everything was so full that there was not even a spare room where the priests could say mass.[7] The delays were increased by the strain on transport systems.[8] Émigrés walked to London from the south coast to avoid long and expensive delays. Some even found daywork on the way, picking hops. A local who lived on the main road from Dover to London wrote that he had

> frequent occasion to see and lament the distresses of these unfortunate men, some almost without clothes, many without money, and not a few hiring themselves out as Day Labourers in the Hop picking. ... We were almost every day upon the road, distributing small alms to such as were travelling on foot to London ... and observing those objects most in need of immediate charity.[9]

Although the initial influx was heavily weighted in favour of the clergy there was still a significant number of other émigrés who arrived in these months. Some were high-society émigrés like the marquise de Bouillé and Mme de Noailles who immediately joined the party of the Prince of Wales in Brighton. These events were reported in the London society press and, eager to prevent any important aristocrats slipping in unnoticed, the press reported almost daily on arrivals from France. Among those mentioned were Talleyrand,[10] Beaumarchais,[11] (both of whom were expelled from Britain – Talleyrand for his suspicious connections and Beaumarchais for buying arms)[12] several Bishops and the duc de Fitzjames and his daughter, who had been obliged to travel disguised as a member of ship's crew.[13]

A particular sensation was caused by the arrival at Shoreham on 17 October of 37 nuns from the convent at Montargis.[14] Nuns were a particular reminder of the evils of popery. Their passage had been arranged by Mrs Fitzherbert herself and upon their arrival in England the Prince of Wales' own carriage was sent for the use of the Prioress.[15] They created quite a spectacle and the beach was reported to be 'a mass of people' curious to see them. But curiosity was the only sentiment the British expressed towards the 'fugitive virgins' and this amazed even the French.

> England proved that virtue and piety oppressed will ever have a claim on her benevolence. The Prince of Wales was at Brighton when these fugitive virgins arrived. His Royal Highness's clemency and bounty were the first pledge of the protection they were to meet

with on their retreat. Enlightenment admired their courage and resolution. They were everywhere treated with that regard which respect inspires, they everywhere met with the most generous support.[16]

The intrigue that surrounded escaping from France and the expense because boat-owners could name their price (and many did) provided plots for stories like the Scarlet Pimpernel. Innkeepers were revolutionary or counter-revolutionary. Boats plied the channel under cover of darkness, and so on.[17] But the romance of the escape stories which the émigrés brought with them to Britain was short-lived. The émigrés came to Britain at the beginning of winter, and, although 1792–93 was not a particularly harsh season, many of them had inadequate clothing and scant financial resources.

It took relatively little time for the seriousness of the émigré situation to be taken in by acute observers. Fortunately for the émigrés, the champions of their cause were some of the most able men in politics. It can never be stressed enough what a herculean task John Wilmot[18] and his supporters faced in trying to convince the British population to dip into their pockets on the émigrés' behalf.

The relief effort grew out of a meeting organised at the Freemasons' Tavern on 20 September 1792. This public meeting was no *ad hoc* affair. The massaging of public opinion beforehand was meticulously prepared and executed by the members of the embryonic committee.

> It is confidently hoped, that a difference in religious persuasion will not shut the hearts of the English Public against their suffering Brethren, the Christians of France; but that all true Sons of the Church of England, all true Subjects of our Saviour Jesus Christ, who are not ashamed in this time of apostasy or prevarication, to confess their obedience to and imitation of their divine Master in their Charity to their suffering Brethren of all denominations – it is hoped that all persons who from the inbred sentiments of a generous nature, cultivate the virtues of humanity – it is hoped that all persons attached to the cause of religious and civil Liberty, as it is connected with Law and Order – it is hoped that all these will be gratified in having an opportunity of contributing to the support of these worthy Sufferers in the case of Honor, Virtue, Loyalty and Religion.[19]

The issue at the centre of public debate was whether or not the émigrés deserved help. Opinions differed wildly about who should receive relief. The main difference came between those who felt that all émigrés should be helped and those who feared that an appeal on behalf of the lay French community would invite such criticism as to destroy the chances of obtaining help for the French clergy. The concern was that the British would refuse to help the French laity, many of whom were former aristocrats, because they held them collectively responsible for the Revolution and were unlikely to be sympathetic. To convince the British public that there were equally deserving members of the laity, aristocrats included, seemed doomed from the outset.[20]

Lord Sheffield,[21] in particular, stressed the case of the entire body of émigrés. Lord Loughborough,[22] who could not see how support for the laity might be achieved, favoured helping only the priests. Both these men were actively involved helping émigrés to settle in Britain. Josiah Wedgwood, the prominent industrialist, well-known for his support of social causes, disassociated himself from the relief subscription as soon as the decision was made to concentrate exclusively on the clergy.[23] Bits of these debates were picked up by the newspapers.[24]

The case of the French clergy took precedence over the case of the French laity not because it was more deserving but because it was more immediate. By the end of August the Bishop of Saint Pol de Léon had already approached the British public and opened a subscription fund account at a local bank.[25] He had 1200 priests enrolled on his relief list, 400 of whom were receiving small amounts of money.[26] This was the point at which the Bishop was introduced to John Wilmot who, with the help of his connections, organised the meeting at Freemasons' Tavern. John Wilmot and the Bishop worked together for the rest of the Bishop's life.[27] They made a good team and their organisation and efficiency made the available funds go much further. But the central aim of providing relief to the French clergy was at the heart of the whole operation. Throughout the emigration, relief for the lay émigré community had a lower public profile than relief for the priests.

The appearance in London of the French priests solicited a number of reactions. Many Britons felt that they should be helped simply because in the normal course of events they were the ones who dedicated themselves to alleviating suffering in others and that it was therefore almost a moral obligation to provide the priests with help when they found themselves in trouble. This was the opinion of Hannah More and it was shared by a large number of people.[28]

> They are entitled to our compassion: and it is but right, that we should attend to their distresses, since foreign countries have been put to the expence of maintaining those refugees from our own island, who for their attachment to an ancient family were, by the rigour of the two foreign reigns, subjected to all the penalties exacted from recusants by the present government in France.[29]

Interestingly enough, the religious issues faded into the background. This was not particularly surprising, but it was unique in the British experience to welcome members of the Catholic clergy into the country and to treat them with compassion. Not all Britons were kind. Londoners, particularly, felt threatened by the French influx and there were concerns that they would take jobs away from the local population.

> What will our industrious mechanics say to the importation of French Refugees? Will not their wives and children suffer by the throngs of artificers who will work at reduced prices or perhaps seduce their supporters not to work at all. [...] Many of those emigrants have repeatedly offered their services in families for their subsistence, regardless of wages.[30]

But what hostility there was was focused at a political or economic rather than a religious level.

There were concerns about groups of priests being seen together talking in the streets, particularly outside the house of the Bishop of Saint Pol de Léon where it was usual for priests to congregate, swapping news of friends or discussing events in France. A code of behaviour was later elaborated which imperiously counselled the French priests to behave in a circumspect manner and not to congregate in groups of more than three anywhere in London.[31] It served to remind them that they were men of principle and ambassadors of their faith.

> In this land of refuge that the Lord had given us for asylum, do not lose sight of the fact that we come here as witnesses to our faith: the cause of our affliction is known; we have said: rather die than soil our consciences with the stain of impiety and perjury; this is what has brought upon us the loss of our property, ridicule, persecution and finally exile.

By November 1792, there were so many senior members of the French clergy in London that supervising the ecclesiastical population was not difficult. Nor was it difficult to verify a priest's credentials and to ascertain whether or not he had sworn allegiance to the Civil Constitution of the Clergy.[32] The Bishop had very little sympathy for priests who had taken the oath. They were not eligible for help from his relief fund and had to apply to other charities for help.

The effectiveness of the Catholic organisation was underlined by the problems encountered later in relation to the French lay community. For example, while the credentials of any priest were easy to check and deception almost impossible because of the number of high-ranking French ecclesiastics in Britain, it was very difficult to check up on details or references given by non-ecclesiastics.

The period from September 1792 until April 1793 is a period of flux. The arrival of a great many émigrés meant that opinions and attitudes were very much influenced by popular images. Rumours about the number of émigrés started to circulate and in turn fuelled the fires of anti-republicanism which resulted in the Aliens Act passed at the beginning of 1793. It was during this time, on the eve of war with France, that the British government made up its mind about the émigré situation, a decision determined in no small part by public opinion.

It can be argued that the most significant contribution the émigrés made to the Counter-Revolution was the image they presented to the British government and public at a crucial point in the crisis. Whatever their shortcomings, they were united in their support for the French monarchy and for the government of the *ancien régime*, which was overturned on 10 August 1792. The image was one of sadness, hardship, distress and stoic determination to endure. Driven from their own country through their refusal to be coerced into submission to a form of government they found abhorrent, the émigrés were people of principle. They found themselves in exile, short of money and of all the other comforts of life but they had their self-respect, and there was nothing the British admired more. To ask the question whether the British government would have agreed to support the émigrés had they not had such a spotless public image is to move into the realms of speculation but the general reluctance of the government to provide the sums committed after 1793 (which were invariably late) rather suggests that had it been at all possible they would have sidestepped the issue.

The passage of the Aliens Act at the beginning of January 1793 is a milestone. Although this act was destined to apply to all foreigners there was no doubt whatsoever whom it was designed to control. The French émigrés were a cause for political concern to the British government. It was not difficult to enter Britain as an émigré and the numbers of émigrés in the country after September 1792 gave rise to concerns that republican/Jacobin spies who wanted to stir up trouble in the British dominions could slip in unnoticed as émigrés and go about their business of undermining the government without interference. Port collectors were instructed to report on the number and general behaviour of émigrés who had arrived in their port in order to ascertain accurate numbers of émigrés in the country.[33] These reports certainly fell far short of the inflated figures in circulation in London.[34] Moreover the collectors reported the émigrés' behaviour to be generally very good and not at all hostile or antagonistic, but this did little to calm public fears.[35]

The émigrés were in fact very vulnerable to accusations and scrutiny of all kinds whether founded or speculative. Moreover the fears which prompted the following remark had little to do with the émigrés or the Revolution but reflected deeper anti-French currents in British society which surfaced in moments of crisis.

> Some tall Frenchmen with their fierce cocked hats and spotted great coats not of suspected but of known ill character continue to parade the streets of London under the protection of the patriotic opposition made from day to day to the Alien Bill. Their time of security is now however short and Britons are not much longer to be insulted by them in the face of day.[36]

The Aliens Act was passed in a very short time.[37] This reflected the political atmosphere which had been created by the appearance of Tom Paine's *Rights of Man* and the intense activity within the debating societies, particularly the London Corresponding Society, which had a network akin to that of the Jacobin clubs and the Society for Constitutional Information where revolutionary activity of a dangerous nature was believed to be thriving.[38] The speed was also indicative of the false sense of alarm stirred up among the politicians. Fox, who was no supporter of the émigrés, adamantly opposed this bill which, he felt, cut across basic human rights.[39] He was not convinced that foreigners presented a threat to national security and urged that a commission be appointed to verify the level of danger before a bill was passed to curtail their movement on British soil.[40]

Fox's and others' reasoned arguments were lost in the panic of the moment. The perceived need for an Act to control the movement of foreigners on British soil predominated, particularly after the

Declaration of 19 November 1792 in which the Revolutionary government offered support and fraternity to all nations wishing to overthrow their oppressors.[41] Grenville was quick to stress the honourable intentions of the bill, which only threatened with deportation those who were a threat to the nation, and therefore the vast majority of émigrés could rest easy and depend on the protection of the British government.[42] The main French émigré newspaper in London, the *Courrier de Londres*, followed the debate on the bill through the house translating the major speeches and, somewhat predictably, gave full details of the arguments against.[43]

> This [the bill] violates the protection that the constitution in this country has always accorded to all foreigners.

> He accused the ministers of ignorance of the affairs and situation in France, he said that if a danger existed on this side, it consisted of their negligence and incompetence.

> The humanity and generosity of the nation, shown in the true colours and to the great honour of the English character, will be arrested and negated by the effects of this bill.[44]

> This country instead of being, as at present, a haven of freedom and protection will become for the unfortunate émigrés a land of bondage that they will flee and hate.[45]

The Public Advertiser pointed out the irony of the situation on 9 January 1793:

> The last importation of Frenchmen are indeed as Mr. Burke said, of that kind from whom little danger is to be expected. Distress and famine have worn them down so that they can be objects of envy only to a lecturer in anatomy.[46]

In fact the bill had two outcomes. On the one hand, it succeeded in imposing a check on the number of émigrés entering the country and their movements within it. This enabled the government to monitor the movements of anyone whom they had reason to suspect and gave them a framework for dealing with 'aliens'.[47] On the other, it imposed enormous amounts of bureaucracy on the émigrés.

The bill obliged every émigré to register at their port of arrival in the country and to obtain a passport stating their name and town of destination before leaving the port. It also obliged ships' captains to declare the names of the émigrés whom they had brought into the country aboard their vessels. Prior to the bill, many captains were unaware of their passengers' identities. The bill made them accountable and punishable by fines for inaccuracies or omissions. Once the émigrés had obained their passports they were required to report to the local Justice of the Peace in the town of destination and declare their address. They were also required to obtain permission before relocating even a few miles. For instance, this letter from Stephen Burney, the Farnham Town Clerk, to Henry Dundas illustrates the sorts of administrative problems of which there are numerous examples affecting both the clergy and the laity.

> Louis Stephen Lucas priest, an emigrant from France, an inhabitant of Farnham under your leave employed in educating youth in the French language having occasion on Sundays to attend Divine Worship at Portsmouth has applied to the Magistrates as well as the Borough as for the County at large for leave to pass and repass from Portsmouth and Farnham on Sundays for the above purpose but the Magistrates not thinking themselves authorised have declined the necessary passport. I am writing therefore for Louis Stephen Lucas, to beg his passing and repassing and to request authorisation to acquaint the Magistrates that you have done so.[48]

This bill caused the émigrés endless problems. It was designed for political not practical reasons and it caused all manner of delays and inconveniences which the émigrés had to endure as well as finance. Despite the fact that it was translated into French and posted in all the ports, so that the arriving French could have no doubt about the formalities required of them there was still much confusion.

> Even the ministerial papers avow that some of the French Emigrants have been very unhandsomely and even unjustifiably treated by the subordinate officers of the Customs-house.[49]

Moreover its effectiveness as a propaganda measure must be questioned because it did little to allay the fears of members of the public about the spread of Jacobinism in Britain. Home office records offer many examples like the following of letters from over-zealous, eavesdropping Britons, addressed to Pitt:

One would have supposed that the Alien Bill would have purged this country of the jacobin French, or at least have prevented them from declaring their sentiments publicly (but it has not). There are hundreds of villains at present in town who pretend to have been officers, and Royalists but if you are to judge by their conversation, they certainly are of a different description, and in the case of an Invasion would be the very first to join the Enemy, and give them every information.[50]

The Aliens Bill was subject to two major revisions, one in 1798 and another in 1802. This level of surveillance of foreigners on British soil was a new departure and posed administrative challenges that were unforeseen at the time of its imposition. The Aliens Office, a branch of the Home Office which was to deal with Alien concerns until its reintegration into the Home Office in 1836, was not in existence when the bill became law.[51] It was created in response to the requirements of this legislation and the *ad hoc* nature of its creation was probably an advantage because it gave it a certain flexibility where émigré matters were concerned.[52] The changes embodied in the 1798 legislation were 'designed to increase the information available to the Aliens Office, to improve documentation, to regularise or extend existing modifications and to close remaining loopholes'.[53] Basically, the original 1793 act was tidied and elaborated in 1798, then in 1802 when the peace had been signed it was simplified to allow traffic to flow more freely in a peacetime environment. The resumption of hostilities in 1803 brought the matter back into Parliament.[54]

So, just how many émigrés were there? Estimates of the total number of émigrés who left France range between 130 000 and 150 000 people.[55] These have been put together from the lists of émigrés in French national and department archives. The sources alone pose many problems of discrepancies and internal inaccuracies. Nevertheless, what they do confirm is that less than 1 per cent of the French population of nearly 29 million emigrated during the Revolution.[56] Emigration was localised and tended to be high in some areas and very low in others. By far the greatest number of émigrés came from the staunchly Catholic royalist areas of West France, from Normandy, Brittany, the Loire and Bordeaux regions but there were other isolated pockets of relatively intense emigration such as from the departments on the Italian border and from Paris itself.[57]

The most difficult thing in relation to the émigrés in Britain is to give an overall figure for the total number of émigrés who sought refuge on British soil in the years 1789–1802. This is mainly because émigrés moved around, and many who were in Britain in 1794 were no longer there in 1799 or in 1802. Annual figures are much more reliable. It is not possible to complete a full set of data for all the years of the emigration but the available evidence points to a figure of around 12 500 émigrés per annum.[58]

It is possible however, to look at contemporary accounts which mention figures and to compare them with numbers in other sources. For instance, in late 1792 it is clear that there was a highly inflated émigré population but that many of these émigrés went on to America or the Netherlands after a short stay in Britain. It is unlikely that the scare-mongering figure of 40 000 which appears in the correspondence of Lord Auckland and in the press ever had any substance.[59]

> Sir, The number of French Emigrants in England at this time cannot possibly be less than 40,000. I believe, if I were to say double that number I should be nearer the mark. The greater part of whom have not brought any property with them. On that account many gentlemen have entered into a subscription for their relief which undoubtedly was very good of those gentlemen. But it can hardly be supposed that we should keep such a number of foreigners in idleness; indeed it would be highly impolitic and not at all charitable.
>
> In many businesses hands are scarce; the farmers in general want men, many of whom would have no objection to employ French men. If some gentlemen would interest themselves in getting the French employed (many of them have been brought up to trades but for want of understanding English and other accounts have no employment) they would, I believe, do more real good than in supporting them by subscriptions; for as the wealth of a nation consists principally in the number and industry of the people if these Frenchmen were to settle here in different employments, instead of being a burden to the public they would be a valuable acquisition.
>
> Perhaps many will agree with me in this when they recollect that many of our manufactures were established by foreigners settling in England, who were driven away from their native country by persecution.
>
> The French are superior to us in many articles which may be a great gain to our nation if some of the emigrants were to reach our workmen.
>
> Their religious and political sentiments need not be a hindrance to their getting employment since they don't understand enough of

1792: The Influx

the English language to disseminate either; when they do, those among us who are religious are well convinced of the superiority of the Protestant religion; those of us who are not religious in all probability will not give themselves the trouble to hear them. As to their politics, it is well known that most of the Emigrants are Aristocrats, therefore, we need not be under any concern on that account.
I am yours &c. B.[60]

Even at this transitory phase, the figure of 20–25 000 seems to be a much more realistic ceiling though even that may be high.[61] Certainly figures from official reports like the accounts from the Port Collectors do not come anywhere near this number. *The General Evening Post* quoted the figure of 6881 of whom three-quarters were clergy so a relatively huge margin of tolerance is required.[62]

This entry in the *Courrier de Londres* is typical of the sorts of sources we are forced to rely upon to support estimations:

If a few individuals have acquired debts, the gold of those who have not done so has none the less remained in this country. Suppose for example that 20,000 Frenchmen have come to England with 25 louis each (which is not an exaggerated figure) that means, that they have brought with them some £500,000. If anyone doubts this, it can be verified by a walk in the main streets of any large town where baskets of louis can be seen on display in the boutiques.[63]

This letter was written to refute the criticism that the French were amassing debts in the capital. Émigré memoirs provide similar clues:

Quand nous arrivâmes à Londres, au mois de novembre 1794, nous y trouvâmes de nombreux compatriotes, on y comptait déjà 15.000 émigrés; un an plus tard le nombre de bannis se montait à plus de 25.000; dans cette noble multitude, il y avait beaucoup de prêtres bretons qui s'étaient exilés plutôt que de prêter serment contraire à leur conscience.[64]

When we arrived in London in November 1794, we found numerous compatriots, there were already around 15 000; a year later the number of émigrés rose to more than 25 000; in this noble multitude there were many Breton priests who chose exile rather than swear an oath which was against their conscience.

In late November Lord Henry Spencer wrote to Lord Auckland:

> A calculation has been made here, I believe by order of the Government, of the French of all descriptions in and about London, and they are found to amount to fifteen thousand. I suppose we shall have some thousands more in a day or two.[65]

Judgement plays a critical role in evaluating the likelihood of accuracy in any given account; Vicomte Walsh was one of those who was prone to exaggeration.

One of the most accurate numeric sources is the diary of John Douglass, Vicar Apostolic of the London District throughout the emigration.[66] As the chief representative of the Catholic Church in London, Bishop John Douglass had an immediate interest in the Catholic émigrés, both priests and laypersons. He had the politically difficult task of reconciling the Catholic community in Britain with the foreign newcomers whose habits and practices were far removed from their own.[67] He was also responsible for codes of behaviour and for the supervision of the French Catholic clergy in London. In September 1792, John Douglass was already a very busy man.[68] Yet with characteristic energy he involved himself in the issues concerning the French clergy and became a key person working closely with the Bishop of Saint Pol de Léon on all matters related to the spiritual and temporal well-being of his new flock. Douglass, like so many of his fellow Catholic priests in Britain, had been educated in France so he communicated easily with the émigrés in their own language. At the height of the emigration English Catholics were often taken aback to find themselves addressed in French in his waiting room. He was well-informed on all matters relating to the French clergy and, from its inception, received regular progress reports from the relief committee. He was also admired and respected by the priests themselves; the abbé Barruel remembering him as

> a prelate distinguished by his piety, his moderation and prudence, residing in London received them (the French clergy) with goodness, he advised them with friendship and edified them by his virtues.[69]

One particular entry in his diary dates from 11 March 1797. It contains a résumé of the number of émigrés in Britain. This entry is particularly important because it is relatively unlikely to be inaccurate.

It does however give a much reduced number from the figures closer to 20 000 which are commonly cited in correspondence dating from 1792–94.

French clergy receiving British Goverment relief	5 000
Lay émigrés including women and children receiving relief	2 950
French clergy not receiving relief	500
Lay émigrés not receiving relief	3 000
Lay émigrés in Jersey	700
Total	**12 150**

Even more important is a second document dated 21 March 1797 which puts the number at 11 940 and contains a more detailed breakdown of its composition.[70] These figures show the nearest that the sources come to reaching consensus.

The major obstacle in estimating the number of émigrés at any given time lies in ascertaining the number who were not enrolled on the relief lists and for whom there are only passing references. Without the passports which they were all obliged to hold there is no reliable record of this other group of independent émigrés albeit that there are a variety of sources like the baptismal records of the French Catholic chapels in London of people who do not appear on the relief lists. From the above note in Bishop Douglass's diary, it can be seen that the important distinctions were between ecclesiastic and lay émigrés and those who were and those who were not receiving relief.

The history of the organisation of the relief for the French émigrés can be broken into two distinct periods. The first involves the months from September 1792 when the charitable committees were formed, until December 1793 when the British government came into the picture. The second is the period from 1794 to 1802 when the émigrés depended on the British government for their subsistance. There is a third period because the emigration did not finish until Louis XVIII returned to France in 1814 but this involved only a group of a few thousand individuals whose names appear on a police list held in the archives of the Ministry of Foreign Affairs, dated 1 September 1807.[71] By contrast with the 12 500 or so émigrés who had resided in Britain annually from 1792 to 1802 this number was comparatively insignificant.

The most important point about the monies collected for the relief of the French clergy and laity in the first period (i.e. September

1792–December 1793) is that the true figure can never be known because the relief in kind of which there were countless and generous examples cannot be quantified in monetary terms. Charles Butler estimated that the donations which never came before the public eye were equal to the larger of the two official subscriptions, which produced approximately £26 000.[72] Through the early months of the Emigration, the British public showed a humanity and a compassion for the émigrés which surpassed anything that could have been inspired solely by the efforts of the various committees.

The committees that were set up when the relief operation first began formed the basis for the Wilmot Committee which later coordinated all monies from the British government destined for the refugees. Initially, three committees were set up. The first two of these, designed to help the clergy, were the Wilmot Committee and the Mansion House Committee convened by the Lord Mayor of London. By the end of October 1792, these two committees had amalgamated to avoid confusion and eliminate costs. The third committee was designed to assist the French laity.

The Wilmot Committee was created in Bloomsbury on 20 September 1792. The founder and key administrator was John Wilmot. His co-organiser in the French community was the Bishop of Saint Pol de Léon. The need for a general subscription was recognised and it was in this regard that Burke wrote the pamphlet entitled *The Case of the Suffering French Clergy Refugees in the British Dominions*.[73] The opening of a subscription was announced in the *London Chronicle*, 13–15 September 1792, naming four banks where donations could be made, and the same entry announced the forthcoming meeting at the Free Masons' Tavern.

The meeting was a great success and by the date of the meeting, £1726-1s-0d had already been received in donations.[74] *The Public Advertiser* pronounced the turnout to be

> not numerous, but highly respectable, several very exalted characters being present. All party motives were disclaimed and the commendable and charitable wish to provide for a persecuted set of people, who have fled for refuge to a country ever distinguished for its benevolence and hospitality, alone prevailed.[75]

On 27 September 1792, the second of the two Committees held its inaugural meeting at the London Tavern. From the very outset it was envisaged that the two committees would work closely together.

1792: The Influx

On 5 October it was agreed that 'as the object of the two Subscriptions is the same it is expedient on accounts to consolidate the two Committees'.[76]

The membership of the Wilmot Committee represented the social and political elite of Britain. The list was headed by the Duke of Portland, the Marquis of Buckingham, Earl Fitzwilliam and the Earl of Radnor. There were 14 members of Parliament[77] and 12 Anglican ministers of whom two, Drs Cooke and Willes, were from Oxford University. Dr Richard Brocklesby and Sir George Baker were prominent physicians, the latter being president of the Royal College of Physicians and one of the King's doctors. From the City came the Lord Mayor Hopkins, Aldermen Combe and Skinner, Brook Watson, later Lord Mayor, Angerstein of Lloyd's and a number of bankers in Edward Forster, Samuel Bosanquet, Sir James Sanderson, Henry Thornton, Sir Richard Carr Glyn and Culling Smith. At least six members were lawyers: Sir William Scott the Advocate-General, Dr French Laurance, Judge of the Cinque Ports, Charles Butler, William Baker, Sir William Pepperell and John Wilmot.[78] The clout this group wielded was formidable. The émigré cause was in the most conservative and most influential hands of the British establishment. The group who championed the laity were similarly well qualified but not quite so well organised.

Sir George Thomas, MP for Arundel, called his meeting at the Star and Garter on 12 September. It was his intention to help women and children but he also mentioned 'several families, one of the first distinction and consequence in France, and who were now actually pawning the last articles of their attire in this country to procure subsistance'.[79] Unlike the Wilmot Committee, this lay committee possessed no ready-made distribution network and there was indecision on how sums would be allocated. This, allied to the fact that they proposed to help the *ci-devant* rich created some scepticism. Nevertheless, money started flowing into bank accounts and, much encouraged, Sir George called a second meeting on 26 September 1792 at the Crown and Anchor in the Strand. This time a committee was created, headed by Lord Sheffield. The lay committee included three MPs, several distinguished bankers and merchants as well as several members of the Wilmot Committee. At this meeting it was clearly stated that the relief was intended for old and infirm men, or women and children and for those clergymen who were not eligible for relief from the Wilmot Committee.[80]

In this way, from the beginning of October 1792, the distinction between lay and ecclesiastic émigrés was formalised by the organisation of the relief. This was no particular surprise but it did cause some confusion among the donors. The very similarity of the Committee titles confused those who were not attuned to the differences between ecclesiastic and lay émigrés. Donors rarely bothered to specify whether they destined their donations to ecclesiastic or lay émigrés and there was a settling-down period during which some donations went to the wrong committee. The records of the Wilmot Committee have been preserved and are now in series T.93 at the Public Records Office at Kew, although an important set of documents and minutes are held at the British Library.[81]

The sums given to émigrés varied initially according to particular circumstances but the Bishop developed an allowance which was adopted as the official relief payment. Outside the clergy, the only men eligible for relief were those under 16 or over 50, excepting the infirm and soldiers waiting to be called up. They received £1-11s-6d per month. Women and girls over 14 years of age received the same amount. Children less than 14 received £1-2s-0d per month. Other men were eligible for relief as long as they could provide a valid medical certificate and men under 50 who had dependent children or wives too sick to look after them were also included. There were also cases for extra payments. Old émigrés in poor health could receive 10 shillings and 6 pence more than the £1-11s-6d each month and émigrés in dire need could apply for a clothing allowance of £2-2s-0d.[82] These payments provided the famous 'shilling-a-day' which is refered to in many émigré memoirs.[83] There were some adjustments made as revisions in 1796–97 of the sums allocated led to a belt-tightening exercise imposed by the government but the allowance which was accorded only to those with no other form of income remained more or less the same throughout the relief period. Some émigrés were favoured due to their standing in the community and consequent obligations, for example bishops, high-ranking naval and military personnel, and magistrates for whom the Bishop of Saint Pol requested special treatment.

> Amongst the émigrés there are a few who by their age, the distinction of their services and the position that they hold in the social order deserve particular treatment and we are pursuaded that the British Government will be happy to make a distinction in the allocation of the aid which has been extended to all those who have taken refuge in Britain from the atrocious and bloody persecution. The British expenses are so great and the number of the unfortunate she

supports so considerable that we could only propose to except from the general category a very small number of individuals chosen from the most distinguished and least numerous class.[84]

Wilmot's committee, although it made an enormous charitable contribution to the welfare of the French émigrés, was unable to sustain the effort. Over £12 000 was collected in the first two months of its existence when public sympathy for the émigrés in London and in British society in general was at its highest. Through the winter months when Britain went to war the income dwindled away but recovered in the spring in response to continued appeals. At the end of 1793 total subscription donations stood at £26 050-13s-2d, but had increased only by only £2500 in the previous eight months.[85] The émigrés could not expect to dominate the list of charitable priorities for ever and in the year after their arrival in Britain there were other needy persons with equally legitimate claims to the benevolence of society. Fanny Burney remarked on the failure of the ladies' committee to secure nearly the amount of support it expected:

> The world is full of claims, and of claimants, for whatever has money for its object, that the benign purpose of these ladies was soon inoffensively thwarted from misapprehension, envy, or ill-will, that sought to excite in its disfavour the prejudices ever ready, of John Bull against foreigners, till his justice is enlightened by an appeal to his generosity.[86]

It was the waning of charitable donations which led to a national church collection on behalf of the French clergy. This method of raising money had not been used since the influx of Huguenot refugees in the mid-1680s. What was unique about this alternative strategy was the irony of Anglican parishes taking up a national collection on behalf of their Catholic brethren. Not only that, but the idea had come from the Anglican clergy themselves.[87] Burke wrote that religion was the foundaton of civilised society:

> The people of England will shew to the haughty potentates of the world, and to their talking sophisters, that a free, a generous, an informed nation, honours the high magistrates of its church; that it will not suffer the insolence of wealth and titles, or any other species of proud pretension, to look down upon what they look up to with reverence ....[88]

Never was this point more forcefully demonstrated than in the support that the Anglican church offered to the French refugees whom they perceived to be the tangible evidence of the evils of Revolution.

The Committee decided to approach Pitt about the possibility of extending this collection to include dissenting congregations. Pitt was quick to support the initiative, which would keep the émigrés from beating on the Treasury door for six months or more. When the Anglican bishops were approached, they stipulated that the King should sanction the collection, which he did in a letter dated 17 April 1793. The sum raised in this fashion was was £40 012-5*s*-11*d*[89] and this only represented the Anglican collections; other donations from dissenting congregations were entered directly into the subscription accounts.

Total charitable relief, including the national church collection, amounts to around £70 000. This is a very large amount of money for the time and it tells us several things about the émigrés and their connections in British society. Without the support that they received from Members of Parliament, from members of the peerage and from interested and influential men of commerce this figure would have certainly been much lower. Exiles, because of their background, understood the workings of pressure and patronage and they had far greater access to men of influence than most other disadvantaged groups in British society.[90] This made an enormous difference to their cause. It is highly possible that without this pressure the British government might not have felt obliged to take on the financial responsibility for the émigrés when they did or indeed at all. Dundas alluded to the pressure being put upon the government in a note in September 1792; he wanted to keep things on an official footing by communicating with the Wilmot Committee rather than personally with the Bishop,

> for otherwise I perceive We shall very soon be implicated to take a more executive part in the business than We intend, ...[91]

4 Soho

Le quartier dans lequel M. de St Blancard avait pris un logement pour nous était assez triste et situé près de Golden Square, et je compris ce que les Français éprouvent en arrivant un dimanche à Londres. Le silence, le peu de mouvement surprend et l'on risque en y arrivant d'être saisi par une attaque de spleen qui se dissipe le lundi par un beau soleil à Hyde Park.[1]

The area in which M. de St Blancard had taken a lodging for us was quite sad and situated near Golden Square, and I understood what the French felt arriving in London on a Sunday. The silence, the stillness was surprising and one risked at first to be overtaken by an attack of spleen which evaporates on a Monday in the beautiful sunshine of Hyde Park.

Soho was a special part of London throughout the emigration. From the earliest point of their appearance in London, émigrés stayed in the hotels of Soho where French was either fluently spoken or readily understood. This area provided a meeting-point where émigrés exchanged information. It was home to the most important French bookshops and publishers in London and it had the added advantage of an established international merchant community.[2] The fact that Marat lived there in the years leading up to the Revolution is indicative of the wide variety of socioeconomic groups and political beliefs covering the spectrum from the wealthy to the wretched, from the staunch Whig to the radical dissident. Its geographic area for the purposes of this study are less exact than the present-day definition. Soho for the émigrés comes to have a metaphorical as well as a physical demarcation. The physical area includes the streets around Golden Square, Soho Square and the whole northern end of Oxford Street where it meets Tottenham Court Road.[3]

Soho was the first destination for most émigrés arriving in the British capital. Rich and poor émigrés alike descended upon Soho in search of contacts, accommodation, news of friends or relatives and they stayed there until they had arranged their next step. The hotels of Soho did particularly well out of their émigré clientèle as this advertisement in *Le Courrier de Londres* in August 1793 suggests:

AVIS AU PUBLIC (Public Announcement)
16 août 1793
HOTEL DE LA SABLONNIÈRE[4]
No 13 Leicester Square, à Londres,

The proprietor wishes to sincerely thank all the customers who have honoured his establishment with their favour and hopes to merit their custom all the more having considerably and agreeably enlarged his hotel, the alterations being of a most elegant and commodious standard.

Its apartments are vast and can accommodate the most numerous families. They are always well aired and consequently healthy. Cleanliness and taste are in constant evidence. There are several dining rooms, the Table d'Hôte, the Restaurant open from one o'clock until midnight where the waiters serve with the greatest attention and care. Prices are very reasonable and conform to all budgets.

Foreigners will find at his hotel all the luxuries and advantages of the situation of the Hotel which is in the centre of London, near the royal palace, the Italian Opera, several theatres and other public amusements. The Hotel offers a range of wines. Many languages are spoken (an uncommon advantage). There are horses, carriages of all description, fresh horses, stabling etc.

NB, the Café of the Hotel is most élégant.

This advertisement alone tells us a great deal about a hotel which was a favourite destination for newcomers to London. Throughout the emigration, it played host to numerous émigrés passing through or dining in the city. It evidently enjoyed great prosperity during this period when it was able to expand. This is also one of the little proofs of the fact that there was still a group of émigrés who enjoyed a good if not high standard of living. This hotel advertised regularly in the *Courrier* during the 1790s so it obviously considered the French community to be an ongoing source of clientèle.

When the Abbé Tardy wrote his guide to London he gave a full description of London eating-habits and customs and mentions two eating-establishments in Soho where the émigré French were particularly well catered for.[5] According to the abbé, a foreigner who did not have his own establishment in London had two choices: he could board with his host, in which case the meals would be included, or he could take his meals in a café or a tavern.

Here is how a middle-class table is usually presented. Meat from the boucherie, boiled or roasted, vegetables cooked in water, never fricasséed, seasoned on the plate with a white sauce or the juice from the meat, potatoes, sometimes a pudding, and cheese for dessert. On some days of the week the roast is cold. Fish is rarely served. This is what you can expect for half a guinea a week.[6]

He goes on to explain that, if this does not suit, the cafés serve, soups, veal stews, cutlets, grills, and fish. But he cautioned émigrés against incurring unnecessary expense.[7]

The Abbé was fond of 'porter'. He wrote that whichever eating option was preferred, the drink was not included. He recommended porter beer which he described as 'the most English drink' and commented that 'a wine d'Oporto seems necessary in the English climate'. Three shillings and six pence (if you returned the bottle) was the going rate in 1799.

In 1739, it was an 'an easy matter for a stranger to fancy himself in France' when he entered Soho.[8] This underlines the essentially French character of the area which was already a favourite address for well-to-do Huguenots, third-generation descendants of the French protestant emigration which took place in the 1680s.[9]

The Huguenots were not overly disposed to welcome their fellow-countrymen with open arms because it was the Catholics who had driven them into exile in 1685 when the Edict of Fontainebleau overturned the religious tolerance proclaimed by the Edict of Nantes. Nevertheless, there were generous individual examples of charity between the old and the new settlers in Soho, particularly in the early period when state aid was not available. It is a tribute to those Huguenots that their compassion for the discomfort and suffering of their fellow exiles took priority over longstanding religious antagonisms.

There were many French lodging-houses and many of the artisans, watchmakers, jewellers and goldsmiths who had businesses in the Soho Square and Soho Fields area were Huguenot craftsmen or their descendants. Golden Square was another very French address and by the mid-1790s many émigrés had swelled the existing French population.[10]

Soho was generally a lay émigré centre. Some priests found lodgings in this area but the expense drove most of them further afield. The Abbé Goudemetz in his letters recounts life in a small community in Poland Street. Seven priests shared a house there and their little *ménage* functioned efficiently. The brothers each had their designated domestic duties, they contributed three shillings each for rent and five shillings a week for food out of their individual allowances and they all took turns at cooking despite having no previous experience.[11] The results were tolerable and he decribes how once or twice a stew didn't work but even in those cases the pot was so full of herbs and spices that it was more of a herbal remedy than a stew. Even this group eventually found that it was cheaper and preferable to leave the fogs of London and to move out into the country.

Despite the fact that almost all those who initially settled in Soho relocated to a cheaper area or left London altogether, there was a constant flow of émigrés through Soho from 1789 until 1814. The diversity of social backgrounds evident in the French population was also a characteristic of its British counterpart. Throughout the eighteenth century Soho had been home to artists and writers, members of the aristocracy and immigrants. Reynolds lived at 47 Leicester Fields, William Hogarth had lived at 30 Leicester Square from 1733 until his death in 1764.[12] William Blake was born there and Fanny Burney spent her childhood in Poland Street.[13]

This great diversity of people, cultures and customs made the French feel more at home in Soho than anywhere else in London. This is reinforced by the statistics. Soho had the highest density of émigré settlement in London.[14] Eighteen per cent of lay émigré families for whom addresses are available lived in Soho and this does not include the 8 per cent for Tottenham Court Road or the 4 per cent for Bloomsbury and Fitzroy Square. Familiar Soho addresses, Old Compton Street, New Compton Street, Wardour Street, Queen Street, Greek Street, St Anne Street, Berwick Street, Denmark Street, Dean Street, and Princess Street figure in the relief lists.[15]

An important émigré in the Soho community was the artist Henry Pierre Danloux. He was a portrait-painter whose clientèle was exclusively drawn from the *ancien régime* elite and he himself was a royalist who had made a conscious decision to emigrate in January 1792 because he had no desire to work in a republican state.[16] He chose London in the hope that he might find ready work in Soho near the famous Reynolds, intending to compete by offering similar portraits at a less exorbitant prices to both the British and the French.

Danloux kept a journal in which he logged his daily list of appointments, sittings and general comments about life among the émigré elite to which he belonged by marriage. His studio, which he set up with meticulous care to appeal to his British clients, in fact became a meeting-place where the *demi-monde* of the emigration could congregate and chat.[17]

Through the closing months of 1792 the studio of Danloux witnessed constant émigré activity.[18] While Danloux did not make his fortune, he kept himself well entertained. On 15 September, he mentions the arrival in London of Talleyrand whose person was less newsworthy than his hairstyle (because he was wearing a pig-tail).[19] He also notes that his arrival followed suspiciously close behind that of Mme de Flahaut.[20] Other names like Peltier, Chateaubriand and Rivarol who stayed nearby at Sablonnières Hotel during his time in London (which was short because English women bored him) are logged and commented upon.

It is in the same context that he mentions Rivarol's dislike of English women that he makes the famous remark about the society of the émigrés, 'Que de nièces dans les bagages de l'Émigration!'[21] (How many nieces there are in the luggage of Emigration!) The emigration provided the opportunity for romantic as well as political escape from the etiquette-ridden confines of *ancien régime* society. The Marquis de Polignac, aged 78, married Mlle de Nédonchel, aged 20, in 1796.[22] This was not an isolated example; even Mme de Staël indulged in a few months of clandestine domestic bliss with Louis de Narbonne at Juniper Hall. The fact that Walpole would not see Mme de Staël because of the scandalous nature of her *ménage* with Narbonne or the Princesse d'Hénin because of her liaison with Lally Tollendal illustrates the rather hostile reaction of the British to the import of libertine values which were so fashionable in pre-revolutionary France.

Danloux reveals much about life in little asides. Talking about Mme de Pusigneux, the sister of Mme de la Suze, he adds:

> Rien en effet trahit chez elle la misère dont on remarque en général l'empreinte chez les émigrés.[23]

> Nothing suggests, in her particular case, the poverty which is generally noticeable among the émigrés.

This remark, made early in 1793, and others like it show just how common poverty was among the émigrés.[24] Danloux himself was not immune to the hardships of emigration. He managed to keep himself in work but constantly struggled with a shortage of cash because so few of his French clients were able to pay the fees they promised. In 1796, he travelled to Edinburgh while the comte d'Artois was resident at Holyrood Palace. He painted members of the royal family and members of the Scottish nobility like the Dalkeith family and returned to London in February 1797 with enough commissions to keep him in work for many months to come.[25]

Lesser artists too set themselves up in Soho as interior decorators and became much sought after. The French reputation for taste even reached the British royal family. Queen Charlotte commented to Fanny Burney that

> there are no people understand enjoyable accommodations more than French gentlemen, when they have the arranging of them themselves.[26]

Soho was also home to the well-known émigré bookshops. Dulau was situated at 107 Wardour Street, near Soho Square. It was opened by a former Benedictine monk who had managed to save the contents of his library and he used them to start a business.[27] It was, after an initial move to more comfortable premises, a large shop with plenty of room for the browsers and loiterers to read and chat. It soon became one of the favourite meeting-places for the émigrés, a centre of gossip and a source of news from France. Dulau edited speeches, pamphlets, poetry and travel diaries which were printed by Cox and Baylis, the only specialist French-language printers in London.[28] He published ecclesiastical works like Chateaubriand's *Essai historique, politique et moral sur les Révolutions anciennes et modernes*, and Abbé Carron's religious works.[29] Another French bookshop, De Boffe, located at 7 Gerrard Street, was also a favourite destination for the émigrés.

The prosperity of these two establishments, of which we know only skeletal details, was due to the intense amount of literary acitivity among the émigrés and the willingness of the British elite to consume what was being written.[30] Most book publications were pre-sold and the lists of subscribers reveal much about the target market. Lally Tallendal's *Mort de Strafford*, for example, had a very impressive list of subscribers, including many important political and literary figures in the French and British community.[31] Print-runs were in the vicinity of 1000 copies, though rarely more than that in a first edition.[32]

Reading and writing were probably the most popular pastimes for the literate members of émigré society. Many émigrés found writing a relaxing way to forget the pressures and hardships of exile. Those who destined their work for contemporary publication usually had political or pecuniary motives but the émigré memoirs alone offer proof of the number of émigrés who sought to justify their own actions to themselves or others through keeping a journal.

Almost all the important authors among the London émigrés lived in Soho. Chateaubriand and the comtesse de Flahaut both lived in the area, but Chateaubriand, after publishing the *Essai historique*, moved from his garret in Holborn to a more elegant address in Marylebone and then finally to Hampstead while the comtesse de Flahaut when she had published her novel *Adèle de Sénange* in 1794, departed for Germany.[33]

Chateaubriand is responsible for one of the most colourful images of émigré poverty. He claimed to have been reduced to sucking sheets to stave off hunger pangs.

> La faim me dévorait; j'étais brulant, le sommeil m'avait fui; je suçais des morceaux de linge que je trempais dans l'eau; je mâchais de l'herbe et du papier. Quand je passais devant des boutiques de boulangers, mon tourment était horrible. Par une rude soirée d'hiver, je restai deux heures planté devant une magasin de fruits secs et de viandes fumées, avalant des yeux tout ce que je voyais: j'aurais mangé, non seulement les comestibles mais leurs boîtes paniers et corbeilles.[34]

> I was eaten up with hunger, I was burning up, sleep had left me; I sucked pieces of linen dipped in water, I chewed on grass and paper. When I went past the baker's shop my torment was horrible. On a bitter winter's night, I stayed two hours in front of a window full of dried fruits and smoked meats swallowing with my eyes everything I saw. I would have eaten not only the foodstuffs but the boxes, baskets and packaging.

The image was undoubtedly embellished but his observations about the émigrés and their society are often very lucid. Chateaubriand brought out the divisions among the émigrés and was not afraid to air them in a critical way, yet he was as quick to make their excuses as he was to blame them.

> Les émigrés françois, comme toute chose en temps de Révolution, ont de violents détracteurs et de chauds partisans. Pour les uns ce sont des scélérats, le rebut et la honte de leur nation: pour les autres, des hommes vertueux et braves, la fleur et l'honneur du peuple françois.[35]

The French émigrés, like everything in time of Revolution, have violent opponents and staunch allies. For some they are scallywags, the rejects, the shame of their nation, for others they are virtuous and brave men, the flower and the honour of the French people.

Soho became home to émigrés from all backgrounds but it housed a significant proportion of the upper-bourgeoisie and the *ancien régime* elite: the comtesse de Flahaut, Rose Bertin (the dressmaker of Marie Antoinette), Marie Françoise, baronne de Joucelles,[36] Mme la marquise de Trayecourt,[37] and Françoise Petit de Maison.[38] It also recaptured for a time through its French inhabitants the fashionability it had enjoyed with the British gentry in the first half of the century.[39]

A further reason for the émigrés to feel at home in Soho was St Patrick's chapel in Sutton Street. It was the first public Catholic chapel to be built in London or in England which was not attached to an Embassy. This chapel was consecrated by Bishop John Douglass on 29 September 1792.[40] It gave the Catholics in Soho a place of worship and created a gathering-point for the French community. As the name suggests, it also served the large and very poor Irish community based there. Rev. Arthur O'Leary, the founder of the the chapel, was a Franciscan friar, who came to London in 1789 and served as a chaplain to the Spanish Embassy. He described the terrible spectacle of poverty of his countrymen in Soho and its immediate neighbourhood.[41]

In 1795, the consecration of the Chapel of La Sainte Croix at 10 Dudley Court, Soho, gave the French émigré community a religious focal point of its very own.[42] It was directed by the émigré priest Abbé Floch and the fact that this chapel was closed in 1802 when the great majority of émigrés returned to France is indicative of its important role during the Emigration.[43] This was one of the first chapels opened for the émigrés and it was understood that they would use their places of worship discreetly in order not to draw attention to their religion.[44]

Throughout 1793, the British government became progressively more involved with the relief of the émigrés. Although not directly financially responsible until December, members of parliament were instrumental in obtaining permission for the settlement of the French priests outside London at the King's House at Winchester.[45] The government also provided fares and assistance payments for those émigrés who were prepared to take passage to America.[46] The willingness on the part of the government to help was partly an attempt to bolster private relief initiatives in the hope of avoiding any more direct involvement.

No. 10 Queen Street was without doubt the best known émigré address in London. It was also a place where émigrés could count on a little sympathy and friendship from people who understood what they were going through. Mrs Dorothy Silburn, landlady of the Bishop of Saint Pol de Léon, was the widow of a cooper and although she had no children she looked after and educated the four children of her husband's brother, two sons and two daughters. Very little is known about her background or upbringing except that she dedicated her life to the service of her church and her community and became 'mother' to countless émigré priests, tending to their needs, listening to their troubles and, to the best of her abilities, finding solutions with limited resources.[47]

Bloomsbury was a well-chosen point situated at a crossroads between Soho and St Pancras where many of the poorer émigrés lived. It was also close to the Middlesex Hospital where the émigrés were allocated two disused wings. This was another reason which added to the importance of Soho for the émigrés. The arrangements made with the Middlesex Hospital to care for the more serious cases of illness among the émigrés provide yet another example of the goodwill and the willingness to cooperate which existed between the British and the French. In April 1793, the Wilmot Committee learned probably through Dr Brocklesby, a member of the governing body of the Hospital, that a ward was to be closed. All efforts were made to secure it for the use of the French émigrés because it was so ideally placed for the French community with the Bishop close by to supervise.[48] By the end of the May, the Committee had secured the use of two wards rather than one and the first was ready for use. As in the case of the government, the working behind the scenes of influential patrons like Lord and Lady Sheffield are apparent in the smoothness with which these negotiations were concluded.

As charge nurse the Committee appointed Soeur Masson, a sister of charity from the diocese of Boulogne whose excellent English and nursing skills made her an obvious candidate. She ran the hospital operation with military precision and her requests to the Board of the Hospital for minor changes to the decor or the dietary regime were rarely refused.[49] When she retired in 1795 (and died in 1798) her role was taken over by the Abbé Blandin who worked equally tirelessly to ensure the comfort of the 24 patients in his charge. Admission was by medical examination by the doctor on duty (although smallpox cases were not admitted) and the comfort of the patients can only be gauged by the reluctance that many of them showed when faced with leaving.

One small proof of the generosity of the Governors of the hospital was their willingness to allow Catholic services to take place in the émigré wards. Indeed, this was arranged by the Anglican chaplain in the hospital who took it upon himself to furnish all the material requirements of a small altar in an appropriate part of the ward.[50] Wine, wafers and candles subsequently appeared in the accounts of Soeur Masson to the Committee.[51] The Middlesex Hospital received émigré patients from 1793 until 1814 and the success of this project can only be attributed to willingness on the part of the French and the British to make it work. Without doubt, the émigré patients whose condition was severe enough to obtain a place in the hospital were the lucky ones.

The Wilmot Committee was reliant from the first on the generosity of pharmacists and doctors in the London area and many were willing to provide their services and medicines free of charge, like this surgeon in Charing Cross.[52]

> Sensible that many of the unfortunate French refugee clergy may occasionally be in want of surgical assistance and being unacquainted with what charitable aids on those occasions they are now supplied with, I will request the favour of your presenting my respects to the Committee informing them of my readiness to attend as a surgeon any of the poor suffering clergy residing West of Temple Bar.[...] I beg it may be understood that together with my attendance (and advice) such medicines as their respective cases in surgery may require, I should also most undoubtedly have them supplied with free of every expense.

The Committee posted addresses of places where émigrés could seek help.[53] A Dr Phipps, an eye specialist, treated the émigrés free of charge until 1802 when he was given a token appreciation of £20 by the Committee.[54] In a letter to the Committee a Dr Saumerez wrote of his inability to cope with the number of émigré patients presenting themselves at his surgery.[55] Sir Henry Walford, King George III's personal doctor, likewise attended to members of the aristocracy like Louise de Polastron, who died of consumption in 1804.

A breakdown of émigré illnesses listed in the Committee records reveals the overwhelming preponderance (48 per cent) of work and stress-related conditions. Medical consultations which were required at the time of the revision of the relief lists in 1796 provide the résumé in Table 4.1 of 85 cases which clearly illustrates this.[56]

Table 4.1 Illnesses among émigrés, 1796

Illness	Number of people	
Weakness/severe weakness (grande faiblesse)	17	
Sick/poor health	16	48%
Feeble sight	8	
Stomach conditions	8	
War wounded	8	
Rheumatism	6	
Scurvy	4	
Lame	4	
Hernia	3	
Cancer	2	
Bladder infections	2	
Fever	1	
Spitting blood	1	
Lung sickness	1	
Gout	1	
Epilepsy	1	
Fracture of the Fibula	1	
Venereal disease	1	
	85	

When the British government agreed to take on the cost of relief to the French émigrés in London in December 1793 it did so on the condition that all monies would be channelled through the Wilmot Committee which had previously assisted only the French clergy. This was done for the purpose of administrative convenience and accountability but also because it took away the need to set up any other form of distribution network. Only much later was Dorothy Silburn reimbursed for the cost of housing the relief operation and equipping an office and a waiting-room for the use of the Bishop.[57]

The payments voted in Parliament were made from the Treasury to the Wilmot Committee (also known as the English Committee) and from there they were paid into a bank account for distribution by the Bishop. The Bishop was not working alone. By this stage, he had some very loyal helpers alongside him and in order to manage payments to the French laity a committee of senior members of the French community was set up to consider the cases of applicants for relief. The

Bishop then delegated the distribution of relief for the French lay community to the French Committee, as it was known, which was based at Nassau Street in Soho, while the French clergy continued to collect their relief from Queen Street. There was another wing to the relief operation and this involved relief payments for émigrés in Jersey which also passed through the hands of the Wilmot Committee and the Bishop but were sent on to Jersey for distribution. In 1796 a significant proportion of the Jersey émigrés were repatriated to the British mainland.[58]

This organisation, while it seems very tidy, was thrown by the sheer numbers of émigrés turning to the Committees for support from 1794 onward. This was particularly noticeable in the case of the non-ecclesiastical refugee population which increased dramatically in 1794. The original grants were set at £7830 per month for the support of 4008 French clergy and at £560 for 375 laypersons.[59] These figures, which in the case of the laity had been set at a very conservative figure precisely in order not to create alarm, quickly became inadequate. To make matters worse, the Committee had not submitted requests to cover any of the extraordinary funding which, with winter at its peak, was also very necessary. By February the number of laypersons had reached 450 and it was estimated that £800 minimum was necessary simply to ensure their survival.[60] On 27 February 1794 Pitt agreed to have the sum increased to £1000 per month but he let it be known that this was seen as a temporary arrangement and that there would be absolutely no more.[61]

It took the personal intercession of the Marchioness of Buckingham on behalf of 400 persons who were without food or heat in the English winter to obtain action from the government.[62] Chateaubriand was not alone shivering and hungry,: there were many whose clothing had worn out, whose shoes had no soles and who had no money for food, let alone coals to make a fire.

The £1000 was increased to £1500 in July 1794 and by the end of the month there were 810 laypersons on the relief list.[63] These included 'several families who had just arrived from Holland [...] in the greatest distress who cannot possibly be relieved by the Committee without additional assistance'.[64] The consequences of the uprisings in St Domingue and Guadeloupe were also being felt in London as émigrés were cut off from their source of income and banks refused credit due to the uncertainties of the political situation.[65] Payments to émigrés in the last six months of 1794 tell their own story.[66]

The haggling between the members of the Wilmot Committee and the government on behalf of the French laity went on. The sum was raised to £3000[67] but by November the Bishop was asking for £3750 for 2295 persons who were on the limits of survival.[68] This increase was granted on the one condition that the list was to be critically reviewed in order to ensure that only those émigrés who had absolutely no other means of income were receiving money. On 17 December 1795 a letter which had been sent from the Bishop to Pitt was read to the Committee.

> Vous êtes instruits depuis plusieurs mois de l'État déplorable d'un grand nombre d'Émigrés Laics et Ecclesiastiques inscrit sur la liste des Secours auxquels l'insuffisance des fonds du Gouvernement destiné à cet objet ne permet de rien accorder et qui en conséquent se trouvent reduits à la plus affreuse misère.[69]

> You have been informed for several months of the distressed state of a great number of lay and ecclesiastic émigrés enrolled on the Relief List. The insufficiency of government funds allocated to this purpose prevents any assistance being offered and they consequently find themselves in the most complete want.

In the same letter the mental strain and the sadness that the Bishop was daily forced to bear are clear.

> Il faut cependant que j'en porte tout le poids. Je sais sacrifier mon temps, tous les agréments de la vie, ma santé même à mes compatriotes malheureux, mais je ne sais pas endurcir mon coeur contre le spectacle toujours renaissant de leur affreuse misère et quand je ne puis leur répondre que par une compassion stérile jugez combien cruel est mon sort.[70]

> In the meantime I carry an enormous burden. I very gladly sacrifice my time, my leisure, even my health to my unfortunate countrymen, but I do not know how to harden my heart before the constant spectacle of their dreadful misery and when I can only respond to them with a sterile compassion, judge how cruel is my fate.

On 22 January 1795 the government informed the Committees that both the ecclesiastic and lay émigré lists were to be closed and that the Committee was to cooperate with the government in order to reduce expenditure.[71] This was the situation in March 1796 when a general re-enrolment on the list of émigrés was called for.

5 Marylebone, Richmond, Hampstead – the High Life

In contrast to Soho, the old parish of St Mary-le-Bone housed the elite of emigration.[1] The early years, 1789–94, were characterised by conspicuous consumption; the latter ones, 1795–1802, by an elegant sufficiency. But throughout the period, the lifestyle of the émigrés who lived in these areas provided a stark contrast with the inhabitants of Soho, Somerstown and St George's Fields. The politics were exclusively royalist or ultra-royalist and this was reinforced by the arrival in London of the comte d'Artois and the duc de Berry in 1799 and the Prince de Condé in 1802.

A contemporary (1792) description highlights the openness of the area:

> The parish lies in the hundred of Ossulston, and is bounded by St. Giles's and St. Pancras on the east, by Hampstead on the north, Paddington on the west, and on the fourth by St. Anne-Soho, St James's, and St. George-Hanover Square. It is eight miles and one fourth in circumference, and it is computed that it contains about 2500 acres of land, of which one third is occupied by buildings, the remainder, extending northward to Primrose-hill, and west to Kilbourn turnpike, is almost wholly grass lands. A few acres are occupied by market gardeners.[2]

Not all newcomers to London were lucky enough to have an address in Bolton Row like the marquise de la Tour du Pin who, even though she and her husband had lost their fortune, were welcomed by her aunt Lady Jerningham in September 1797 after their escape from France in the weeks following the Fructidor coup. But there was nevertheless a significant proportion of émigrés who managed comfortably through the émigré years even though they had to make adjustments to their former lifestyle.

The royalist elite of the Emigration, many of whom lived in Marylebone, have borne the brunt of much criticism. History has recorded their pettiness, their intolerance and their lack of flexibility in the wake of what we know to be one of the greatest upheavals of all time. Historians in particular have pointed to the great disservice the émigrés did themselves in being unable to agree upon anything and, although they were all clear on wanting to restore a monarch, the form of government to be established in the new France was far from a matter for consensus. In seeking a target for their disappointments, they reproached each other.

> La société des émigrés, ainsi que toute réunion d'hommes jetés hors de leur voie, contenait bien des ferments de discorde. Le malheur, les jalousies, l'inaction, l'attente d'un avenir meilleur, souvent improbable, dont on désespérait tous les soirs, après l'avoir annoncé tous les matins, ajoutaient leur triste contingent au lot de misères commun à toute société humaine. Le dévouement était classé par des coteries d'intrigants; l'un avait émigré trop tard pour des gens aussi purs; l'autre avait continué à siéger à la Constituante à une époque où tel déclarait qu'il n'était plus possible de s'y montrer. On reprochait à ceux-ci d'avoir combattu encore l'étranger à Valmy et à Jemappes, avant de s'exiler, à ceux-là de rendre quelque justice aux d'Orléans.[3]

The society of émigrés, like any gathering of men thrown off their course, contained many seeds of dissent. Unhappiness, jealousy, inaction; the wait for a better future, somewhat improbable, despaired of every night after having been anticipated every morning, added a heavy contingent to the load of miseries common to all humankind. Devotion was classed by the whims of intriguers: this one had emigrated too late for such purists, that one had kept his seat in the Constituent Assembly at a time when so-and-so said it was no longer acceptable to be seen there. This one was accused of having fought the enemy at Valmy and at Jemappes before emigrating, that one was accused of crediting Orléans with a little justice.

The foundation for some of these accusations can be found in the émigrés' own mémoirs. Émigré society was more petty and vindictive than the Parisian society they had left behind because the strains of exile had increased social pressures. Madame de la Tour du Pin confirmed this.

Après trois jours de résidence à Londres, je constatai que je n'aurais aucun plaisir à y demeurer davantage. La société des émigrés, leurs caquets, leurs petites intrigues, leur médisances m'en avaient rendu le séjour odieux.[4]

After three days in London, I confess that I took no pleasure in staying there any longer. The society of the émigrés, their tales, their petty intrigues, their nastiness had made the stay quite odious.

She uses expressions like 'full of pretentions', and 'ferocious aristocrat', adjectives like 'haughty' and 'intolerant' to describe émigré women in London. The duchesse de Gontaut expressed a similar desire to leave London as soon as possible.[5] Some of the émigrés, women and men, for whatever reasons undoubtedly displayed these characteristics. Mallet du Pan regretted

cet indomptable esprit de discorde, de malignité et de despotisme qui dévore les réfugiés.[6]

this indomitable spirit of discord, of nastiness and despotism with which the refugees are eaten up.

Mme de Boigne remembered:

Le mélange d'anciennes prétentions et de récentes petitesses était dégoûtant.[7]

The mixture of old pretentions and recent nastinesses was disgusting.

Mme Danloux commented about the absurdity of émigrés entertaining lavishly and giving balls yet this too obviously took place with some frequency.

On parla ensuite du luxe des femmes émigrées qui étaient à ce bal; on dit que cela faisait un contraste frappant avec la simplicité des quelques Anglaises qui s'y trouvaient. Nous convîmnes tous qu'il était bien ridicule que les émigrés donassent des bals.[8]

We talked about the finery of the émigré women who were at the ball (given by Mme Dillon) and remarked that there was a striking difference between this and the simplicity of the few English women who were there. We all agreed that it was ridiculous for the émigrés to be giving balls.

Entertaining on this scale can be seen as a protection mechanism against the disintegration, of their fortunes, of their social expectations, of their rank and nobility; in short, of their world. It also had a political context because they were, or saw themselves as, the representatives of court society who had a duty to uphold the dignity of the French crown even though that crown was lying in the dust.

> Il se trouvait à Londres quelques personnes à qui des circonstances heureuses avaient conservé une partie de leur fortune, ou du moins des ressources momentanées. C'était la partie élégante de l'émigration; là on montait à cheval, on allait en cariole; là se trouvaient des jeunes femmes suivies, recherchées, comme elle l'eussent été à Paris, et des jeunes gens aussi occupés de plaire qu'ils avaient pu l'être quand les succès auprès des femmes étaient l'affaire la plus importante de la vie.[9]

In London, there were a few people who were lucky enough to have kept something of their wealth and had funds at their disposal. This was the elegant set where there were fine horses, carriages, young women who were sought after just as they had been in Paris and young men as obsessed with their own pleasures as they had been when the conquest of women had been the most important activity in life.

The pretensions of the sort described by the duchesse de Duras and the marquise de la Tour du Pin are difficult to explain. They had their origins in the rejection of the social changes which had been brought about by the Revolution and were compounded by an uncertain future which bred collective insecurity. William Windham, reflecting on this, wrote:

> We abuse the emigrants for their hostility to one another. What sort of charity shall I feel for the Dukes of Bedford, the Plumbers, the Cokes and other large lists that I could name, when we meet in exile and beggary in some town on the Continent?[10]

Marylebone had a density of émigré settlement of similar proportions to Soho. Twenty-nine per cent of émigrés who received relief registered themselves as having Marylebone addresses. Ten per cent of these lived around Manchester Square and 5 per cent near Portman Square.[11] With the Marylebone addresses went a mind-set that was invariably royalist if not ultra-royalist and a baggage of shared and self-perpetuating prejudices. This was the faubourg Saint Germain of emigration:

> La noblesse française émigrée habitait à Londres des quartiers très différents. Sur les bords de la Tamise, nous avions comme sur la Seine le faubourg Saint Germain et le Marais; le faubourg Saint Germain d'outre-mer, c'était West End, Manchester Square, Portman Square, Baker-street, Portman-street, Dorset-street, Spring-street et King-street.[12]

> In London, the French émigré nobility lived in very different areas. On the banks of the Thames we had, as on the banks of the Seine, the faubourg Saint Germain and the Marais, the overseas faubourg Saint Germain: it was the West End, Manchester Square, Portman Square, Baker Street, Dorset Street, Spring Street and King Street.

Like Soho, Marylebone had been an area of Huguenot settlement but, at the time of the Huguenot emigration, it had been a village on the edge of London and it had been chosen because it was relatively close to Soho, separated only by Oxford Street. Several Huguenot families were involved in flower-cultivation to the north-east of the High Street and the area became known as the Jardins Français. There was a Huguenot church in Hogg Lane and this attracted other Huguenot refugees to the area.[13]

Marylebone became known as Normandy to Londoners after the name of the tavern in the High Street, The Rose of Normandy, so called because many of the locals originally came from there. By 1792, Marylebone had lost the bohemian autonomy which characterised it throughout the greater part of the eighteenth century and had been subsumed by the city. The creation of the squares, a characteristic of Georgian architecture, was an important detail for the émigrés, as two squares, Portman and Manchester, were home to the émigré French aristocrats, and it was in King Street, just off Portman Square, that they built the French Chapel Royal.

The Chapel of the Annunciation was also known as the Chapelle Royale de France or the French Chapel Royal because, shortly after its consecration in March 1799, the comte d'Artois took up residence nearby in Baker Street. This chapel was special because the French community provided the money and most of the labour for the building work. A London resident remembered:

he used to stroll through the Mews to watch French priests at work, digging the foundations, carrying the bricks, sawing the wood – a curious sight were their shovel hats and their black and white bands – all chatting gaily in their native tongue.[14]

And it is mentioned in many of the émigré memoirs:

> Dans une ruelle aboutissant à cette dernière rue, des nobles ouvriers avaient élevé et bâti de leurs mains un temple au Dieu qui soutient les exilés; la chapelle de King Street existe encore aujourd'hui et le prince de Polignac, avec grande convenance, en avait fait la chapelle de l'ambassade de Sa Majesté très chrétienne. Après le bannissement les Français dont l'exil avait fini, et qui venaient revoir l'Angleterre, s'empressaient d'aller prier dans cette église de leurs mauvais jours.[15]

> In a little street which gave on to Portman Square, noble workers had built with their own hands a temple to the God who supported the émigrés. The Chapel in King Street still exists today and the Prince de Polignac very appropriately has made it the chapel of the Embassy of His Very Christian Majesty. After the emigration, the French exiles who came back to England hastened to go and pray in this church of their dark days.

Unfortunately this unimposing little chapel was demolished in 1978.[16] Unimposing it may have been, but it had been consecrated by one of the highest representatives of the French Catholic Church, the Archbishop of Aix, Jean-de-Dieu Raymond de Boisgelin, and welcomed no less than three Kings of France to worship or mourn within its walls. Charles Philippe, the comte d'Artois, later Charles X, worshipped there regularly. The list of those who attended the funeral of Louis XVIII's wife, known as the comtesse de Lille, on 26 September 1810, attests to its importance and to its historical significance now lost.[17]

> This remarkable little chapel, so full of history, yet tucked discreetly away in a backwater behind Portman Square (where the French Embassy was once situated) was finally closed in 1911. Its last ministering priest, Father Louis Tourzel, who died in 1910, was there thirty years and was made a Canon of Westminster Cathedral. The chapel itself survived for another couple of generations – playing

the strangest variety of roles as a furniture warehouse, a day nursery, a mortuary chapel, a Protestant prayer-room, a synagogue and a sound-recording studio.[18]

This would seem like more than sacrilege to the aristocratic Frenchwomen of impeccable pedigree who not only arranged the flowers and washed the altar cloths with their own fine hands but whose beautiful needlework adorned the pews.[19]

> Mesdames de Saisseval, de Vaudreuil, de Certaines, de Sommery et de Grandval et plusieurs autres grandes dames était chargées de décorer le sanctuaire et d'entretenir le linge sacré des autels.

> Mdes de Saisseval, de Vaudreuil, de Certaines, de Sommery and de Grandval and other great ladies were responsible for the decoration of the sanctuary and preparing the linen for the altar.

By 1799, the date of the opening of the Chapel of the Annunciation, the aristocratic quality of the inhabitants of Marylebone had undergone some very big changes. The lifestyle of the early days of emigration had disappeared almost completely. Émigrés who had come to the area hugely wealthy with rents and income from their colonial properties in Saint Domingo or elsewhere, and who had initially impressed London society with their sumptuous taste and lavish entertaining, had since been humbled by the events of the war and the disappearance of their fortunes. Many émigrés were reduced to some kind of commerce in order to supplement their income and aristocratic women in particular found themselves very well equipped to turn their accomplishments into profitable endeavours.

One émigré woman who left copious and highly emotive memoirs was Mme de Ménerville, the wife of an officer in the Prince's army, who lived during her time in London at 30 Little Marylebone Street near Manchester Square.[20] She described how she and many women sold their work in a little shop which was set up at the instigation of the Marchioness of Buckingham in order to spare the émigré women the embarrassment of selling their work themselves. The Duchesse de Gontaut also mentions this shop and describes how grateful the émigré women were to be able to take their work and price it themselves 'evitant avec soin tout ce qui pouvait humilier leur délicatesse'[21] (carefully avoiding anything that might offend their delicacy).

The High Life

In fact, it was not very long before émigré society had adapted to the necessity of work and integrated it into the rhythm of their daily life. It is not surprising therefore that the sort of work the émigrés found to do reflected their aristocratic tastes and employed their existing skills. Fortuitously, plain white muslin embroidered dresses were the height of fashion and highly sought after. These were relatively easy to make and very profitable.[22] Embroidery was put to many uses, making fashion accessories and all manner of little trinkets which sold very well. Straw hats were the other important fashion accessory which the émigrés turned into a blossoming trade. The hats, which sold for 25 shillings apiece,[23] were a feature of the emigration and are probably the best-known product of émigré labours in London.

But there was more than just work involved. Very soon émigré life revolved around the morning spent in the *atelier* or workshop.

> On arrivait vers les onze heures du matin. Là nous faisions des chapeaux de paille, non tressée, comme la paille de Livourne, mais entière, blanche et brillante; des fils de laiton liaient ensemble regulièrement tous ces brins de paille, qui s'arrondissaient sur des formes de calotte, en s'aplatissant en passes sur des feuilles de carton. En travaillant sans trop de distraction, on pouvait faire son chapeau en trois jours.[24]

> We arrived about eleven o'clock in the morning. There we made the straw hats, not plaited like the ones from Livourne but using the raw straw whole, white, and brilliant; threads of wire held all the strands together which were rounded to form the crown then layered flat on heavy card. Working without too many distractions you could make a hat in three days.

Walsh goes on to describe how the young, because they generally spoke better English than their elders, were given the unenviable task of going and selling the hats to the hat shops in the city.[25] He remembers clearly the haughtiness of the shopkeepers which he calls their '*sot orgueil*' (silly pride) and it is obvious that for a well-born émigré, even or perhaps more so for a teenager, the experience of finding himself at the mercy of a common shopkeeper was one of the hardest things in the world. The clergy did not like selling their work much either and they persuaded the Wilmot Committee to do it for them.[26]

The *ateliers* of emigration were social institutions. They provided the émigrés with an outlet for pent up feelings, shared griefs and aspirations.

The company of others lightened the gloom and despair of personal circumstances and played an important role in helping the émigrés both to cope with the strains of prolonged exile and simply to pass the time.

> Après le dîner tous les pauvres exilés, occupés comme moi le matin, se rassemblaient, tantôt chez l'un, tantôt chez l'autre, suivant les quartiers qu'ils habitaient. Il y avait beaucoup de sociétés différentes d'après les anciennes relations, les liens de parenté, de province. Chacun était près de ses amis. La rue que j'habitais et les environs de Manchester Square réunissaient mes plus intimes relations. On avait adopté chacun un jour. Ma société était en général, jeune et aimable; les femmes faisaient de la musique. On jouait peu, on causait, on riait beaucoup; on faisait de la politique; on parlait du gouvernement à établir en France, des hommes à y employer. Des projets d'avenir, de paix, de bonheur, nous occupaient tous. La patrie était au fond de toutes les pensées de tous les discours de tous les coeurs.[27]

> After dinner, all the poor exiles who were occupied like me in the morning gathered at one or other's house according to the areas where they lived. There were many different social groups based on old friendships, family ties or provincial loyalties. Everyone was near their friends. The street where I lived and the area around Manchester Square housed all my dearest friends and relations. We had all booked a day. The members of our society were young and vivacious, the women were musical. We didn't gamble much, we chatted, we laughed a lot, we talked politics, we discussed what form of government France ought to have and which men should be involved. Projects for the future, for times of peace and happiness occupied us all. Our country was central to all thoughts, all discussions and all hearts.

This need for society and for companionship created a unity and a sense of common destiny which drew the little French community of Marylebone together. Mme de Ménerville, describing the dark winters of 1795, 1796 and 1797 in London, comments:

> Je n'ai jamais retrouvé une société aussi franchement unie (tous les interêts, toutes les opinions, tous les désirs étaient les mêmes) aussi distinguée par l'esprit, les talents, les bonnes manières, une conversation plus charmante ni des soirées qui valussent celles que nous

passions à Londres dans de pauvres salons, mal meublés, auprès d'un feu de charbon, éclairé par une petite lampe ou deux chandelles. Des jeunes et souvent très jolies femmes, vêtues d'une robe indienne, coiffées d'un méchant chapeau de paille, déployait une gaieté, une grâce, une aimabilité enviées des Anglais.[28]

I have never since come across a society so frankly united (all the interests, all the opinions, all the wishes were the same), as distinguished by intelligence, talents, good manners, a conversation more charming or evenings which were more memorable than those which we spent in London in humble salons poorly furnished, beside a coal fire, lit by a little lamp or two candles. Young and often very pretty women, wearing an indian cotton dress and a cheeky straw hat possessed a gaity, a grace, an aimiability that was envied by the English.

Some émigrés turned their hobbies into lucrative pastimes with more success than others. The Duc d'Aiguillon found work copying music for the director of the Opera because it had been something that he had loved as a child. Michael Kelly let him do it anonymously and he was paid one shilling per sheet, the same rate as any other copyist.[29]

The art of painting was a valuable asset. Many émigrés set themselves to painting miniatures, which were popular and sold particularly well. The duchesse de Gontaut and her husband both painted miniatures. She describes how she had taken lessons in Rotterdam, and when they ran out of money in London she painted brooches with intricate scenes.

M de Gontaut suivit mon exemple; mais les amours poétiques n'étaient pas son genre de peinture; il peignait des sujets burlesques qui furent fort recherchés et s'en amusait lui-même. Ma mère faisait de petits ouvrages en frivolité en tapisserie, et le temps passait vite.[30]

Monsieur de Gontaut followed my example but poetic love was not his genre. He painted burlesque subjects which were very sought after and amused him too. My mother tapestried pretty little objects and the time passed quickly.

This is not the only instance where the initiative was taken by a woman. It was the women who began the hat industry and the men were soon involved either in the production or in going to the market at Cornhill to buy the straw. Everyone had a job to do.

> maris, amants, poursuivants, tous sont occupés activement ... à courir dans Holborn pour y acheter la paille ... Le Chevalier de Puységur ... son gros paquet de paille sous le bras me dit avec un air consterné, 'J'arrive de Holborn, le diable emporte les femmes et les chapeaux de paille ...'.[31]

> husbands, lovers, followers, everyone had a job to do ... running off to Holborn to buy the straw. The Chevalier de Puységur ... his great bundle of straw under his arm, said to me with great vexation, 'I am just back from Holborn, the devil take women and straw hats!'

Both men and women taught music. In order to do this women were sometimes required to go to the home of their pupils 'la robe retroussée dans ses poches et un parapluie à la main'.[32] The image of a well-born émigré woman, in this case the comtessse de Boisgelin, 'her dress stuffed into her pockets' to keep it out of the mud 'and an umbrella in her hand' is tantalisingly comic.

Some émigrés managed to make a comfortable living this way. Monsieur Brillaud de Lonjac, 103 High Street, Marylebone inserted this advertisement into the *Courrier de Londres* in 1793:

> Resident in London for two years, and out of gratitude for all the encouragement he has received from the nobility of his country, Monsieur B. has the honour to offer his humble talents to all the respectable French families exiled in this city. He proposes to offer, three days a week, to a limited number of people, group lessons in singing, the English guitar and accompaniment.[33]

Music lessons and tuning pianos were a favourite way to make money but it was not common for émigrés to make their fortunes out of concert music. The Italians had a monopoly. Danloux mentions a Mlle Mérelle, a talented young harpist who had made the mistake of trying to make her living. She gave concerts which were sparsely attended, in freezing venues, and was thrown into the debtors' prison for a debt of 15 guineas. Luckily for her, somebody told the comte d'Artois, who paid her debts.[34] The comte de Marin, a talented violin player, was an exception; he had an established reputation before he came to London and managed to be successful. He gave charity concerts to raise money for émigrés who were not as fortunate as himself.[35]

One famous émigré who lived and worked in Marylebone even though he did not belong to the elite was Sebastien Érard. Like Danloux in Soho, Érard had emigrated to avoid the commercial impact of the Revolution on his business because he was dependent on the aristocracy to buy his musical instruments. In 1794, he patented the Érard Harp in London and went on to become a maker and supplier of fine harps and pianos to the aristocracy.[36] He returned to Paris in 1796 and with the exposure he had had to English piano-mechanisms he made the first grand piano or clavecin using the English system which he had refined and perfected. He returned to London in 1808 where he revolutionised the harp by designing the double-action harp, which by the addition of semi-tones allowed a greater musical range. This new harp was launched in London in 1811 and, in that first year, Érard sold instruments to the value of £25 000. Érard had businesses in London and Paris and politics impinged very little on the dazzling success of this talented craftsman. His London firm[37] was inherited by his nephew Pierre Érard and survived throughout the nineteenth century to be bought in this century by the Morley Brothers, and Érard harps are still among the most sought-after concert instruments. The records of the Érard business dating back to 1802 were recently auctioned at Sothebys.[38]

Émigrés were resourceful. Some even found quite novel ways of making their living. Jean Gabriel Peltier, a flamboyant émigré journalist, capitalised on the English fascination for the guillotine. He had a miniature of the guillotine made in walnut and, for the price of a crown for the front seats and a shilling for the rear, he advertised the gruesome spectacle: 'Today we guillotine a goose, tomorrow a duck.'[39] It seems that this macabre spectacle appealed, because several other émigrés followed his example and made quick profits.

Both Montlosier and Mallet du Pan lived in Marylebone. Montlosier, who arrived in 1794, had lodgings at the Edgware Road end of Marylebone Road, and Mallet, who did not arrive until 1798, lived initially in Woodstock Street, Cavendish Square. Although the politics of these men were out of tune with the beliefs of most of the royalist inhabitants of Marylebone it was, like Soho, a place where émigré news arrived promptly and politically right in the thick of things. Royalist spies and couriers were equally well represented. Charles-Alexandre de Calonne, Louis XVI's finance minister from 1783 to 1787, lived there after 1795.

The other common way for émigrés to make money was through theatre readings. Reading aloud was a common and popular form of entertainment practised throughout genteel society in France and Britain, so commercialising on a dramatic talent was an obvious way to rectify 'un embarras financier'.[40] The sorts of plays offered are indicative of the market for French theatre in British society. Classic French theatre, the plays of Corneille, Racine and Molière, were lightened by farces with names like *l'Anglois à Paris* or *Le Gentilhomme campagnard, l'Anglois à Bordeaux*.[41] These readings were advertised in the newspapers and audiences were signed up by advance subscription for several sessions. It has been suggested that English theatre was not to French taste and this, if true, may have boosted the success of some of these ventures.[42] Monsieur le Texier, a former *fermier general* (or Director of the Tax Farming operation which was so famous for its corruption in France before the Revolution) was one of a number who read Corneille and Racine to audiences in London.[43]

For the inhabitants of Marylebone privations were limited and work, to the extent that it was necessary, was integrated into an enjoyable social round. Mme de la Tour du Pin knew several émigré women who never appeared in society but instead worked for their living.[44] This was not the case for most Marylebone women: they went to their *ateliers* in the mornings and entertained each other in the afternoons and they managed to survive comfortably.

Moreover, although there is only disparate evidence of such activity it is plain that service industries sprang up as the émigré community grew.[45] Mme de Guery kept a famous ice-cream parlour in Oxford Street, and a M. d'Albignac made his fortune tossing the salads at fashionable parties. There are several versions of this story but at least one individual made such an entertainment of tossing the salad that he became sought after and very soon needed an assistant to organise and carry his condiments, different types of vinegars, caviar, truffles, anchovies, meat juices, yolks of eggs and so on, and he was soon able to afford a carriage.[46] Walsh lists a whole group of nobles by name who adopted trades: bookbinding, painting miniatures, publishing, tailoring, teaching (everything from Latin to fencing and draughts), selling wine, and even coal.[47] But as this list suggests, they were discerning in their choice of activity and generally did not not favour occupations which they considered demeaning.

Outside London a number of fashionable areas found favour with the émigrés. The village of Richmond, because it was a favourite destination for the British upper class, was the single most important centre of French settlement. Émigrés would have endorsed Mary Russel Mitford's description of

> that fairy land, which has so little to do with the work-a-day world, and seems made for a holiday spot for ladies and gentlemen – a sort of realization of Watteau's pictures! The Hill is grown rather too leafy – too much like Glover's pictures – too green; it wants crags, as Canova says; and really looked better when I saw it last in the winter. But the water and the banks are beyond all praise.[48]

From the earliest days, when Mme de Boufflers moved in and set about recreating her Paris salon peopled with admirers and émigrés alike, Richmond became a very prestigious émigré address.[49]

> The village of Richmond is distinguished for its beautiful situation upon the banks of the Thames. It lies in the hundred of Kingston, at the distance of about eight miles from Hyde-park-corner. The parish is bounded by Mortlake, Kew and Petersham. The land which is not inclosed either in the park or the royal gardens is principally arable; the predominant soil is sand, but in some parts of the parish there is clay and gravel.[50]

Horace Walpole described it in 1791 as 'une véritable petty France'.[51] Madame de Cambis wrote in September 1792:

> Nous avons icy la Princesse de Tarente dame du palais de la reine, qui a été huit jours en prison à l'Abbaye, qui a été jugée par cette infernale tribunal du peuple, et qui a été sauvée par miracle. La Duchesse de Maillé autre dame du palais, fille du Duc de Fitz-James et de ma belle soeur est aussi avec nous, elle était, le 1er août, avec la reine, vous jugez comme nos conversations sont intéressantes, nous nous rassemblons tous les faits et nos récits et nos questions ne finissent point, nous nous séparons le coeur serré et cependant nous recommençons le lendemain.[52]

> We have here the princesse de Tarente, lady-in-waiting to the Queen who was eight days in the Abbaye prison, who was judged by the infamous people's tribunal and who was saved by miracle. The duchesse de Maille, daughter of the duc of Fitz-James and of my sister in law, another lady-in-waiting, is also with us. On 1 August she was with the Queen. I leave you to judge how interesting our

conversations are; we assemble the facts and our discussions and our questions are endless. We part with heavy hearts and yet the next day we start all over again.

With the exception of Lally Tolendal, whose constitutional leanings and lodgers were tolerated by the royalists because of his impeccable social credentials and his friendship with Mme d'Henin, the French inhabitants of Richmond were exclusively royalist.[53] The Hill and the Green were favourite addresses but many émigrés were drawn to Richmond simply because of its peace and its prettiness. Women on their own especially found this part of the countryside less threatening than the city of London. Many of these women lived quietly, embroidering dresses to eke out their modest incomes and patiently awaiting the moment when they could return to their homes.[54]

Because rents were so expensive, entertainments were necessarily simple. Émigrés did not have large homes so The Castle Inn provided an appropriate venue for the émigrés to return hospitality without incurring vast expense and great enjoyment was obviously had there:

> For Richmond news les voici. Snow had his concert at the Castle the night before last and when it was over a string of his harpsicord burst, for the poor man was arrested. Mr. and Mrs. Darrell on the Hill, are cousins to the Darrell's of the Vale. They live in the house that was built for the Duke of Ancaster. They are very good kind of people; they have an assemblée and a bread and butter ball once a week on a Friday. It begins soon after seven and ends soon after eleven, French and English old and young.[55]

Amélie de Biron, Mme de Boufflers' daughter-in-law, was guillotined in 1794 after returning to try to save family possessions. Her death affected the whole Richmond community because she played the harp exquisitely and had provided entertainment on many occasions. She was said to play like Orpheus: Horace Walpole, when asked, regretted that he had never had the pleasure of hearing Orpheus so he was not in a position to comment.[56] Her death was a great shock to the émigré women because they did not imagine that the revolutionary legislation was going to be applied to them.[57]

The princesse d'Henin, Mme de la Tour du Pin's aunt, whom she described as being dominating to a point of tyranny, was one of the key figures in Richmond.[58] Fanny Burney, who was not family, found her charming. She and M. de Lally made a special trip to visit the d'Arblay home during a stay at Juniper Hall.[59]

The particular characteristic of the Richmond French population was its stability, which was missing in other places of émigré settlement in Britain and elsewhere. Like Mme de Boufflers many émigrés settled for their entire stay in exile in and around Richmond.

One of the reasons that so much has been recorded of this community at Richmond is that it figured not only in the diaries of the émigrés themselves but it was also frequently mentioned in the correspondence of Horace Walpole, Edmund Burke and George Selwyn. Horace Walpole lived at Strawberry Hill and was among the group of British francophiles who frequently entertained the French. His own links with Parisian society and his lasting correspondence with Mme de Deffand drew him invariably to the vibrant company which was to be had whenever the subject of politics could be avoided.

> I sat yesterday morning a great while with the Fish's friend Mme de Roncherrolles. Entre nous, I like her much more than any of the whole set. She has neither *du brillant dans son esprit, ni une infinité de grace dans ses manières, je l'avoue, mais, elle est sans prétensions, et avec beaucoup de bon sens, même de la solidité, et elle est instruite suffisamment*. Mr. Walpole ne lui donne pas la préference. He must have something de l'esprit de l'Academie, &c., something of *a caractère marqué. Je ne cherche rien de tout cela je suis content du naturel et de trouver une personne raisonnable, honnête et de bonne conversation*. She is going for a week or more to Lady Spencer's at St Albans.[60]

The Duchess of Devonshire, who had a house at Chiswick, was loved by the French. She gave balls and entertained them and was particularly fond of the poetry of Jacques Delille.

> De toutes les notabilités anglaises, celle qui recherchait le plus la société française était la duchesse de Devonshire; les émigrés l'aimaient beaucoup et lui savaient gré des égards qu'elle temoignait aux Bourbons; elle n'avait rien dans ses manières de la froideur de son pays; elle comprenait les arts, en parlait avec entente et sans nulle pédanterie; elle savait beaucoup; elle était poëte et détestait les bas-bleus; en revenant d'Italie, elle passa par le mont Saint Bernard, et frappée des grands et magnifiques aspects des montagnes, elle avait redit en beaux vers ses 'impressions de

voyage', que l'abbé Delille traduisait aussitôt avec sa pureté et son élégance accoutumées.[61]

Of all the British aristocrats, the one who sought French society the most was the Duchess of Devonshire. The emigrés loved her and they were grateful for the attention and repect with which she treated the Bourbons. She had none of the customs or the haughtiness of her country, she understood the arts and spoke about them without any pretensions. She was well-educated, she was a poet and detested blue-stockings. Returning from Italy she went by way of Mount Saint Bernard and, struck by the grandeur and magnificence of the mountains, she drafted in verse her 'impressions of the journey' that Abbé Delille translated with his accustomed purity and elegance.

The Duchess was mentioned by many émigrés with warmth, gratitude and admiration. Mme de la Tour du Pin remembered;

> un grand déjeuner d'émigrés dans sa délicieuse campagne de Chiswick; sa soeur, lady Bessborough, un beau dîner à Roehampton, où elle passait l'été dans une maison ravissante. Nous fûmes priés à ces deux réunions, et j'y allai avec plaisir, quoique je fusse grosse de sept mois et demi.[62]

> a sumptuous dinner in her delicious country residence at Chiswick. Her sister Lady Bessborough, [hosted an equally] elegant dinner at Roehampton where she was passing the summer in a beautiful house. We were bid to both these gatherings and I went with pleasure despite the fact that I was seven-and-a-half months pregnant.

Many émigrés were buried in the Richmond cemetery also known as the Vineyard burial ground. Among them where Mallet du Pan, who died in the house of his friend Lally Tolendal on 10 May 1800, and Louisa Frances Gabriel d'Alsace Chimay, Vicomtesse de Cambis, who died on 27 January 1809.[63]

Closer to London but descidedly less fashionable, Chelsea offered seclusion from the city and summer entertainments. During the years of the Revolution Chelsea was changing rapidly. In 1792 much of it was still open countryside but it became increasingly built up as the century drew to a close and many émigrés lived there.[64] In 1798 Chateaubriand evoked the pleasure of dining at Chelsea with the poet Fontanes.

The High Life

Nous dînions souvent dans quelque taverne solitaire à Chelsea, sur la Tamise, en parlant de Milton et de Shakespeare: ils avaient vu ce que nous voyions; ils s'étaient assis, comme nous, au bord de ce fleuve, pour nous fleuve étranger, pour eux fleuve de la patrie. Nous rentrions de nuit à Londres, aux rayons défaillants des étoiles, submergés l'un après l'autre dans le brouillard de la ville. Nous regagnions notre demeure, guidés par d'incertaines lueurs qui nous traçaient à peine la route à travers la fumée de charbon rougissant autour de chaque réverbère: ainsi s'écoule la vie du poète.[65]

We often dined in a solitary tavern in Chelsea on the Thames and talked about Milton and Shakespeare. They had seen what we saw, they had sat as we did, on the banks of this river, for us a foreign river, for them a native one. We returned to London after dark by the fading rays of a few stars which were subsumed one by one by the fog of the city. We made our way home guided by dubious rays which barely lit the road through the reddish coal smoke hanging around each lamp post; such is the life of a poet.

It was obviously still countrified but the short distance separating it from the city conferred an autonomy and gave it a great appeal to visitors. The Ranelagh gardens were also closeby.[66] The French loved these gardens in the summer and the fact that entertainments were advertised in the French newspapers and the gardens themselves so meticulously described by the Abbé Tardy attest to their popularity.[67]

A more lasting contribution of the French in Chelsea was the important part played by the abbé Voyaux de Franous in establishing a Catholic parish and organising funds for the building of St Mary's Chelsea, which (although not the original church building) survives to this day.[68] Baptismal records for the parish date back to 1804 but the chapel was not consecrated until June 1812. The abbé stayed on in Britain and served the Catholics of Chelsea until 1840 despite several offers of handsome positions in the re-established French Church from the restored monarchs Louis XVIII and Charles X.

Hampstead was also much loved by the French. Within easy distance of Marylebone, it enjoyed patronage of the émigré elite but the community which grew up there lasted longer than the emigration, essentially due to an ecclesiastic, the Abbé Morel, who stayed on after 1814 as the local priest.

The village, which, from its beautiful situation, is one of the most noted in the neighbourhood of London, lies on the side of a hill, about four miles from St Giles's church. The fine views of the metropolis, and the distant country, which are to be seen from the heath, and from most parts of the hill on which the village is situated, are not the only beauties of the scene; the home landscape, consisting of broken ground, divided with inclosures, and well planted with elms and other trees, is extremely picturesque. Such attractions of situation, so near to the metropolis have always drawn together a great number of occasional visitors, for whose accommodation several places of public entertainment have been established.[69]

It was hardly surprising therefore that the émigrés were drawn to this pretty place and encouraged to spend what they expected to be a short time in such an agreeable setting. The duchesse de Saulx-Tavannes wrote:

Mon oncle avait loué pour nous une jolie maison à Hampstead, village situé à trois milles de Londres. De vastes prairies l'en séparaient alors et maintenant (1830) une seule rue semble l'y réunir. Plusieurs familles françaises s'y étaient déjà établies, mais on s'y voyait peu, il n'y avait pas de réunions, l'abattement était extrême. J'aurais préféré habiter Londres où je me serais trouvée avec des personnes de connaissance, cependant je me résignai.[70]

My uncle had rented a pretty house in Hampstead village which was about three miles from London. Vast expanses separated it then, and now (1830) a single street joins the two. Several French families were already established there but we saw little of each other. There were few parties and a very depressed atmosphere reigned in the French community. I would have preferred to live in London where I would have found people I knew but I resigned myself.

Other émigrés were among the visitors to Hampstead:

J'allais souvent me promener à Hamptel, village très près de Londres; j'y trouvais M Chaumont de la Galaisière, ancien intendant de Strasbourg, l'homme le plus aimable que j'aie connu, ses trois filles si distinguées, Mmes d'Escayrac, de Tourville et d'Autichamps, la bonne Mme de la Rivière, sa fille la comtesse de

Canillac. Je voyais souvent à Londres la duchesse d'Uzès, née Châtillon (la dernière de ce grand nom) qui m'avait comblée de bontés dans toutes les villes où nous nous étions rencontrées; Mmes de Chavagnac et Mme de Rosilly, leur soeur. Les évêques d'Uzès, de Montpellier et de Coustances, Mgr de Talaru avait pu à cause de la proximité de son diocèse faire passer quelques fonds en Angleterre. Il avait loué un appartement qui contenait un grand salon chauffé et ouvert toute la journée pour les prêtres de son diocèse qui avaient tous émigré; il en retenait tous les jours quatre à dîner, les uns après les autres.[71]

I often went to walk at Hampstead a village very near to London. I joined M. Chaumont de la Galaisière, a former Intendant of Strasbourg, one of the most charming men I ever knew, and his three lovely daughters, Madames d'Escayrac, de Tourville et d'Autichamps, the good-natured Mme de la Riviere and her daughter the Countess of Canillac. I saw a lot of the Duchess d'Uzès in London (the last of the great name) who was so very kind to me in all the towns where we had occasion to meet, of Mmes de Chavagnac, and Mme de Rosilly, their sister. The Bishops d'Uzès, de Montpellier and de Coustances, Monseigneur de Talaru who, because of the close proximity of his diocese, had been able to get funds out of France. He had taken a house with a large sitting room which was heated and open for the priests of his diocese who had all emigrated and each day he invited four in turn to dine at his table.

Saint Mary's, Church Row, Holly Place is the present-day survivor of a Catholic chapel opened as early as 1796 by the Abbé Morel.[72] Although the tomb of the Abbé Morel is still in the church the close connection between the church and the émigrés has long been forgotten. In the early 1800s, it was one of the most flourishing Catholic parishes in London and the French made up a significant proportion of its congregation. It seems likely that Mrs Francis Crewe, the organiser of the Ladies' Committee for Emigrant Relief, was instrumental in bringing Morel to London because he lived from 1792 to 1796 in Sussex where the Crewes had a country estate. The Abbé Morel, who died in 1852, devoted the rest of his life to the parish he had helped to establish.

The devoted pastor hid the once hunted priest. Yet something of the Frenchness seems to have rubbed off. There seems to be a whiff of garlic in Holly Place. I remember hearing someone call St Mary's 'The French Chapel'. The Abbé, I feel sure, would have liked that.[73]

There were other spots close to London which the émigrés loved. The 'delicious little village of Stock' was the destination for several families of émigrés whom Walsh describes as the 'least poor' of the emigration. In the summer of 1794 they decided

> quitter la fumée de Londres et d'aller respirer aux champs un air pur, un air qui leur rappelerait un, celui de la France....[74]
>
> to get out of the smog of London and take in the air of the countryside, a pure air, one which would remind them of that of France.

The following description of that holiday demonstrates the romanticised nostalgia, typical of émigré memoirs:

> Nous passâmes un délicieux été dans notre humble cottage et pour tous ce fut un véritable bienfait que l'air pur de la campagne; sur les prairies plus vertes que dans aucun autre pays; sur les champs si bien cultivés; sur les arbres d'une si luxuriante végétation, il manquait sans doute de ces lueurs chaudes et colorées de notre soleil de France; mais entre l'atmosphère des campagnes d'Angleterre et celle de Londres il y a une immense différence. On étouffe sous l'épais brouillard de la grande cité; et c'est chose curieuse, par un des rares beaux jours de ce climat, quand au-dessus des villages, des hameaux et des grandes résidences seigneuriales, vous apercevez un ciel à peu près bleu; c'est chose étrange, disons-nous, que de voir un lourd et noir nuage immobile et permanent sur un point de l'horizon; ce nuage vous indique l'emplacement de la moderne Tyr, et marque ainsi l'endroit d'où s'élève la fumée de ses cent mille cheminées. Cette sale respiration de l'immense ville fait toujours tache sur le beau ciel de ses environs.[75]

We spent a delightful summer in our humble cottage and the country air did us all good. We missed the warmth and the hot colours of our own French soil but between the countryside of England and the landscape of London there is an immense difference. No country has fields so green or better-cultivated or trees of a more luxurious vegetation. One stifles in the thick smog of the large city, but curiously, there are rare fine days in this climate, when above the villages, hamlets and great houses, you can see an almost blue sky. It is very strange, we said to ourselves, to see it from the other direction and to see this heavy black cloud permanently fixed at a point on the horizon which marks the docks and thus the place from which rises the smoke of a thousand chimneys. This dirty breath of the huge city always makes a stain on the beautiful sky around it.

The émigrés also savoured what Louis Philippe described as the 'peace of Twick' where the young future King of the French lived with his brothers between 1800 and 1808 and where he would return when the storms of the 1848 Revolutions drove him into exile a seond time.[76]

In 1808 the Chevalier de Broval, aide-de-camp and private secretary to Louis Philippe, sustained a correspondence in 1808 with Mrs Forbes, a neighbour during the season in Twickenham whose company, and particularly that of her daughter, the duc had enjoyed.[77] He describes their disappointment at the Forbes' decision to remain in Aberdeen rather than come to London:

> Je ne doute presque plus Madame que vous n'ayez renoncé à venir à Londres cet hiver. J'en suis sincèrement affligé. Que de fois je vous y ai désirées, et comme les bontés des deux voisines de Twickenham m'y auraient été sensibles! Daignez me dire, pour me consoler un peu, qu'elles se portent bien et qu'elles sont aussi heureuses qu'on peut l'être dans ce triste monde.[78]

> I no longer doubt, Madame that you have renounced your plans to come to London this winter. I am sincerely grieved. How many times I have wished you here and how often I have appreciated the generosity of my neighbours at Twickenham. Be so kind as to tell me, to console me a little, that they are well and as happy as one can be in this sad world.

This correspondence continued when the princes left London for Malta. The comte de Beaujolais, the duc's younger brother, had tuberculosis and his return to health required the warmth of the Mediterranean climate. They did not leave, however, without writing their regret at the loss of their friends, and the chevalier de Broval was particularly asked to express the regret of the duc himself.[79]

The duc de Montpensier died at the end of June 1808 aged only 29, and, with the death of the comte de Beaujolais in 1807 less than a year earlier, this left the young duc d'Orléans the only surviving member of the Orléans family. On the 18 July 1808, the Chevalier de Broval lamented, 'ô Twickenham! qu'en est devenu ce tems?' The correspondence between the comte de Broval and Mrs Forbes betrays the closeness of this relationship.

> Mde. de Vaudreuil que j'ai vue l'autre jour, croyait Miss Forbes mariée. Je l'ai persuadée du contraire. Mais s'il y a au monde quelqu'un digne d'elle, et d'acceptable à ses parens à quoi donc songe-t-il? Quelle triste et indolente créature ce doit-être malgré tout le mérite que je suppose qu'il a pour la mériter! Soyez sûre que je ne lui pardonnerai de la vie, à moins qu'il ne l'ait pas encore vue, et qu'il ne puisse la voir. [...] Si toute la pûreté, le mérite solide, les talens et de ce naturel qui fait la grâce, étaient sacrifiés à un mauvais mari (which God forbid!) je ne m'en consolerai jamais.[80]

> Madame de Vaudreuil whom I saw the other day believed Miss Forbes to be married. I persuaded her of the contrary. But if there is in the world somebody worthy of her and acceptable to her parents, who can it possibly be? What a sad and indolent creature must this be in spite of all the merit he must have to merit her. Rest assured that I would not forgive him in this life unless he has not yet seen it and may never do so. [...] If all the purity, the real merit, the talents and this natural ease which make up her grace were sacrificed to a bad husband (which God forbid) I would never console myself.

The duc d'Orléans was not the only French prince to find Englishwomen attractive. The liaison between the actress Amy Brown and the duc de Berry is well known.[81] She was a British actress whom the duc de Berry fell in love with in London and they had two daughters, Charlotte Marie (b. 1808) and Louise Marie (b. 1809), to whom the Duke was devoted and, if the memoirs can be believed, with whom he spent a great deal of time. The duc de Berry was assassinated leaving the Opera on 14 February 1820, and it was his dying wish that his two illegitimate British daughters be recognised as his children. They were naturalised on 10 June 1820 in accordance with this wish and their half-brother, *'l'enfant du miracle'* Henry, duc de Bordeaux was born in the same year.

Life for the émigrés became localised and personalised in a way which would have been unimaginable in Paris. It is no accident that refugee society in places like Richmond, Twickenham and Chiswick was dominated by women and shaped by their desire to live in a way which involved as little alteration as possible to their accustomed pleasures and tastes.[82] It was also recognised as a haven of elegance and intimacy by British women.

> Who can describe the almost inconceivable mélange of a true female gossip; where dress and music, dancing and preaching, pelisses and beaux, flowers and scandal all meet together, like the oil and vinegar of a salad?

Change for some like Madame de la Tour du Pin was stimulating and she was one who found her life in Richmond very dreary (*fort monotone*). She prided herself on finding her own solutions; during the voyage to America she had taken a pair of scissors and, against her husband's wishes, cut off her long hair. When she threw it into the sea she observed that with it went 'all the frivolous ideas that my beautiful blond curls had inspired'.[83]

Women, whether rich or poor, timid or adventurous, learned to be strong and practical in emigration – something that none of them found easy. It is hardly surprising that we find Fanny Burney reminding her hero in *The Wanderer*

> That where the occasion calls for female exertion, mental strength must combat bodily weakness; intellectual vigour must supply the inherent deficiencies of personal courage; and that those, only, are fitted for the vicissitudes of human fortune, who, whether female or male, learn to suffice to themselves.[84]

Country society provided a buffer against the unavoidable reality of Revolution and the changes it had wrought in all the émigrés' lives. Informality of the sort described at the soirées at the Castle was a happy compromise between the luxury of their former life and the austerity of their émigré existence. Even Mme de Boigne, usually so critical of London, was captivated by the British countryside.

> On a pu voir partout des rues qui ressemblent à celles de Londres, mais je ne crois pas qu'aucun pays puisse donner idée de la campagne en Angleterre. Je n'en connais point où elle soit autant en contraste avec la ville. On y voit un autre ciel, on y respire un autre air. Les arbres y ont un autre aspect, les plantes s'y montrent d'une

autre couleur. Enfin c'est une autre population, quoique le costume de l'habitant du Northumberland ou du Devonshire soit parfaitement semblable à celui du promeneur de Piccadilly.[85]

One can see streets which resemble those of London anywhere, but I do not believe that any country could give an idea of the English countryside. I do not know anywhere where there is such a contrast between the country and the town. You see another sky, you breathe a different air. The trees have a different aspect and the plants a different colour. In truth, it's a different population despite the fact that the dress of an inhabitant of Northumberland or Devonshire is perfectly similar to that of the stroller in Piccadilly.

6 St Pancras, Somerstown and Saint George's Fields – the Low Life

De l'autre côté de la Tamise, dans la partie de Southwark et Somerstown la physionomie de l'émigration était plus grave, plus austère et plus triste; là ce n'était plus le monde de cour, c'était le monde de province, moins léger et moins rieur.[1]

On the other side of the Thames in the areas of Southwark and Somerstown the physiognomy of the emigration was more serious, more austere and infinitely sadder. Over there, it was no longer the world of the court, it was the world of the provincial émigrés, much less light-hearted, and less gay.

Vicomte Walsh, though he was mistaken about the geography, was accurate in his judgement. As the socio-economic geography of émigré London evolved, these squalid areas were adopted by the poorest refugees. There were several groups who were particularly drawn to these localities: the widows of Quiberon, the war-wounded or infirm, the provincial nobility who were trying to make slim resources go even further, the elderly and the ecclesiastics.[2] There were also a significant number of French domestic servants who lived in these areas either with their former employers or independently of them.

These were the poorest émigrés of all and many of their stories were tragic. Insanitary accommodation, lack of heat in winter and long hours working under inadequate light all took their toll. Many émigré women died in childbirth or from the most simple complications caused by the cramped or unhygenic conditions in which they lived. Old people remained in bed because they could not dress or look after themselves unaided.

Every emigration has its casualties, some more tragic than others. But for the genuine refugees of Revolution, those with no other source of assistance and nothing left to sell, exile in London had no metaphysical element; it was a cold, harsh reality and only the lucky ones survived. Many members of the French clergy lived in these areas and the distinction between lay and ecclesiastic tended to fade into the background, overshadowed by the abject poverty and by the need to help each other.

St Pancras was one of the first areas to attract poor émigrés.[3] It was attractive because the French were given the use of an Anglican church there and although in theory church services had to be taken by an Anglican minister, when it came to burials or services of particular sentimental value the Anglicans withdrew and left the French to worship without interference. At a time when there were no other churches available to the French Catholics, this was an act of great charity and compassion.

The duchesse de Gontaut lived in St Pancras for a year, 1794–95. Their house:

> n'avait d'autre vue que le cimetière catholique, cette dernière demeure de nos pauvres compatriotes. La cloche lugubre, quelques pleurs répandus sur ces modestes tombes, serraient bien souvent le coeur.[4]

> had no other outlook than the Catholic cemetery, this last resting-place of our poor compatriots. The gloomy sound of the bell, a few tears scattered on these modest tombs, tore at your heart.

The St Pancras cemetery was an important churchyard for the émigrés. Many noble Frenchmen were laid to rest there, including the Bishop of Saint Pol de Léon in 1806.

> On this day was buried at St Pancras the Reverend John François de la Marche. High mass was sung for the repose of his soul at the French Chapel of the Holy Angels, London Street, Fitzroy Square by the Bishop of Vannes, *corpore presente*, on the foot or lower end of the coffin was placed a white mitre covered with black gauze and a gilt crossier covered as the mitre with black gauze, the pectoral cross and a violet Stole. After high mass and the funeral obsequies, the corpse was taken out to the Hearse and carried to St Pancras.[5]

The Bishop was in good company; among the other French émigrés to be buried at St Pancras were the Bishop of Coutances (1798), the Bishop of Tréguier (d. 1801), the Bishop of Noyon (d. 1804), the comte d'Hervilly (d. 1795), the comte de Montboissier (d. 1797), the marquis de Bouillé (d. 1800), Louis Charles Bigot de St Croix (d. 1803) and the comtesse de Polastron (d. 1804).[6] The émigrés were partly responsible for filling up the cemetery. In 1801 it was noted that there had been around 30 French priests buried there for some years past and, in 1802, there were 32 burials.[7] There are varying explanations for the preference of St Pancras church as a burial place for Catholics.[8] One of them is that there were links with a chapel dedicated to St Pancras in the south of France where masses were said for the souls interred at St Pancras in England.

> The church and the churchyard of Pancras have been long noted as the burial place of such Roman Catholics as die in London and its vicinity. Many persons of that persuasion have been interred at Paddington, but their numbers are small when compared with what are to be found at Pancras, where almost every headstone exhibits a cross, and the initials R. I. P. (Requiescat in pace), which initials, or others analogous to them, are always used by the Catholics upon their sepulchral monuments.[9]

As in the case of St Pancras, the Saint George's Fields French community grew up around a chapel. By 1800, there were eight Catholic chapels in London, among them 21 Prospect Place, Saint George's-in-the-Fields.[10] It was the chapel of Notre-Dame, opened on 1 June 1796.[11] This was an area of particular squalor in the late eighteenth century. Stagnant puddles and the absence of sewers were listed in a medical report in 1836 as some of the most immediate problems. Yet many émigrés lived south of the river in Saint George's Fields and Southwark.

> Dans ces quartiers 'infashionables', les logements étant beaucoup moins cher, les familles et les prêtres, qui n'avaient par jour que le schelling du gouvernement anglais pour vivre, s'y étaient portés en foule. Là beaucoup de nobles familles de la Bretagne, de l'Anjou, du Poitou, de la Saintonge, et du Midi, mosaïque vivante de vieux officiers et de vieux magistrats, de femmes de conseillers et de femmes de chevaliers de Saint Louis, de jeunes filles et de chatelaines douairières, de jeunes hommes et de vénérables prêtres, de femmes de chambre et d'anciens domestiques qui ne recevaient plus de gages mais qui servaient toujours avec le même zèle leur maîtres appauvris par la fidelité et par l'honneur.[12]

To these 'unfashionable' areas, lodgings being much less expensive, families and priests who had only the shilling a day from the British government flocked in droves. There were many noble families from Brittany, Anjou, Poitou, from the Saintonge and the Midi, it was a living mosaic of old officers, old magistrates, of parlementaires' wives, of wives of Chevaliers de Saint Louis, of young women, of dowagers, of young men and respectable priests, of ladies' maids, and old servants who were no longer paid but who served their impoverished masters with the same zeal out of loyalty and honour.

The inhabitants of Saint George's Fields were particularly hard-hit by the disastrous expedition to Quiberon Bay in July 1795 where, as well as those lost in the fighting, almost all those taken prisoner were executed in accordance with the Émigré laws.[13] The émigré regiments carried in British vessels made up the entire force of the expedition. British troops who were due to follow if the operation went well never entered the conflict. The French émigré regiments with names like the Loyal Emigrant and Royal-Louis were to link up with local resistance forces or *chouans* in an attempt to make a landing on French soil. The Quiberon peninsula provided a geographically suitable landing place and a technically defensible bridgehead to the mainland but a series of breakdowns in communications, and the difficulties of coordinating scattered forces spelt disaster and that disaster, for the French émigrés taken prisoner, was fatal.[14] Not the least of their difficulties was the inability of the royalist émigrés to work on an equal footing with their social inferiors, the *chouans*, who took their name from the owl-call they had once used as a signal.[15]

> Everything, except their hatred for the Republican forces, separated the Émigrés and the Chouans. There was too great a contradiction between the two. The first, dressed in their red uniforms, highly-trained and well-armed, could only despise this swarming, screaming, drunken rabble who recited rosaries, brandished pitchforks and let off their guns just for the fun of it.[16]

Quiberon was a psychological turning-point for the émigrés. When the émigré regiments left London they did so taking the hopes and prayers of the entire émigré community with them.

> Les femmes pleuraient et priaient, et la chapelle catholique n'avait jamais été si remplie de fidèles que depuis l'annonce du départ. Là devant les saints autels, les epouses et les mères les filles et les

soeurs des partants criaient au Seigneur: 'Dieu veillez sur ceux qui vont combattre pour la croix et les fleurs-de-lis; soyez leur guide et leur bouclier.'[17]

The women wept and prayed, and the Catholic chapel had never been so full of the faithful as since the announcement of departure. There, before the altars, mothers and wives, daughters and sisters of the departing supplicated their Lord, 'God speed those who fight for the cross and the fleur-de-lys, be their guide and their shield.'

For those émigré families who were struggling to survive in the poor areas of London, Quiberon was to be the end of their ordeal. The failure of this long-anticipated expedition to recapture France for the royalist Bourbon cause was devastating. And for the widows of Quiberon, many of whom lived in Saint George's Fields, it was a crushing blow.

Les malheurs effroyables de Quiberon avoient jeté un grand nombre de familles dans la plus dure position; les moyens de subsistance, dont quelques-uns s'étoient jusqu'alors soutenus, étoient épuisés, le secours qu'ils avoient reçu de leurs compagnons d'infortune, les ecclésiastiques françois, qui partageoient avec eux la foible somme qu'ils recevoient du gouvernement avoit cessé, en conséquence de l'arriéré des paiemens au moment où les nécessités de la vie avoient rehaussé de plus de moitié, et les conséquences de ce délai de paiement en des circonstances aussi dures auroient été terribles sans la bienveillance et l'intelligence de nos gens de métiers et des autres personnes avec qui la dureté de leur infortune avoit donné à ces malheureux étrangers des rapports de circonstance, et qui leur donnèrent crédit, souvent même partagèrent avec eux leurs propres ressources.[18]

The dreadful misfortunes of Quiberon had plunged a great number of families into the deepest distress. The means of subsistence by which they had so far survived were exhausted, the relief which they received from their fellow refugees, the French clergy, who shared with them the feeble sums which they received from the Government, had ceased as a consequence of these payments falling into arrears – this, just at the time when the cost of living had gone up by more than half. The effects of this delay in payments in such difficult circumstances would have been terrible without the charity and kindness of the working class of people who, drawn to these foreigners by a common bond of suffering, gave them credit and often shared with them even their own resources.[19]

The news of the disaster was received with stunned disbelief in London but as the truth of the accounts was confirmed dismay turned to despair. Almost all the diarists of emigration described the shock that Quiberon caused the London émigrés. Every family had lost a husband, a son or a close relation in the fighting at Quiberon or the executions afterwards.

> Notre société à Londres fut donc cruellement frappée au coeur quand la nouvelle toute sanglante du désastre de Quiberon lui arriva. Parmi nous tous ce ne fut alors qu'une douleur qu'une consternation, qu'un désespoir général. Presque toutes nos familles comptaient une ou plusieurs victimes dans le combat du fort Penthièvre, dans la mêlée de la plage et dans la trahison d'Auray.[20]

> Our society in London was cruelly struck to the heart when the freshly bloody news of the disaster at Quiberon arrived. Among us there was only grief, consternation and general despair. Almost all our families counted one or several victims in the fighting at fort Penthièvre, in the scramble on the beach and the betrayal of Auray.

There was more than just general despair.

> La consternation fut affreuse parmi nous lorsque la nouvelle du désastre de Quiberon parvint à Londres. Les listes des morts, des malheureux prisonniers arrivèrent les uns après les autres. Nous voulions espérer que beaucoup de nos amis de nos frères avaient pu se sauver. Mais bientôt, le gouvernement nous donna le cruel éclairissment que chacun cherchait avec une curieuse anxiété.[21]

> Our grief was dreadful when the news of the disaster at Quiberon came through in London. The lists of the dead and of the unfortunate prisoners arrived one after the other. We wanted to hope that many of our friends and our brothers had managed to escape. But soon, the government broke to us cruel news that everyone was waiting for with a curious anxiety.

Mme de Ménerville goes on to talk about families in Somerstown which she calls Somersfield and by her vagueness reveals just how

The Low Life

great a gap separated the émigrés of Marylebone from those of Somerstown and Saint George's Fields.

There were women who went insane. A Madame d'Aiguille went mad upon hearing of the death of her husband who had been mercilessly shot like any other prisoner at Vannes despite a distinguished military career in the American war. His wife left her two children and wandered through the London streets calling his name. The two children were rescued by a neighbour who heard their cries. The mother disappeared and was never heard of again.[22]

The accounts of Mme de Ménerville are not reliable because they are so highly embellished but there are other reports of distraught émigré women going mad under the strain and the clergy described how the news of Quiberon compounded the other problems émigrés faced in London at that time. The way the Committee coped with these cases was to put them in the care of a priest but this too had its problems. Abbé Duheron wrote of his patient that she had an inordinate appetite and she ate all the time otherwise her state was uncontrollable.[23] There were a number of émigré cases in Bedlam. Placement in asylums was difficult because applications had to be sponsored by the parish but in some cases the Bishop of St Pol was able to use his influence.[24] The Bishop of Ely arranged for some cases to be accepted at St Luke's, Old Street in St James where he was a governor.[25] There is evidence of great compassion on the part of the Committee towards these sad cases and their care. A return fare was paid for a patient to be accompanied to hospital in London from Southampton and John Wilmot himself personally visited patients in private asylums. It is difficult to ascertain just what percentage of these patients were women because gender is not always specified but the sources rather suggest that a high number of them were. In one case a young woman was obliged to share a bed with a stranger in an asylum. When John Wilmot investigated this and found it to be true and in keeping with the accommodation rate of 12s per week paid by the Committee, a special payment was made to give her a bed of her own.[26] In cases where extra money was not available, there was recourse to individuals like the Duchess of York who supplied the required funds.[27]

When a noble woman died of hunger in Saint George's Fields questions were asked and the seriousness of the situation became brutally apparent. British women, some of whom were wives of Wilmot Committee members and well-informed about the situation of the refugees, were appalled that a woman of noble birth could die such a miserable death. They made inquiries and these only served to uncover the true scale of the problem. Women in particular were on the verge of starvation or worse and many children were living in inhuman conditions for want of food, clothing or both.

Up until this point, these women, who were all from the British upper class, had confined their charitable acitivities to fund-raising concerts and bazaars for the relief of the émigrés without getting any more closely involved.[28] Now, horrified by what they had discovered, they destined their aid solely for the women refugees who needed the most basic assistance. Under the leadership of the Marchioness of Buckingham and the patronage of the Duchess of York, they issued a pamphlet promoting their cause. The original has not suvived but parts of it were quoted by the Abbé Lubersac including examples of several particular cases.

1. Mme de L... who had gone mad following an awful birth. She had just been admitted to the hospital of St Luke leaving five children, the oldest 7, without any provision.
2. Mme de D... dead of hunger. She left a paralysed husband and three sons without any clothes and all three sick.
3. Mme de P... heavily pregnant without any money.
4. Mme de R... in the last stages of consumption, her husband partly disabled as a result of an old wound. They could not look after themselves and they had no money.
5. Mme la comtesse de B... was sick, her husband who was an old man suffering from gout could not leave his bed. They were without food or medicine.
6. Mme de B... had been left without anything with five children who were completely naked.[29]

The members of the women's committee organised a relief in kind which provided assistance to these women. They provided beds, linen and blankets to women who were pregnant and clothes for the children. Food and medical aid they provided as they could. Very little trace of this assistance survives but it is quite obvious that at a crucial time during the winter of 1795–96, when many émigré women were in desperate need of assistance, the British women were there to help or to do what they could for the émigrée's physical comfort.

The first thing they did was to prioritise the recipients of relief. In the first and most needy class they put all the widows of Quiberon, who would receive ten pounds per annum. Secondly they turned their attention to all the young women aged between 6 and 14 (around 150) whom it was proposed to bring up and educate to become useful members of society. The cost was not to exceed ten pounds per person. In the third category they placed the sick, the old and infirm, pregnant women and women who had just given birth, as well as little girls under 6. The needs of this class would necessarily vary but in general it was expected to be around 6 or 7 pounds per year per person.[30]

The total monies needed to operate these three categories was £2500 and it was this sum that it was hoped would be raised among the women of Great Britain. Dr Charles Burney, (Fanny Burney's father) who was the secretary for the Ladies' Committee presented their Plan to the Wilmot Committee. In principle it was very simple, although it proved to be a little less so in practice as had been the case in 1793:

> Each of these Ten will fix upon Ten Others, taking care to choose those resident in different parts of the Country, and who have different connexions. By this means there will be one hundred Ladies to collect in various parts of the Kingdom and if each can procure 200 Subscribers [which supposing the Choice to be well made does not seem impossible] the whole will amount to £20,000
>
> The First Ten Ladies are to get the proper papers printed and sent to those of their nominations. They will also give information which shall be procured from time to time for carrying on the Plan. This will not be very difficult each lady having to correspond with ten persons.[31]

The population of Saint George's Fields was, as Walsh observed, very mixed. There was little that these émigrés had in common besides their misfortunes and their stoic perseverance in the absence of any alternative. Most had already been receiving relief but the Quiberon expedition brought to light just how inadequate that relief really was.

There were some local tensions. The British population of Saint George's Fields was as poor as its French counterpart. Poverty bred resentment and religious fears as well as compassion. Bishop Douglass recorded an incident which took place on 3 June 1800:

> In the chapel St George's Fields a noise and species of riot happened last Sunday (Whitsunday) afternoon. Three fellows went into the chapel during the singing of the psalms at Vespers and were observed to be looking all about with more than common curiosity:

at length one of the three went into one of the Confessionals and drew the curtain before him; on being asked what he was doing there, and drawn out by one of the congregation he used improper language; then asked what they were singing, what language, if French or Italian? When told it was Latin he said to the man the collector at the door – do you understand Latin? Some more words of abuse and a scuffle ensued: on which some Irishmen in the chapel came to the assistance of the Collector and the fellow was driven out but not without charge to a constable who let him go. The three fellows were it is said Presbyterians.[32]

Tensions inevitably existed between the émigrés and the British poor who resented the presence of the refugees in London. Predictably too, the most vehement polemics against the French were written in the context of the threat posed by the refugees to the work prospects and charitable options available to the local poor. As early as September 1792 newspapers started to bear witness to this hostility. An observer wrote of his profound regret

> that the lower class of people act with much barbarity to those poor Frenchmen who have taken refuge in this land of liberty. It was with much concern that I felt for a coach-load of these unhappy emigrants who were passing over Westminster Bridge in my sight. It is shameful that they should be treated with such illiberal language.

What must remain surprising throughout is the fact that these outbursts of anti-French feeling were not more widespread and tended to be silenced by the British themselves without any reference to the émigrés. This symbolic role of the refugees as martyrs of a British cause after their entry into the war in 1793 is particularly important. Even among the poor there was recognition that the French émigrés were fighting for the survival of their honour and their society as they knew it and, in the wake of the writings of Paine, many Englishmen imagined themselves easily in the refugees' position.

The French settlement at Somerstown is another particular example of 'self-help'. Both Saint George's Fields and Somerstown had their populations swollen by the arrival of the émigrés who were repatriated from Jersey in 1796.

Émigrés on Jersey had been a source of problems for the British government from the start. They were difficult to administer and their relations with the islanders were chequered. They were eligible for relief, which was channelled through the Wilmot Committee and sent by the Bishop of Saint Pol de Léon to local representatives of the French community on Jersey for distribution, but the problems were similar to those facing the émigrés in London, particularly in relation to the lay population. In July 1796, with an invasion of Britain looking imminent, it was decided to repatriate émigrés on Jersey and Guernsey to Britain.[33] This was an unpopular measure because it cost the émigrés who had established themselves their crops and anything else they had acquired which they could not easily transport with them or sell at short notice. A paltry £1 per head was allowed for removal expenses.[34]

The months of June to September 1796 witnessed a heated correspondence between the different parties representing the émigrés and the government, who had very different priorities. The concern of the government was not for the welfare of the émigrés but for the strategic situation in case of invasion. The details of the evacuation were secondary though they were forced to acknowledge some of the difficulties involved.

The comte de Botherel, who was the administrator of relief to the émigrés in the Channel Islands in 1797, pointed out some of the problems. There were concerns about the continuity of relief and the continuation of extra payments which had been obtained from the government but could not be supplied by the Wilmot Committee. The initiatives and expenditure which could not be recouped were stressed:

> They have adopted a branch of industry or commerce, they have acquired the tools, the crafts and the animals. They have made great sacrifices in the hope of improving their future prospects.[35]

He also stressed their efforts to integrate themselves into the local community and to win the confidence of the locals. They had taken on financial obligations which they could not pay off quickly. They could not hope to obtain a fair value for anything they had to sell under these conditions. The hidden costs of reinstallation in Britain, of regaining the ground they had made in the Islands was not taken into consideration and was a cause of general despair. There were hidden costs too, associated with travelling, that could not be recouped under the arrangements. Furniture could not be transported. Perhaps worst of all, the delays of relief payments were only adding to the distress.

This inadequate picture of the distress that the émigrés are going through illustrates the extent to which their frustration is due to the effects of the order to evacuate which has been so suddenly given. Is it necessary to add that this order comes at a time of grief when many fathers of families and young men of good faith have so recently perished in an expedition which took with it the last savings that these families had.[36]

Of the 1300–1400 lay émigrés resident in the Islands only 350 came to Britain and all settled in London. The efforts of the comte de Botherel and the Wilmot Committee did obtain the compassion which they sought from the government in relation to the human impact of the policies it was making. The terms were modified and provisions were made but the net result was still evacuation at short notice for many Jersey refugees.

The duc d'Harcourt, in a letter to Lord Grenville, tried to suggest practical solutions. He asked that their possessions should be transported free of charge, that they should be exempted from customs duties, that they should be accorded two months' relief allowance to cover the move, that their relief payments should be paid in London exactly as they had been in the Islands, without re-enrolment or revision, and that they should not be able to be prosecuted for default on debts which they could not pay under the circumstances of their evacuation.[37]

The realities of the relocation were softened only a little for the Jersey inhabitants who came to swell the numbers of poor émigrés in London. The majority of the Jersey émigrés settled in Somerstown. It was a new area of London a long way from the centre of the city and the rents were significantly cheaper. Prior to these arrivals it had been a favourite area for the clergy.[38]

The Jersey émigrés stamped their identity on Somerstown. The Abbé Guy Toussaint Julien Carron in particular became a leading figure of the London emigration. He was an ecclesiastic who, like the Bishop of Saint Pol de Léon, had a flair for organisation but he had the distinct advantage of youth and energy on his side. Carron had set up schools in Jersey and had played a central role in the French community there. When he came to London he took a larger group of refugees, both lay and ecclesiastic, under his wing in Somerstown and set out to provide them with spiritual and temporal guidance. He was described as the Vincent de Paul of the emigration.

Carron fund-raised and organised with great energy. He established pharmacies and hospices for the French community as well as libraries and seminaries for the priests. And in doing so he provided the émigrés with a an invaluable sense of community, purpose and identity. He also provided individuals with jobs in the community which left them little time to dwell on their sad situation.

His compassion for the small and the sick led to the creation of several institutions. He created a hospice for women; those who were

> hors d'état de pouvoir être secourues dans le facheux état de la maladie, et de graves infirmités, où souvent elles se trouvoient comme abandonnées dans leurs chambre et sans secours absolus.[39]

> beyond help and a captive of some sickness or grave infirmity where often they found themselves abandoned in their rooms and absolutely without care.

This was run by pious women who devoted themselves to the care of the sick with the dedication of nuns. With equal compassion he saw to the comfort of the elderly priests; those

> plus de sexagénaires, devenus infirms, qui supportoient, avec une sainte résignation, leur état de souffrances, restés sans moyens de se faire secourir dans leurs chambres.[40]

> over sixty, who had become infirm and who put up with their suffering with a saintly resignation and were without care or the means of providing it in their rooms.

The Abbé Carron took two adjoining houses at the Polygon in Somerstown and acquired all the necessary equipment and furniture, about 40 beds, tables, utensils, and so on. His ability to overcome problems was legendary. It was this sense of community forged by the abbé Carron which Delille evoked in his poem.

> Salut ô Sommerstown, abri cher à la France!
> Là, le malheur encor bénit la Providence;
> Là, nos fiers vétérans retrouvent le repos,
> Et le héros instruit les enfants des héros:[41]

7 Educational Pursuits

> Le marquis sémillant au comptoir est tranquille;
> Plus d'un jeune guerrier tient le rabot d'Émile;[1]

In 1945, John Nef, History Professor at the University of Chicago, noted that of all the nations which had been invaded the course of the Second World War, the French had been able, very successfully, to continue their intellectual and scholarly activity both at home or in exile.[2] This remark provides a key to understanding the role of intellectual pursuits in French exile culture which was as important for the émigrés of the French Revolution as for those of 1940.

Education was a central theme of the emigration in Britain. Émigrés not only provided an unprecedented number of teachers for British educational institutions but they also provided a new market, with numbers of French émigré children being sent to British schools. This twofold relationship of both supply and demand sets education apart from other aspects of life in emigration.

Education also cut across class barriers. Rich émigrés sought to place their children in British establishments, the modest sought to work in them and for the French clergy the preoccupations of teaching were a tonic for the stresses of exile. From their British hosts, there was a certain resignation. *The St James Chronicle* recorded in September 1792:

> We shall now have the swarm of seminaries in the neighbourhood of London cheaply and promptly supplied with teachers [...] and the great desideratum in the modern education of our women [...] the knack of chattering bad French shall be happily obtained.[3]

The education of their children was a source of great anxiety. The older émigrés were aware that their children of all ages were being deprived of the education they would otherwise have received had they grown up in different and more normal circumstances. By late 1794, there were many children whose physical needs alone were taking priority over their other requirements but it was painfully obvious to certain members of the émigré community and to supporters in the British community that it would not do to let these children grow up wild with no education whatsoever.

Women in particular were doubly sensitive to this gap in their children's life and the heavy toll that this lack of education might have later when they all hoped they would return to France to gather up the threads of their old life. Senac de Meihan wove this theme into his novel:

> Who could have told me ten years ago when I lost the duke whom I sincerely loved, or when, three years ago, I lost my little Charlotte, that there would come a time when I would regard their death as a blessing for them and almost as much of a blessing for me. Who could assure me that the Duke ardent, passionate in his tastes for new ideas would not have been a democrat or that he would not have been one of the victims devoured during the awful days which surpassed those of the St Bartholemew. How would he have been able to resign himself to poverty and to the humiliation that accompanies it, impatient, proud as he was? What would I have done with my Charlotte who would today be 14 years old? Forced to leave her sometimes in order to concentrate on my work and my little industry, how could I have guaranteed the formation of her mind? And if things in France do not get better, what would the future hold for her? For someone brought up with the tastes and sentiments of her station, how could one suppose that one so young could impose reason over memory without suppressing it completely and resign herself to such disappointments without being crushed. This is what my reason sometimes tells me in order to calm the grief of her loss. But my heart knows better and I sometimes imagine Charlotte sharing my work, taking care of me, and I imagine her as a dear companion to whom I could open my heart, as the object of an affection which by its nature and vivacity would provide solace for the most sensitive and active soul.[4]

Mme de Ménerville was another woman who worried about the education of her daughers and the harm that the emigration might be doing to their advancement:

> Mes filles grandissaient; leur éducation me donnait des soucis; leur précoce intelligence y répondait si bien! J'envoyais les deux aînées à une petite école et, bientôt, elles parlèrent anglais de manière à me servir d'interprètes. Je l'apprenais aussi; j'avais pris des leçons en

France; je l'entendis bien vite mais je n'ai jamais pu le parler étant continuellement avec des Français.[5]

My daughters were growing up. Their education was a cause for concern because their precocious intelligence responded so well to encouragement. I sent the two eldest to a little school and soon they spoke English well enough to interpret for me. I learnt too. I had taken lessons in France and I could understand well but I never had the opportunity to speak, being constantly in French company.

And the comtesse de Flahaut set out to write her first novel in order to finance the education of her son. She was acutely aware of the responsiblity and inwardly proud of being able to provide the necessary funds from her own activity:

Seule dans une terre étrangère, avec un enfant qui a atteint l'âge où il n'est plus permis de retarder l'éducation, j'ai éprouvé une sorte de douceur à penser que ses premières études seraient le fruit de mon travail.[6]

Alone in a foreign land, with a child who had attained an age where it was impossible to delay his education any longer, I was happy to think that his first studies were the fruit of my work.

There were cases where fathers took on the responsibility for their children's education, as Madame de Boigne testifies:

My father, who was retired, took full charge of my education. I worked regularly for eight hours each day at the most serious things. I studied history, and I was fascinated by works on metaphysics. My father never left me to read alone, but I was allowed to read anything as long as he was with me. He would have feared the formation of false ideas in my young head if his wise reflections had not been there to stop them. To compensate perhaps, my father added a few books from his tastes on political economy and I enjoyed them very much. I remember the laughter of M. de Calonne when the following year in London he found me reading a volume of Smith's *Wealth of Nations* for recreation and this was the first time that I became aware that my tastes were unusual for a girl of fifteen.[7]

In the early years of the emigration, 1793–95, English schools made substantial gains from the infusion of French children and many children experienced the austere boarding schools in the north of England referred to by Balzac.[8] The fact that British schools advertised in the French newspapers suggests that the upper echelons of the French community were a target market.

ÉDUCATION PARTICULIÈRE POUR L'ACQUISITION DES LANGUES MODERNES

A Rugby, dans le comté de Warwick, on prend en pension un petit nombre de jeunes Messieurs, qui sont principalement instruits dans les Langues, Française, Allemande et Italienne.

Le prix de la Pension, en comprenant le blanchissage, etc, raccommodage du linge, ainsi que l'usage d'un cheval, est de 100 guinées par an. On paye 6 guinées en entrant, indépendamment de la pension. Les jeunes Messieurs étrangers, pour lesquels l'acquisition de la Langue Anglaise peut etre un objet digne d'attention sont admis aux même conditions.

S'adresser par lettre à M Wratisau à Rugby

NB Si l'on n'exige pas l'usage d'un cheval le prix est alors de 80 guinées.[9]

The young Vicomte Walsh spent several years in an English boarding school.[10] His memories of it were mixed and he wrote of being a lamb amongst the wolves.[11] Adèle de Flahaut later congratulated herself for being a 'barbarous mother' and sending her son to a similar establishment because the rigorous learning discipline and language skills he acquired there served him all his life.[12]

There were many schools in London in this period and the frequency with which they opened and shut was indicative of their reliability as employers. One French priest wrote:

> J'ai de la plus grande aversion à résider dans les écoles. J'ai l'air bilieux, étriqué, ma maigreur devient extrême, ma taille petite et mince n'est pas propre à en imposer sur les jeunes gens. [...] En général il est très vrai de dire que la place de maître de français dans une pension est la plus désagréable de la maison sans exclure celle du dernier domestique.[13]

> I have the greatest aversion to living in schools. I appear bilious, stooped, extremely thin and my sickly figure is not fit to impose on young people. In general it is true to say that the post of schoolmaster

in a boarding establishment is the most disagreeable in the house not excluding that of the most lowly domestic.

Another wrote of being

excédé d'ennui, de fatigue et de dégoût et qu'il ne pourrait pas continuer à exercer un métier qu'il croyait qu'il aurait bien fait de ne point entreprendre.[14]

beside himself with boredom, tiredness, disgust and he could not continue to perform a job which he believed that he would have done well not to undertake in the first place.

There were many schools on the edge of the city in places which were considered conducive to learning. Chelsea and Hammersmith were considered to be ideal places for schools, as the air was fresh and clean. The émigrés marvelled at the ingenuity of the British when it came to growing vegetables and fruit in their cold, damp climate and it was in places like Chelsea and Hammersmith that examples of this kind of cultivation could be found.

Après avoir vu Hyde Park, St James's Park, Green Park et Regent's Park nous sortimes de Londres pour voir les belles serres de M. Lee au joli village de Hammersmith. Malgré les brouillards et le froid du climat, nous y vîmes des milliers de fleurs et des fruits en maturité. Rien n'enseigne aussi bien que la nécessité: les Anglais voyant que leurs étés et leurs automnes ne peuvent mûrir leurs pêches et leurs raisins, ont appelé l'art à leur secours, et un riche habitant de la Grande Bretagne voit servir sa table des fruits bien avant nous.[15]

After we had seen Hyde Park, St James's Park, Green Park and Regent's Park we left London to visit the greenhouses of Mr Lee in the pretty village of Hammersmith. In spite of the fog and the cold of the climate we saw thousands of flowers and ripe fruit. Nothing creates like necessity: the English, knowing that their summers and autumns could not ripen their peaches and grapes, have enlisted the help of the arts and a rich inhabitant of Britain can serve fruit on his table well before we can in France.

It was in this healthy setting that the marquise de Macnamara with the support of the Relief Committee opened her school for émigré girls.[16] The initiative came from the Marchioness of Buckingham who was concerned to provide penniless young émigré girls with the education and skills necessary to enable them to earn their living.

> Réunies dans une maison spacieuse à Hammersmith, ces jeunes demoiselles y reçurent l'education la plus soignée et la plus complète. On y avoit en vue de former tout à la fois et la vertueuse chrétienne, et la mère de famille utile, instruite: grammaire, langue angloise, géographie, quelques arts agréables, tels que le dessein, la musique, etc. s'y joignoient aux talens utiles; et il n'est aucune branche de travaux propres aux femmes qu'on n'y cultivât, tels encore que broder et coudre, occupations ordinaires du sexe: tellement que ces différens exercices, sagement distribués sous la prudente direction et par le tendre zèle de Mde la marquise de Macnamara, qui étoit à la tête de cette bonne oeuvre, accoutumoient, peu à peu, les jeunes demoiselles à l'habitude si précieuse de ne laisser aucun instant vide, et de les consacrer tous au développement de connoissances et de talens utiles.[17]

> Housed in a spacious dwelling in Hammersmith, these young ladies received the most careful and complete education. Attention was taken to give them the preparation of a virtuous Christian life and to prepare them for practical and educated motherhood. Grammar, English language, geography, a few gentle arts like painting, music, etc. were included alongside the useful ones. No necessary part of a woman's education was neglected; they learnt to embroider and sew; the ordinary occupations of their sex. Under the wise direction and tender care of the Marquise de Macnamara who was in charge of this good work, the young girls acquired the habit of never being idle and channelled all their energies into cultivating useful talents.

This school operated for six years but in 1801 it was closed and its pupils and their mistress were moved to the girls school set up by the Abbé Carron in Somerstown.[18]

Like Hammersmith, Chelsea was considered to be a good place for schools. It was

> pleasantly situated up the banks of the Thames, which is supposed to be wider in the adjoining reach than in any part west of London-bridge. The church is two miles distant from Buckingham-house, but the village extends almost to Hyde-park-corner, including a considerable part of Knightsbridge.[19]

Mary Russell Mitford attended a school at 22 Hans Place Chelsea, run by Monsieur de St Quentin, former secretary to the comte de Moustiers.

> He knew many emigrants of the highest rank, and indeed of all ranks; and being a lively kind-hearted man, with a liberal hand and social temper, it was his delight to assemble as many as he could of his poor country-men around his hospitable supper table. These suppers took place on Saturdays, and were followed by tric-trac and reversé.[20]

She was sent to this school in 1797 at the age of 10 from her parents' home in Reading – a redbrick house on the London road – and she obviously remembered her school days with pleasure:

> No 22 Hans Place a small square into which you turn on the right hand out of Sloane Street as you go from Knightsbridge to Chelsea. It was then just finished and the houses bright fresh newly painted looking into a garden full of shrubs – flowers were in no slight request among persons of modest incomes and gentle condition. One of the largest No. 22, had been taken by M. de St Quentin, a well-born, well-educated and well-looking French emigrant for the purpose of setting up a ladies school, which perhaps of all the schemes adopted by any of his suffering and ingenious co-mates in exile for the relief of their necessities appeared the most extraordinary and least likely to answer. He made the attempt however and it succeeded. He was assisted, or rather chaperoned in his undertaking by his wife, a good natured, red-faced, French woman, much muffed in shawls and laces; and by Miss Rowden, an accomplished young lady, the daughter and sister of clergymen who had for some years been the governess in the family of Lord Bessborough. M. de St Quentin himself taught the pupils, French, History, Geography, and as much Science as he was master of; or as he thought it requisite for a young lady to know. Miss Rowden with the assistance of finishing masters for Italian, Music, Dancing and Drawing superintended the general course of study; while Mme de St. Quentin sat dozing either in the drawing room with a piece of work, or in the library with a book in her hand to receive the friends of the young ladies or any other visitor who might chance to call.[21]

Not all the British gentry were so quick to take advantage of French schools. There were many schools which opened and closed during this period because staff were readily available and wages were cheap.

Life in the lesser schools could really be quite distasteful, as Chateaubriand among others found out. In Bath this protest against émigré schools was made:

> Are not Schools daily advertised in this City, at enormous Prices? Are not Languages, Painting, Drawing, Music and other Employments usurped by Foreigners to the Ruin of our own Countrymen? What may not be the Consequence, by thus *Sapping* the *British Citadel*, when an opportunity offers to join in the general assault? Surely this is another *Norman Conquest* by *insidious attack*, and too much encouraged by the torpid acquiescence of unsuspecting Englishmen.[22]

One of the British patrons who was most involved in the relief operation and most committed to the restoration of the French monarchy was Edmund Burke. In the aftermath of Quiberon, he had another reason to empathise with the dreadful grief of the émigrés because he had just lost his only son. The story goes that he went to visit the two children of Mme d'Aiguille who had been given to the care of a servant;

> Il demanda à l'aîné qui avait six ans, 'Voulez vous être mon fils?' 'Non', repondit l'enfant, 'je veux toujours être celui de mon pauvre papa et rester Français.' 'Oui tu resteras Français,' dit en pleurant M. Borck, 'et je veux que tu sois digne de ton père'.[23]

He asked the eldest who was six years old, 'Would you like to be my son?' 'No', replied the child, 'I want always to be the son of my poor papa and stay French.' 'Yes you will stay French,' said Burke in tears, 'and I want you to be worthy of your father.'

Whether this incident actually took place is doubtful but Burke was intimately involved with the Quiberon affair and its impact on the émigrés. It was as a result of this that he managed to obtain funding for a project to provide a school for the boys who had lost their fathers at Quiberon or in the service of the *armée des princes*. He believed that these children should be educated so that they could provide a new generation of leaders for France and an alternative to another generation of revolutionaries. Instead they were

> growing up in poverty and wretchedness, and inevitably mixed with the children of the lowest of the people, in the miserable lanes and

alleys of London, in which the poverty of their parents obliges them chiefly to reside. ... From wretchedness and bad company, the transition is easy to desperate vice and wickedness. In this bad society they grow up without any sort of education. ... If providence should restore them to their country, they will be utterly incapable of filling up their place in society; – no small calamity to all nations, to have France the receptacle of noble or ignoble barbarians. ... If they are to remain in perpetual exile, they are nothing less than trained to Botany Bay or the gallows.[24]

This was only a beginning. The Penn School which Burke founded could only cater for a very limited number of boys. It was, nevertheless, an unparalleled initiative in the experience of the emigration in Britain. Honour and the need to nurture the new generation of royalists was the prime motivation for this school. The Comte d'Artois was its patron and he often travelled the 28 miles from London to distribute the prizes at the graduation ceremony. He took a sincere interest in the school and its pupils who were the sons of his most loyal and impoverished devotées.[25] Today the school no longer exists, the last pupils dispersed in 1820, and the house it occupied has long since disappeared.

Although Burke conceived the Penn project as early as 1794, he had to wait until the end of 1795 after the Quiberon disaster before he got any progress from government on funding. The school house near Beaconsfield had been acquired in 1793 for the French clergy but in the event the clergy were housed elsewhere, so it was left empty. Burke wanted £1000 in start-up costs and £50 per month over and above the guinea per month that was received by each school-child. The relief payments for the pupils were made directly to the school. Burke and the Bishop of St Pol de Léon squabbled over the curriculum because the Bishop didn't want any British teachers and Burke wanted a 'good dash of English education'.[26]

Yet letters like the following reveal just how important it was to the loyal fraternity of émigrés to obtain a place in this institution which represented so much of what they were fighting for.

No date, To the Prince de Bouillon,
The many kindnesses you have shown me to date led me to hope that you might do me a great favour. At the moment a school is being formed in London at the expense of the British government for the education of French boys. They are taking them from the

age of 7 to 14 years. My two sons are eligible. One is eleven and a half, the other is nine and a half. I dare to hope, my prince, that you might generously write to recommend that they be placed. There will be many applicants so I would beg you to do it as soon as possible because I have no doubt about their case being successful with your support and my gratitude could only equal the profound respect with which I have the honour to be ... etc. LISCOET[27]

Like the two boys of the Marquis de Liscoët who received places, the other sixty names on the list of the first pupils at the school represent the first families of the *ancien régime*.[28]

The school was directed by an ecclesiastic, the Abbé Maraine.[29] He had been recommended to Burke by the Bishop of Saint Pol de Léon and had spent 20 years as the superior in a seminary college in Rouen, emigrating to Britain in 1791. He was loved and admired by the boys whom he taught and it is clear that they regarded him as a father-figure. When he returned to France in 1820 he took the remaining students back with him.

The school opened in April 1796 and from that date until the death of its founder on 9 July 1797, was a personal project which Edmund Burke referred to as his nursery. He lived nearby and there are many references to the fact that he saw to all the little extra needs of the boys himself and sent food from his kitchens to vary the daily fare.[30]

The Penn school, which was seen as a particular monument to Burke, was kept going after his death by the intercession of influential political friends like the Duke of Portland.[31] Yet from the correspondence between the director of the school, the Abbé Maraine, and the members of the Relief Committee it is clear that it was a great struggle to keep the school viable and the number of pupils dwindled away.

The Abbé Maraine's dedication to the school and to the boys who were in his charge was complete, but after Burke's death he faced obstacles on all fronts.[32] He had no direct line of report and could only appeal to his friend Dr Lawrence King to intercede with the Committee on his behalf, and when the Committee themselves were not receiving the monies promised from the Treasury on time, his case was a long way down the order of priorities. His correspondence with King reveals just what a panoply of problems, both academic and administrative, running the refugee school presented.

The supervisor of the Penn School estimates that the time when consideration is being given to new masters for the school is the appropriate time to represent the indispensable necessity of increasing their number. He deems it appropriate to detail the problems he has encountered along with his two colleagues and how it has been impossible to advance the students as far as he would have hoped in their studies without extra assistance. In short, sixty young persons, which has always been their number, require more attention than three masters can provide. But if one considers that the sixty young people are of different age and different learning capacity and that they have come with more or less instruction, that some do not know how to read and write while others, while a little more advanced, are not at the same stage and that in order to avoid wasting their time it has been necessary to divide them into six or seven different classes, it is easy to appreciate the problems that with the most active enthusiasm and the most robust health we have not been able to overcome. We have reached a situation where the large group made up of boys from nine to twelve years more or less have only just started to learn their grammar.[33]

The most basic day-to-day issues were affected by delays in payments from the Treasury which should have come via the Relief Committee. The boys' clothing was worn-out and Maraine's attempts to instill into the boys the importance of a clean, neat appearance were thwarted by the financial silence from his directors.[34]

Having received no news from Mr. Nagle whom I have written to twice in order to represent the needs of the school, I address myself to you with confidence. It is more than four months since I received any money from the Treasury, neither the masters, nor the servants, nor the suppliers have been paid and the latter group have just come to demand the payment that is their due. I do not know what to tell them. They say they will not go on supplying the school. You have been kind enough to tell about a month ago that the government has agreed the money. Dare I ask you to see Mr Woodford and to have us paid a part of the promised sum because we are in the most pressing need.[35]

In May, he was still waiting; in July, he hardly dared show his face at Penn after a trip to London which was without result. The suppliers had not been paid for the present month and the school already owed them five months accounts.[36] On 4 June 1802,

You would do us a great favour if you could obtain from the Treasury the arrears due to the school because, for a long time now, I have been in great financial distress.[37]

The roll had gone down due to émigrés returning to France and, in September, he writes of not replacing a housekeeper but making do with two servants. He was still waiting for payment in November and had received only £250 from the Treasury for the current year:

It is simply impossible for me to defray the current expenses with such a modest sum.[38]

The survival of the school was more due to the perseverance of the Abbé Maraine than any action on the part of the British government, which again reflects the whole approach to refugee relief. With his strong direction, the school managed to keep going and sums from the Treasury were eventually paid albeit months late.[39] Some of the pupils at the Penn school remained in England when their families returned to France in 1802 in order to avoid service in Napoleon's armies. A letter from one former pupil of Penn School to another in 1820 gives an example of the strong school spirit among *les Pennois* as they referred to themselves and there was also a great sense of attachment to Britain, their home by adoption.

j'irai faire une tournée en Angleterre, c'est une paix qui me plait toujours infiniement. J'aime John Bull, j'aime les beef-steaks et comme dit Lord Byron j'love [sic] a porter beer as well as any.[40]

The clergy were very involved in education. Teaching, although a preferred profession for many of the lay members of the French community, was a special preference for the clergy. Their religious training made them particularly suited to teach subjects like languages, Latin, Greek, French and other academic subjects. Yet ecclesiastics were often treated badly in British schools. They complained to the Committee not only about their conditions of work but also about the calibre of the minds they had to teach. A priest wrote that his students 'have little taste for the application demanded by the study of a language whatever it may be and often cease taking lessons'.[41] He also complained about the miserable remuneration. Competition for students was also fierce. At Worcester, which apparently had no tutors,

Abbé Toussaint was able to secure only four pupils because another ecclesiastic had preceded him by a week.[42]

Charles de Broglie, a son of the duc de Broglie, came to London in 1801. The skills he required of the dozen or so fellow clergymen who taught in his school were the ability to teach languages (Latin, Greek, English, Italian and Spanish), sciences and

> talens propres à diriger l'éducation d'une nombreuse jeunesse, destinée, par sa naissance, à remplir, un jour, les professions honorables en tout genre qu'on exerce dans un État tel que la France se trouvoit avant la révolution.[43]

> skills appropriate to direct the education of young people destined by their birth to fulfil one day the functions of the honorable professions that might be required in a state such as France was before the Revolution.

Not all school projects were successful. This school initially set up in Kensington ran into financial problems and moved to Hammersmith. Charles de Broglie was imprisoned for debts in 1806 but the school survived and was still going in 1814.[44]

A small number of ecclesiastics were lucky enough to obtain secure school positions, which made their circumstances quite comfortable. The Abbé Tuvache taught grammar at Winchester.[45] The Abbé Duclos who had more than 50 pupils lived in at Eton and was able to entertain his friends.[46] Abbé Brémont stayed for seven years in Monmouth, teaching in two schools and from the £40–£50 salary was able to furnish a *'petit maisonette'*.[47] The Abbé Doublet taught for ten years in Shaftesbury and supplemented his income by saying mass.[48] There were a few who managed to succeed in education outside the school environment. A priest in Bath was able to earn enough during the season to keep him for the rest of the year.[49] Émigrés were also appointed to private families as tutors[50] and some were even employed as travelling tutors to young men making the Grand Tour.[51]

The other striking success story was the Abbé Carron in Somerstown where he created schools whose reputation for excellence was noted all over London. It was,

> grâce à lui, des écoles s'étaient élevées comme par miracle pour la jeunesse émigrée des deux sexes.[52]

thanks to him schools for young émigrés of both sexes were built as if by miracle.

He harnessed the best talents the French community could provide for teachers. Messieurs de Ramédon de Guéry, de Houx de Lancesseur and de Godefroy and Mesdames de Kersalio, du Quengo, Tuffin, de Villiers, de Couëssin, de Boisriou, de Trémereaux, de France de Landal, de Mansigny, and de Cornullier-Lucinière are mentioned by name as teachers in the Abbé Carron's Somerstown schools.[53]

> Avec ce noble personnel, les écoles de l'Abbé Caron acquirent bientôt une telle renommée, que les familles anglaises catholiques de distinction y envoyèrent leurs filles. Il y venait même des élèves de l'Inde et de l'Amérique. ... Des fils de Georges III, ayant entendu vanter les écoles françaises de l'Abbé Caron, voulurent assister à une distribution de prix où ils se trouvèrent avec nos princes français.[54]

> With staff of this quality the schools of the Abbé Caron soon acquired a reputation which encouraged the British Catholic families of distinction to send their daughters. There were even pupils from India and America. The sons of George III, having heard the praises of the Abbé's school, offered to attend the prize-giving, where they appeared beside the French princes.

His major task was to provide for the children of this community, many of whom had lost their parents and become orphans in the saddest circumstances. Some of these children he adopted and provided for himself. He made his schools pay by taking British children as well as those of the émigré families he was responsible for.

> When some of these unfortunate children became all of a sudden orphans very young losing both father and mother and finding themselves abandoned in a foreign country, it was this charitable and kind spiritual father who took them in with open arms and adopted them as his own ... and to this day, he has some of them still at his schools and in his charge.[55]

The schools of the Abbé Carron which were opened in 1796 disappeared with the end of the emigration. The boys' school had 60 pupils and the girls' school 40 and by 1801, at the height of their short existence, there were as many as 70 students in each establishment situated at 1 and 3 Phoenix Street respectively.[56] There were also children from English and Irish Catholic families enrolled in these schools. In 1805, the Abbé Carron was even accused of proselytising and had to defend himself before the Bow Street magistrates' court. The following account of the incident appeared in the diary of Bishop Douglass.

> Abbé Carrron has been sent to Sir Richard Ford of the Office at Bow Street by order from Lord Hawkesbury, Secretary of State for the Home Department, to answer to some charges made against him for receiving children of Protestant parents into his charity school. Sir Richard Ford received Mr. Carron into a private room of the House and had a handful of letters and papers in his hand containing the accusations. Abbé Carron answered that he took no children of Protestant parents without a petition in writing of the parents praying him to receive their respective children into his school, and as for grown up people, whom he had received into the Catholic church, it was by their own desire. He never sought to make converts; but when anyone spoke to him and wished to be instructed in the Catholic religion, he could not refuse to instruct them, and receive them into the Catholic church. The modesty with which the Abbé spoke in answer to several charges pleased Sir Richard so much, that he tore the papers he held in his hands, and threw them into the fire. Sir Richard even allowed him to take children of Protestant parents into his boarding school saying they are rich and will not become Catholics; but that the poor ... accordingly the worthy Abbé does not take any Protestant children into the charity school.[57]

A letter from Louis XVIII, dated 12 May 1797, recognised the Abbé Carron's work, his dedication to the young and the debt of the émigré community to him.

> Vos jeunes élèves apprendront par vos leçons, et surtout par vos exemples, à aimer et à respecter Dieu, à connoître et chérir les véritables lois de notre patrie; ainsi vous aurez doublement mérité d'elle, et je serai heureux, un jour, de pouvoir vous en récompenser dignement: soyez en attendant bien persuadé, Monsieur, de ma sincère estime et de tous mes autres sentimens pour vous. Louis.[58]

Your young pupils will learn, by your lessons and your example, to love and to respect God, to know and to cherish the true laws of our country. Thus, you have doubly deserved her thanks and one day, it will be my pleasure to be able to reward you appropriately. In the meantime, be assured of my sincere esteem and of my great admiration for you. Louis.

8 Politics – Their Own Worst Enemies?

> Vous avez trop raison sur nos pauvres émigrés. La révolution a duré trop longtemps pour la mesure commune du courage humain qui n'est que la résignation des âmes fortes. Le malheur les a aigris. Le dèsoeuvrement a fait fermenter toutes leurs misérables passions.[1]

> You are only too right about our poor émigrés. The Revolution has lasted too long for the common measure of human courage which is nothing other than the perseverance of strong-minded people. Misfortune has made them bitter. Inactivity has given rise to all manner of destructive passions.

Authors who have written on the subject of the émigrés have often found themselves at a disadvantage because there are so many preconceived and contradictory ideas about the role of the émigrés in the struggle to overthrow revolutionary France. Since as early as 1792, ideas and opinions have been in circulation about what they should have done or what should have been possible, leaving the reality seriously compromised. The very title of a pamphlet by Calonne, entitled *Pensées sur ce qu'on a fait et qu'on n'aurait pas dû faire; sur ce qu'on aurait dû faire et qu'on n'a pas fait; sur ce qu'on devrait faire et que, peut-être, on ne fera pas*[2] (Thoughts on what we have done and what we ought not to have done, on what we ought to have done and have not done; on what we ought to do and perhaps will not do) indicates the level of critical analysis they indulged in. This particular work was a clever mixture of Burke and Boissy d'Anglas.[3] In short, Calonne proposed that the most experienced statesmen and the best informed parties should produce a plan with two objectives: first, to show that a limited monarchy was the form of government best suited to a grand empire, and second, to present a detailed analysis of how and why this solution would work for France. He thought the French people needed convincing on four key issues:

(1) that the restoration of a monarchy would not necessarily entail a complete return to the *ancien régime* nor would it advocate a return to the constitution in effect in 1792.

(2) that property was the inviolable and sacred right of every citizen and that, therefore, there was a need to redress the injustices which had been committed.
(3) that the financial crisis must be solved in order to reassure against the threats of total bankruptcy, taxation overhauled, and money in circulation controlled.
(4) that religion needed to be revitalised. The plan would advocate a return to the basic principles of Christian belief, necessary for all civilised societies. It would subsidise the expenses of the dominant cult without being exclusive and assure the subsistence of the clergy.[4]

Calonne was not alone in evolving a plan for the French state as it would be after the Revolution under a restored monarchy; there were plenty of political amateurs publishing untried solutions to France's problems. These authors, however, often failed to appreciate the extent to which the Emigration and Counter-Revolution were central to the survival of the Republic.

> In a world increasingly divided into the innocent and the enemies of the people, the salvation of the former depended on the extermination of the latter, who had chosen to forfeit their claim to be treated as members of the city.[5]

There was not only an ideal city of the Revolution; the émigrés too had their own metaphorical Sparta which did not equate to any reality, political or economic, past or present. With all their human and financial limitations they were a long way from the image of crusading *chevaliers de Saint Louis* struggling to restore Bourbon France that many of them aspired to be.[6] The popularity of the Bourbon cause, particularly as the Emigration turned long-term, benefited from the fact that Louis XVIII was the only candidate who represented the absolutist tradition and the cult of the Bourbons, both of which were as vague as the terms suggest. At the centre of the royalist movement the person of the king mattered less than the cause he represented, and hence the anomalies, which are made explicit in this comment:

> It is infuriating to see such a man at the head of a cause that one would like to support. One wonders how he could have decided to escape and with what intention – to put himself at the head of a nobility flocking to him from all parts and whose efforts he negates

by giving in to the intrigues of Mme de Balbi his mistress whom he has carted along with him? Monsieur, who asserted the the position of Regent of the Kingdom during the captivity of the King, has the confidence of all the ministers of Europe, his nobility offers him the sacrifice of their possessions and their life for the restoration of the kingdom of which he represents the head of state. This same man forgot the dossier which had all the negotiations of highest secrecy. He left it at Verdun and by this inconceivable stupidity he caused the loss of those who had shown him the most devoted loyalty. And it's this man who could be our King. When one thinks about it one is tempted to turn republican rather than be politically associated with people of this sort. Thus I am closer to republicanism than to the Constitution itself because the makers (of the Constitution) all come from this former group.[7]

The harshness of this judgement, which reflects not only the acrimony many émigrés expressed about the influence of Mme de Balbi on events at a crucial time in the conflict, but also contains a highly critical appraisal of the ineptitude of Louis XVIII, underlines the crisis management which characterised émigré government in the early period and arguably throughout the Emigration. Mme de Balbi was the mistress of Louis XVIII (then the comte de Provence) during his stay in Coblenz and her extravagant behaviour was a subject of much censure.[8] The leadership qualities of Louis XVIII also came under fire. Yet this kind of severe criticism has to be juxtaposed with the fact that many émigrés realised only too well the shortcomings of their cause:

Combien je préfère ces salons anglais où l'ont dit tant de mal de nous, et où je me sens si utilement humilié de mon insuffisance.[9]

How infinitely I prefer the English salons where much is said against us but where I feel so rightly humiliated by my own inadequacy.

Factions within the Emigration often predated the Revolution and criticism was rife between different socio-economic and religious groups. This reflection on the behaviour of the non-ecclesiastic population in London made by a priest is typical of the level of vehemence and vindictiveness with which the factions assaulted and accused each other:

Ce qu'on voyait de Français à Londres et aux environs (je ne parle pas des ecclésiastiques) étaient ou des émissaires de la propagande parisienne, ou des membres de l'Assemblée constituante, venus, les uns pour souffler le feu de la discorde et de l'insurrection, les autres pour chercher un asile contre la fureur des monstres qu'ils avaient enfantés, et qui annonçaient très ouvertement le dessein de dévorer leurs pères.[10]

The French in London (I am not referring to ecclesiastics) were either emissaries of Parisian propaganda or members of the Constituent Assembly, who had come, some to stir up the fires of discord and insurrection, others to seek asylum against the fury of the monsters they themselves had created and who openly threatened to devour their parents.

Throughout the Emigration London was home to a group of highly literate men, ecclesiastic and non-ecclesiastic, who were fully prepared to justify their actions in print. Journalists, ex-politicans and *gentilhommes* were committed to re-establishing a government in France based on tradition and reason *à la Burke*, invariably a monarchy, but few outside the princes' entourages were in favour of *ancien régime*-style absolutism.

There were in London a group known as the *constitutionnels*, those who wanted to see a British-style constitutional monarchy established in France.[11] Among them were Mounier, Malouet and Mallet du Pan, Montlosier, Lally Tolendal and the journalist Jean-Gabriel Peltier. For a short time, Madame de Staël reinforced this faction. They disagreed wildly about the parameters of such a constitution yet, without exception, they were committed and prolific writers.

A barrage of works appeared in London in the last years of the eighteenth century on the subject of the Revolution by both British and French authors. Among these Malouet's *Défense de Louis XVI*, and Mounier's *Recherches sur les causes qui ont empêché les Français de devenir libre* were among the first. In 1795, Lally Tolendal published a persuasive *Défense des émigrés* which was read from one end of Europe to the other by the elite and, although addressed to the French people, had far more success among those audiences where Lally was preaching to the converted.[12] It did not appeal to the staunch royalists because it accepted and even praised the creation of the Republic. It was essentially a plea for clemency before the abject injustice of the laws against the émigrés which condemned them all outright, irrespective of their crimes. The *Défense* systematically highlighted the absurdity and injustice underlying the émigré laws which labelled the émigrés 'traitors' and 'cowards' without any further qualification.[13] He constructed an elaborate defence of the cause starting with the most obviously innocent émigrés.

> Women. Great God! Women guilty of cowardice or treason. ... The whole body of society is bound to protect the mothers of families, the wives, the sisters, the female friends who support or cement or embellish the social bond. The coward is he who abandons them; the traitor he who gives them up.[14]

He lambasted the Jacobins for targeting innocent children, for making them take responsibility for their situation and for obliging them

> to be the absolute masters of their own conduct to be perfect men in short at TEN YEARS OF AGE![15]

And he poignantly pleaded the case of

> The child, whom a widow, a father or a daughter overwhelmed with despair, has carried away with her at her bloodstained bosom and who has not yet heard of the calamities of its country nor of the massacre of its family, the child conceived in sorrow in exile and who drinks more of the tears than the milk of its wretched mother is already attained by this murderous law.[16]

Expressed in dramatic language, this was the sad truth for many émigrés. He also bemoaned the fact that even children who had not emigrated were equally vulnerable.[17]

He wanted to see the removal from the criminal lists of all émigrés who had not borne arms.[18] He vehemently attacked the Jacobins, whom he accused of wanting to keep the émigrés as a whipping-horse for all the crimes of the Revolution.[19]

> FRENCHMEN if you wish to believe the truth rest assured that the JACOBINS ALONE brought on this war, that they ALONE declared it, and that they ALONE wish to continue it.[20]

He appealed to the citizens of the French Nation to put the evils of the Revolution behind them, maintaining that honest men had no other objective than peace.[21]

You must have it for without it, the best composed legislative body can do nothing and with it it can do anything. Yes, certainly Europe is in want of peace and all people demand it. Yes, England is in want of peace and her inhabitants call for it. But no country in the whole world stands so much in want of it as France.[22]

Lastly, Lally employed all his literary skills and his formidable knowledge of eighteenth-century literature to provide the *Défense* with an eloquence which drew its strength from historic premises dear to the revolutionaries like this quote from Rousseau:

It must not be supposed that an arm can be wounded or cut off without the pain being felt in the head: and it is not more credible that the general will should consent that one member of the state, whoever he may be, may wound or destroy another, than it is that the fingers of any man, in possession of his reason, should be employed to put out his eyes.[23]

Fanny Burney's enthusiasm for this work was typical of the reception it solicited among the moderate royalist émigrés throughout Europe. The British were particularly receptive because by 1797 not only were they aware of, and regretted, the suffering of women, children and priests in their midst but it was the best of solutions because this work advocated the establishment of a limited monarchy on the English model:

I think never more by any writing I ever read: there is a nobleness of mind and of style, of thought and of expression, so strikingly combined, that eloquence has rarely seemed to me so natural, and never more penetrating. That any country can voluntarily throw away such a statesman, such an orator, such a citizen! You know how forcibly I was struck by M. de Lally Tolendal from the first: you will therefore not wonder I am now quite enthusiastic for him. Warmth and sensibility such as his, joined to a candour that seems above all prejudice on any side, or for any party, or purpose, or even wish, make me reverence now as before I admired him.[24]

In contrast to the enthusiasm for his writing expressed above, Mme de Boigne described him, admittedly years later, as a professional whiner.[25]

By the time of the second coalition, it was clear that Britain would have a central role in deciding or influencing the form of government that would be restored in France.[26] Until the arrival of Napoleon as Emperor of the French and the birth of the King of Rome (his son by his second wife Marie-Louise of Austria) there were only two probable options for a restoration. The royal house of Bourbon or the rival house of Orléans. Louis XVIII, the younger brother of Louis XVI, who assumed the title of King in 1795 upon the death of the young son of Louis XVI in the Temple prison, was the Bourbon claimant. His own marriage was childless but his younger brother the comte d'Artois had two teenage sons, the duc d'Angoulême and the duc de Berry, to assure the succession. In 1799, in exile in Mittau, the eldest, the duc d'Angoulême, married his cousin the only surviving child of Louis XVI.

The house of Orléans, which had seen its senior member Philippe Égalité go to the guillotine a few days after Marie Antoinette, was represented by his son who had defected into emigration with Dumouriez. Louis-Philippe, who would later rule France from 1830 to 1848, had fought with the Republican army at both Valmy and at Jemappes.[27] From 1800 onward he lived in London and was in close contact with his cousin, the comte d'Artois. The relationship was friendly and they enjoyed the hospitality of the Prince Regent and his circle of friends. He and his two younger brothers were based at Shot House in Twickenham. Louis XVIII, who rather envied the position of Artois in London, close to the British government at the centre of all the counter-revolutionary activity, came to Britain late in 1807 but the British government saw to it that he resided outside London because they were not yet prepared to openly support a Bourbon restoration. Louis Philippe himself seemed to accept and support the prospect of a Bourbon restoration. He was on good terms with and respected Louis XVIII who was walking a diplomatic tightrope with dignity and patience, both virtues a legacy of his time in exile.[28]

It was not until after the Restoration that Louis Philippe broke out of the émigré mould and moved progressively closer to the camp of the liberal opposition. The monarchy of Charles X, the comte d'Artois (1824–1830) retrenched in ultra-royalism in the face of mounting challenges from a rapidly industrialising French Nation, and a restlessly liberal Assembly convinced him that absolutism was out of step with the times.[29] Louis Philippe, due to his comparative youth and late emigration (1792), represented the *compromis bourgeois* between the ultras and the liberals and, in 1830, the aging General Lafayette brought it about.[30]

It is therefore not surprising that within the royalist ranks of emigration during the years 1795–1814 there were deep divisions about allegiances, about the future of French government, about the future monarch. In the Declaration of Verona Louis XVIII made no concessions to the constructive changes which had been brought about by the Revolution but instead announced his intention to turn the clock back. Never more so than with the language of the Declaration of Verona he destroyed the chances of reconciliation between the ultras and the moderate monarchists:

> You must renounce the dominion of those treacherous and cruel usurpers who promised you happiness but who have given you only famine and death: [...] You must return to that holy religion which had showered down upon France the blessings of Heaven. [...] You must restore that government which for fourteen centuries, constituted the glory of France and the delight of her inhabitants; which rendered our country the most flourishing of states and yourselves the happiest of people ....[31]

Just as it had been disastrous to expect Louis XVI to embrace the 1791 Constitution it was unrealistic to expect Louis XVIII to contemplate constitutional government. His entire formation and culture persuaded him of the truth of the above statement, which sowed the seeds of 1830 in 1795.

Dissatisfactions and frustrations were aired with monotonous frequency. The émigré community in London was as reflective of these divisions as the settlements anywhere in Europe and, as Britain became more and more important in the struggle to contain Republican ambitions, London became more and more politically complex.

This political complexity was due not only to the sensitivity of the parties involved but also to the sheer breadth of the conflict. The emigration provided a crossroads for European politics because it was uncomfortably suspended between the internal politics of the French Revolution and the external politics of the European powers. This was a situation which required professionals rather than amateurs simply in order to understand the interests of the parties involved which after years of war and exile were embittered, self-interested and avaricious in the extreme whether on a personal or national level.

Sooner or later all parties were disappointed and denied the role in the settlement of French affairs which they would have liked. The British government kept everybody guessing much to the gall of the *constitutionnels* or *monarchiens* who dearly wanted to be involved.[32]

L'abbé Maury wrote to the comte d'Antraigues that Mallet du Pan was not interested in a constitution that was not of his making, which was a fairly accurate assessment.[33]

> The monarchiens in London found themselves reduced to the position of powerless observers deprived of direct influence in the political life of their country. It is none the less true that they brought to bear with an exceptional pressure and perseverance a discordant voice in the ranks of the émigrés and it is this contribution to the counter-revolutionary debate which gives them their interest and their historical identity.[34]

French newspapers in London played a special role in the struggle against Revolution but they were limited by the financial and political limitations which hampered all small independent newspapers in the late eighteenth century.[35] After the fall of Robespierre censorship in France was relaxed a little but under the conditions of war it was re-imposed and under Napoleon it became charged with the force of a religious inquisition.

Therefore the existing French newspapers based in London which had a European circulation assumed a privileged position and became independent critics of imperial policy in a way impossible for those in France. Under these conditions the French newspapers, the *Courrier de Londres*, the *Courrier d'Angleterre*, the *Mercure Britannique* and the *Ambigu* in particular gained a status and a notoriety they would not otherwise have enjoyed. Through the mid- to late 1790s their circulations had been generally insignificant but with the advent of Napoleon and a change in editorial direction they all received a new lease of life and their modest circulations flourished.[36]

The *Courrier de Londres* was a direct descendant of the *Courrier de L'Europe*. It was essentially a political paper although it published advertisements, letters and miscellanea. Its focus was the French National Assembly and the British Parliament. Its bias was moderately constitutional but it was read by the entire French population in London either first or second hand as it was readily available in reading rooms and bookshops. From 1792 to 1797 it was edited by the abbé de Calonne, brother of Charles Alexandre de Calonne, the ex-finance minister of Louis XVI, who lived in Sloane Place, Chelsea.[37] On 1 August 1797 it was taken over by Montlosier, who had run his own paper, *Le journal de France et Angleterre* for six months. The two papers merged and Montlosier assumed the editorial direction of the *Courrier*.[38]

Montlosier was an eloquent and confident *constitutionnel*. Even before Lally's *Défense des émigrés* appeared, he had published his *Vues sommaires sur les moyens de Paix pour la France pour l'Europe, pour les Émigrés*.[39] In it he maintained that the émigrés were in a better position than the coalition to continue the war because they at least could lose nothing more. He argued that, as long as they remained in exile, they provided an important focus for patriotic hostility and, were they to return to France, that hostility would cease to exist.

> In many ways, the émigrés are in a more advantageous position to continue the war than the coalition, because they have nothing to lose; and this is their strength. The émigrés would have been able to believe themselves to blame if they had not acquitted their debts of loyalty. Today, it is only in continuing to outlaw them that the revolutionary government can make them dangerous; restored to their hearths they would not be.[40]

In the political climate directly preceding the *coup d'état* of Fructidor this was a logical argument. But Montlosier also showed how aware he was of the enormous complexity of émigré society and the profound differences which separated the world of the émigrés from Republican France. He wrote:

> If, through their conduct, their doctrine, their attitudes, they can behave in such a way as to take advantage of the situation; if a sincere renunciation of grandiose and ancient prerogatives, of deep-seated and grounded resentments, can be achieved; if they are capable of entering the circle of others, without always obliging others to enter theirs; if they can show themselves to be the sincere friends of France who want order, and not those who want to perpetuate the confusion and the calamities; if they can see beyond this state of mind where there is only complete lack of hope or a situation where they will recover absolutely everything; in a word, if they want to undeceive themselves about the false principles with which they constantly persuade themselves that good will come from evil, that it is through hell that they will reach happiness: the émigrés will put themselves back in a competitive situation; they will find in France as many allies as there exist fair men.
>
> Finally, if our princes themselves would assume these attitudes; if they would study the current situation in France instead of focusing on an impossible return and show some willingness to enter into

arrangements which might suit them, the monarchy could regain some favour.[41]

The editors of these newspapers constantly showed as much naivety as the émigrés they criticised in regard to the likelihood of any kind of rapprochement between the Bourbons and the liberal ideas which dominated French politics throughout most of the nineteenth century.[42] The royalists remained wedded to old prerogatives even though they were divided about exactly what those prerogatives were:

> For the rest of the revolutionary decade the programme of 23 June[43] would represent the most that the princes who led the forces of counter-revolution were prepared to concede should they regain power. Many of their followers were proved unwilling to go even that far, dreaming of a complete restoration of the old regime and they in turn would bitterly resent the arrival in counterrevolutionary ranks of men whose break with the hated movement came later, sometimes much later, and who until the moment of defection had accepted its work or tried to arrest its course from within. From the start counter-revolution was no more of a unity than the revolution it opposed.[44]

Not only was compromise unlikely, but more importantly, the princes who had returned to absolutist tradition as set out in documents like the Declaration of Verona had nothing to gain from negotiating with the republicans and weakening their already fragile support from the governments of Europe. As far as they were concerned, their only hope lay in affirming the Bourbon tradition and staunchly maintaining their claim to the throne of France.[45] The fact that this alienated the moderate element of the French political nation was an irony which served only the journalists who could see the absurdity of the situation, especially in the political context of the Second Directory, which had survived only by purging its Assemblies first of one faction then of the other. In September 1797 (the *coup* of 18 Fructidor) the moderate royalists who had gained an election majority were neutralised by illegal force, then in May 1798 (the *coup* of 22 Floréal) the same tactics were used on the radical Jacobins in the Directory's bid to establish the Republic as the political institution of the property-owning bourgeoisie. The Directory citizens, whose voting rights were more firmly based on property-owning than on the discriminatory active and passive distinctions of the 1791 Constitution, were far closer in many ways to moderate monarchy than to republicanism particularly when it had to accommodate Jacobinism.[46]

Whether or not they acknowledged the unsuitability of Louis XVIII to assume the leadership of post-revolutionary France, the exile newspapers exploited all the mileage to be had out of the ironies of this situation. The *Ambigu* in particular made itself the mouthpiece of the satirical response. Vehemently opposed to the Napoleonic regime, it poked fun at all aspects of the political situation and praised the British system with its reliance on law.[47]

The most important consequence of these rifts and factions within the emigration is the negative impact that this has had on the historiography of the French Revolution.

> Historical judgement has always been rather severe, and rightly so, concerning the political action of the émigrés, or rather more precisely of the counter-revolutionary emigration led by the King's two brothers.[48]

In books which are widely used as texts for French Revolution courses throughout the English-speaking world the legacy of these differences is a blanket condemnation of all émigrés whatever their political beliefs. This portrayal reflects two centuries of bias and these sources alone will affect another generation of students before any significant changes are made.

> But by itself the counter-revolution of the émigrés could not amount to much. With no money and minimal foreign support, its helplessness was only underlined by the Prince de Condé's quixotic plan to invade the country at the head of a column of gentlemen.[49]

> By their own efforts the bickering émigrés never had any chance of arresting or moderating, much less reversing the march of events in France. All they sometimes succeeded in doing by their antics, was to help push things to greater extremes – which only the more crass among them expected to advance their cause.[50]

The language of these two historians leaves little doubt about their opinion of the émigrés as a group. This is, of course, the common fallacy. French historians are only slightly more cautious:

> The émigrés made a great stir, but they were not universally supported; according to the accounts still available to us they hardly present a flattering picture of the French aristocracy. They were not

the kind of men who inspired confidence; they displayed inordinate ambition, and the allegiance shown by the Comte d'Artois towards his brother was, to say the least, equivocal. None of this was likely to help them to be taken seriously.[51]

This illustrates the dilemma facing post-revisionist historians in relation to émigrés. If they acknowledge the importance of the Emigration they must be prepared to defend their opinion against two hundred years of republican academic tradition to the contrary. It must never be overlooked that the first histories of the Revolution were written by French liberal Republicans even if their brand of republicanism seems tame by contrast with later nineteenth-century strains. Thiers, Michelet, Lamartine and Louis Blanc are among the forerunners; Michelet in particular, who was responsible for popularising the Revolution, wrote of émigrés in terms of black and white, they 'emigrated or they resigned themselves' and this view, which allows for no other position, recurs again and again in the writing and speeches of those who were members of government in post-restoration France.

In 1797, William Windham expressed his personal opinion about the French émigrés at the time of the revision of the Alien Bill. It was an opinion which was bound to be favourable due to his many contacts in émigré society but it was also measured and fair.

> The body of French emigrants ought, in his opinion, to be considered as consisting of men, many of whom had made great sacrifices for their loyalty and attachment to their ancient Government; many of them the respectable representatives of all that remain of the clergy, nobility, magistracy and propriety of the land.
>
> They had a claim to be considered not merely as suffering individuals but also in their collective and representative capacity which made them of still greater consequence.[52]

1802 marks a turning-point in the political make-up of the Emigration because many of the émigrés who held moderate political positions were able to return to France and to support the imperial regime. They were encouraged to do so by Napoleon who tempted them with conciliatory policies, places at court, and other concessions which many émigrés, who desired nothing more than to return to their homes and to assess the damage, were happy to accept.[53] The Concordat signed with the Pope in 1801 had brought to an end the ecclesiastic emigration for all but the most inveterate monarchists among the clergy and from all corners of Europe priests flocked back to France.[54]

The significance of this return has been ignored in the historical assessment of the Emigration. The small group which remained in exile and unconditionally supported the restoration of the Bourbon monarchy, although a minority of the émigré population, have had a preponderant and unrepresentative impact on the political history of the Emigration.[55] After the restoration of Louis XVIII the Emigration became a metaphor for all that was held to be inflexibly Bourbon and absolutist in the extreme.

The Archbishop of Aix summed up this position rather nicely when he consecrated the French Chapel Royal in London in 1799 and bishops were among those who remained in exile and refused to acknowledge the Concordat. Ironically, however, in this case, it was this same man who preached the *Te Deum* for the celebration of the Concordat in Paris in 1802.

> Plutôt mourir ... mes chers enfans, que de violer jamais dans le cours de votre vie le pacte de vos pères, le pacte pour nous inviolable et sacré de la religion et de la monarchie. Vous êtes instruits par nos infortunes, comme par notre fidélité, nos parens n'avaient pas reçu dans leur génération naissante, les leçons qui vous sont données chaque jour par les événements. Ils n'avaient point vu leurs pères, leurs frères, leurs concitoyens victimes de la révolte et de l'impiété; le crime usurpateur portant une main sacrilège sur le plus vertueux des souverains; leurs princes dans l'exil et leur roi légitime, centre nécessaire de tous les intérêts de l'Europe, sans autre pouvoir encore que le pouvoir inaliénable de ses talens, de ses vertus, et de ses droits; ils n'avaient pas été ravis dans leur enfance, arrachés du sein de leur patrie à travers les ruines des palais, des maisons et des temples; et que seriez vous devenus, ainsi que nous-mêmes dans ces jours de proscription, si la Providence n'avait pas marqué notre asile au sein de cette nation hospitalière et sous ce roi Protecteur de l'étranger et du citoyen, dont les vertus personnelles ont étouffé dans ses États le germe des revolutions et dont la puissance étendue aux extrémités des deux mondes, est devenue par la sagesse, le courage et la victorie, le conseil, la defense et la force de tous les souverains et de tous les empires. Vos parens tranquilles et fortunés sous le toit paternel et dans la terre natale n'avaient point appris par les épreuves cruelles de leur premières années quelle

était l'indissoluble union des intérêts et du devoir de l'église et de l'État. Votre éducation est formée tout entière du spectacle des grands malheurs et de l'exemple des grandes vertus: la monarchie vous a voué à la religion sur les débris du trône et l'amour de vos rois est le serment que la religion vous fait prononcer sur les débris des autels.[56]

Better to die, my dear children, than ever in the course of your life to violate the pact of your fathers, a pact which is for us the inviolable and sacred pact of religion and of monarchy. Learn from our mistakes, as from our loyalty. Our forefathers did not have the advantage of the lessons which are daily given to you by events. They have never seen their fathers, their brothers, their fellow countrymen victims of revolt and impiety; the usurping crime bringing a blasphemous blade down on the most virtuous sovereign; their princes in exile and their legitimate King the necessary focus of all the interests of Europe, without any other power except that of his talents, his virtues and his rights. They have not been deprived of their childhood or torn away from their country across the ruins of palaces, houses and churches. What would you have become during these days of exile, if Providence had not given us an asylum in this hospitable nation and under the protection of this King, champion of foreigners and citizens, whose personal virtues have snuffed out the spark of revolution and whose power extends to the extremities of two continents, who has become through wisdom, courage, victory, good counsel, the defence and the force of all monarchs and all empires? Your relations, calm and fortunate in their own homes on native soil, have not learned through bitter hardship in their early life the indispensable link of duty and loyalty which binds church and state. Your education is completely fashioned around the examples of intense misfortune and great virtue. The monarchy has made you swear allegiance to the Church on the ruins of its throne and the love of your King is the oath that the Church obliges you to swear upon the ruins of its altars.

It was this faction who triumphed in 1814 despite that fact that their triumph was stage-managed by the governments of Europe, led by Britain. Precisely how many of the Bourbon supporters shared the opinion of Mme de Boigne who maintained that she was far more anti-bonapartist than pro-Bourbon, we will never know.[57] But many, like the author of these lines, were inflexibly royalist or anti-revolutionary:

Vous voilà donc sous l'écoutille
Du grand vaisseau républicain
Et la victime et l'assassin
Ne feront plus qu'une famille.[58]

    The unrepresentative nature of the historical portrayal of the emigration is an important stumbling block in any attempt to do justice to the sincere, committed and honourable nature of the vast majority of émigrés. These individuals were not prepared to accept the promethean destiny of the Revolution as the fate of all France. They were not all reactionary, as much of their writing proves. Many acknowledged the good that had come out of the early years of the Revolution and many were prepared to acknowledge, at least in theory, that there were some benefits to be derived from republican government. Royalist supporters were forced to take up ideological positions which were more extreme than they might have wished. Those prepared to voice opinions other than the politically correct ones in emigration had to sustain the ostracism that invariably followed. Yet it was 'a universal truth that the bloodthirstiness of the Terror repelled all French citizens, émigrés and patriots alike', and there were other moments between 1794 and 1814, such as the eve of the *coup d'état* of Fructidor, when a rapprochement seemed likely or even achievable. These opportunities melted away, either suppressed by the revolutionary government like Fructidor, or wasted like the Declaration at Verona. Montlosier was right to draw attention to this.

    Lastly, the perception of the émigrés from inside France was locked in stalemate. Fears about the threat posed to the Revolution by the Counter-Revolution necessarily included an assumption that all émigrés wanted the resurrection of the Bourbon monarchy. This assumption was based on rumour and served very effectively to annihilate any potential for compromise between the two parties. As Lally pointed out, it was not in the interests of any of the revolutionary governments to concede any justice to the émigrés. By maintaining them as the instruments of the evil that currently afflicted France they shifted the blame away from themselves to a party which was unable to defend itself before the French people; just as, on an individual level, émigrés were legitimately stripped of their property so they were unable to defend themselves before the emerging political nation. Even contemporaries were not deceived and this opinion of Arthur Young's is but one example:

It has been repeatedly asserted, that the Government of France has done nothing in violation of the rights of property, except with relation to emigrants, who were considered as guilty for the act of flying: but is it not palpable, that filling prisons on suspicion, by arbitrary commitments, and emptying them by massacre – that the perpetual din of pillage and assassination – are calculated to fill men with alarm and terror – and to drive them to fly not through guilt, but horror? By your murders you drive them away, and then pronouncing them emigrants, confiscate their estates! And this is called the security of property. The cry of aristocrat or traitor is followed by immediate imprisonment or death, and has been found an easy way of paying debts. Upon my inquiring of a correspondent what was become of a gentleman I had known at Paris, the answer was, that he was met in the street by a person considerably in his debt, who no sooner saw him than he attacked him as a traitor, and ordered him to gaol. No known massacre was committed in that prison, but my acquaintance was heard of no more. It is easy to conjecture what became of the debt.[59]

9 Émigré Writers and Writing about Émigrés

In any consideration of the literature produced and inspired by the Emigration it is useful to distinguish between the writing with a direct political purpose, like Lally's *Défense*, and that which had an indirect political purpose, like Chateaubriand's *Génie du Christianisme* or Mme de Staël's *Corinne*. This allows the reader to separate the polemical literature with a more limited lifespan from those works which are considered to belong to the 'literature' of the early nineteenth century. After the Restoration, there was no need to continue the propaganda assault on the Republic which effectively put the émigré press out of business. It was not until the 1830s that renewed attacks on émigrés in a different and new political climate prompted a fresh burst of political writings and memoirs. It is, therefore, in the literature (not only French but also British) which goes beyond the chronological dates of the Revolution and Empire that the legacy of the emigration can be more fully appreciated. Chateaubriand and Mme de Staël are examples of writers whose émigré connections have been considered unimportant but whose émigré experiences shed much light on their work.

It is not possible in this short chapter to do justice to these authors but I will attempt to illustrate how integrally their writing was affected by their contacts with the émigré world. Other émigré writers who had an impact on their contemporaries in Britain and France were the abbé Delille, Jean Baptiste Cléry, the abbé Carron and the comtesse de Flahaut. These writers wrote for a reading public divided into the refugee society in London and Europe, the British upper class and their fellow countrymen and women in France.

Much has been written about the little colony at Juniper Hall.[1] The house was rented by Louis, comte de Narbonne with funds provided by Mme de Staël and it became home to several members of the *constitutionnel* faction in exile, Madame de la Châtre, François, comte de Jaucourt, Mathieu de Montmorency, and Général Alexandre d'Arblay. Mme de Staël's arrival in Britain early in 1793 was an important event in émigré society.

Mme de Staël's arrival in England had been delayed until January by the birth of Narbonne's child.[2] Her husband was in Brussels and it was difficult for her to find a socially acceptable excuse to remain. After the departure of Mme de la Châtre at the beginning of 1793, she implored Narbonne to find a mistress, someone not too pretty, who could provide a disguise for their *ménage*. The diversion Narbonne sought was fortuitously provided by Fanny Burney and her sister Mrs Susanna Philips. Fanny's diary from late 1792 and 1793 recounts life among this group of émigrés which included visitors like Talleyrand and Malouet, and in July 1793 her marriage to Alexandre d'Arblay, one of Lafayette's trusted aides-de-camp, perpetuated the link.

Fanny Burney is an honorary émigré and, as in the case of Chateaubriand and Mme de Staël, her writing is better understood, particularly her novel *The Wanderer*, with a knowledge of her personal links in emigration.[3] Burney was not an obvious marriage choice for an impoverished émigré: she had no fortune and only a very small annuity of £100 per year.[4] She and d'Arblay survived on the income from her novels which, by 1796, when *Camilla* was published, was enough to allow them to build a small cottage. Theirs was a love match and its plainly apparent imprudence was pointed out by her father:

> As M. d'Arblay is at present circumstanced, an alliance with anything but a fortune sufficient for the support of himself and partner would be very imprudent. He is a mere soldier of fortune, under great disadvantages. Your income, if it was as certain as a freehold estate, is insufficient for the purpose; and if the Queen should be displeased and withdraw her allowance, what could you do?[5]

The Burney family were intimately involved with the French émigrés. Both Fanny's sisters knew and entertained émigrés and her father was closely involved with Relief effort. Sarah, who lived at Bradfield near Bury St Edmunds, 'lived upon French politics and with French fugitives where she seemed perfectly satisfied with foreign forage'.[6] Susanna, who lived at Mickleham, a stone's throw from Juniper Hall, at times found herself wishing she did not know there was such a country as France.[7]

It was in a letter from Susanna, dated September 1792, that Fanny first learnt of the arrival of the French inhabitants of Juniper Hall which was to change her life. Mrs Philips wrote that

> two or three families had joined to take Jenkinson's house Juniper Hall, and that another family had taken a small house at Westhumble,

which the people very reluctantly let, upon the Christian-like supposition that, being nothing but French papishes, they would never pay.[8]

The tenants of the small house were Mme de Broglie and her son Victor:

> This poor lady came over in an open boat with a son younger than my Norbury and was fourteen hours at sea.[9]

This was the beginning of endless visits and a close relationship with Mme de Staël which was based on mutual respect for each other's ability and further cemented by the fact that Burney was no society beauty but a woman of similar talents to those she described in her friend:

> She is a woman of the first abilities, I think, I have ever seen; she is more in the style of Mrs.Thrale than of any other celebrated character, but she has infinitely more depth, and seems an even profound politican and metaphysician. She has also suffered us to hear some of her works in MS., which are truly wonderful, for powers both of thinking and expression.[10]

Fanny, like all well-bred young English women in the late eighteenth century, was rather naive and completely oblivious to the nature of the liaison between Mme de Staël and Narbonne, which was common knowledge in London. Even when her father, who was concerned about the social repercussions of his daughter's association with these émigrés, enlightened her, she was still somewhat disbelieving.

Mme de Staël who, in her turn, described Fanny as 'la meilleure et la plus distinguée' of women wrote:

> Il faut laisser l'injustice aux hommes malheureux; il faut qu'ils s'occupent des personnes quand ils ne peuvent rien sur les affaires; [...] il faut tout ce qui est ordinaire et extraordinaire dans une pareille époque, et se confier au tems pour l'opinion publique – à l'amitié pour le bonheur particulier.[11]

> We must leave injustice to the unfortunate, they have to turn their attention to people when they can do nothing about events. [...] everything that is ordinary must be extraordinary in an era such as this, and we must put our confidence in time, where matters of

public opinion are concerned, and in friendship, for those of individual happiness.

The friendship and respect of these two women for each other's society was lasting and the links created at Juniper Hall in 1793 inspired warm memories for the rest of their lives.[12] It is not surprising that they were drawn to each other. They shared and articulated in their novels a vision of the role of women in society which was more emancipated and more egalitarian than the society they themselves would ever know.[13]

In order to placate appearances, Mme de Staël spent much of the month of March 1793 in London visiting friends, among them the comtesse de Flahaut, who was writing her first novel, *Adèle de Senange*, with the editorial advice and assistance of Talleyrand. In April, Mme de Staël was in Richmond to hear the first reading of Lally Tolendal's play *Le comte de Strafford*, which was an important occasion in the émigré community because its themes were those of personal loyalty and political integrity, which were central to the emigration.

During her stay at Juniper Hall, Mme de Staël wrote *De l'influence des passions sur le bonheur des individus et des nations,* a work which was published in 1795 but remained incomplete. D'Arblay spent his time recopying her manuscripts, functioning much as Mme de Flahaut's 'vraie machine à écrire' but, in his case, for his own pleasure and amusement.

Mme de Staël left Surrey on 25 May 1793. Narbonne stayed on at Juniper Hall in the company of d'Arblay until the latter's marriage in July. In November, he too moved out of the house and the episode came to an end. But for Mme de Staël the memory of her short stay in Britain never faded and in the letters she wrote to Fanny Burney there is a yearning for the peace and tranquillity which characterised not only the English landscape but the domestic culture of the British nation.

These opinions are central to her novel *Corinne* which juxtaposes the French and the British character in its two heros.

[Le comte d'Erfeuil] avait des manières élegantes, une politesse facile et de bon goût; et dès l'abord il se montrait parfaitement à son aise. [...] il était doux obligéant, facile en tout, sérieux seulement dans l'amour propre, et digne d'être aimé comme il aimait, c'est-à-dire comme un bon camarade des plaisirs et des périls.[14]

> [The comte d'Erfeuil] had elegant manners, an easy politeness and good taste. From the very first he seemed perfectly at ease ... he was gentle, obliging, considerate, serious only about his vanity and worthy of being loved only as he loved, that is to say, as the travelling companion of pleasures and perils.

He admired in his friend Lord Nevil

> sa résignation et sa simplicité, sa modestie et sa fierté lui inspiraient une considération dont il ne pouvait se défendre. Il s'agitait autour du calme extérieur d'Oswald.[15]

> his resignation and his simplicity, his modesty and his pride inspired in him an affection that he couldn't help. The composure of Oswald made him restless.

In regard to his attachment to France,

> il était exempt des préjugés qui séparent les deux nations, parce qu'il avait eu pour ami intime un Français, et qu'il avait trouvé dans cet ami la plus admirable réunion de toutes les qualités de l'âme.[16]

> He did not share the prejudices which separated the two nations because he had had a very good friend who was a Frenchman and he had found in this friend the most admirable composition of human qualities.

When Oswald (Lord Nevil) entered Rome;

> il ne sentait que le profond isolement qui serre le coeur quand vous entrez dans une ville étrangère, quand vous voyez cette multitude de personnes à qui votre existence est inconnue, et qui n'ont aucun intérêt en commun avec vous.[17]

> He felt only the profound isolation which grips your heart when you enter a strange town, when you see this multitude of people who don't know you and with whom you have nothing in common.

The echoes of emigration resound through this novel, which likens years spent on foreign soil to trees without roots.[18] When Oswald returned to London, il fut frappé de l'ordre et de l'aisance, de la richesse et de l'industrie qui s'offraient à ses regards; les penchants, les habitudes, les goûts nés avec lui se réveillèrent avec plus de force que jamais. Dans ce pays où les hommes ont tant de dignité et les femmes tant de modestie, où le bonheur domestique est le lien du bonheur public, Oswald pensait à l'Italie pour la plaindre. Il lui semblait que dans sa patrie la raison humaine était par-tout noblement empreinte, tandis qu'en Italie les institutions et l'état social ne rappelaient, à beaucoup d'égards, que la confusion, la faiblesse et l'ignorance.[19]

He was struck with the order and the ease, with the richness and the industry which he found before him. The habits and customs, the tastes that he was born with reawakened more strongly than ever. In this country where the men show so much dignity and the women so much modesty, where domestic happiness is the key to public happiness, Oswald could only think of Italy with pity. It seemed to him that everywhere in his country there was the noble trace of human reason whereas in Italy the institutions and the society in many ways evoke only confusion, weakness and ignorance.

The description of Italian politics is of course a thinly veiled critique of the French system and Italy thus served as a political metaphor. But it is Oswald who conveys the depth of Mme de Staël's admiration for the British which goes beyond the political system.

Oswald en arrivant à Londres, retrouva ses amis d'enfance. Il entendit parler cette langue forte et serrée qui semble indiquer bien plus de sentiments encore qu'elle n'en exprime; il revit ces physionomies sérieuses qui se développent tout à coup quand des affections profondes triomphent de leur réserve habituelle; il retrouva le plaisir de faire des découvertes dans les coeurs qui se révèlent par degrés aux regards observateurs; enfin il se sentit dans sa patrie, et ceux qui n'en sont jamais sortis ignorent par combien de liens elle nous est chère.[20]

Oswald, arriving in London, found his childhood friends. He heard spoken that strong and guttural language which seems to suggest many more sentiments than it expresses. He welcomed these serious countenances which transfigure themselves immediately when heartfelt affections triumph over their habitual reserve. He rediscovered the pleasure of divining the secrets of hearts which only reveal themselves by degrees to acute observers. Finally he felt at home, and those who have never been away are not aware how precious that feeling can be.

The novel *Corinne* was written in 1805–6 and published in 1807. It was a huge success and its topicality made it the toast of the season. *Corinne* was Mme de Staël in a beautiful form instead of her own rather unattractive masculine appearance. Various characters from the novel were identifiable contemporary figures. The character of Mme d'Arbigny was undisguisedly the comtesse de Flahaut, which suggested that the connection with the Emigration was deliberate and desirable. Oswald was loosely based on Benjamin Constant, who had spent his childhood in Edinburgh.

Mme de Staël was censored, despised and exiled by Napoleon, which led her to remark that men in France were unable to become sufficiently republican to be able to cope with independence and natural pride in women. She nevertheless suffered from this humiliation combined with her unfortunate lack of looks and complained that as soon as a woman is spoken of as a distinguished person the public in general turns against her.[21] This served to heighten her esteem for the British and their attitudes towards women. On receiving the news of Burney's marriage to d'Arblay she wrote:

> tous mes regrets, comme toutes mes espérances, me ramènent en Surrey. C'est le paradis terrestre pour moi – ce le sera pour vous, je l'espère.[22]
>
> All my regrets and all my hopes draw me back to Surrey. It is an earthly paradise for me and I hope it will be for you.

Her stay in Surrey she remembered passionately and nostalgically and, of Norbury Park in August 1793, she wrote:

> Dans cette retraite [...] j'ai trouvé quelque tems un asyle loin des crimes de la France, et des préjugés que l'horreur qu'ils doivent causer inspirent à tous ceux qui n'ont pas la force de résister aux extrêmes contraires. Le respect, l'enthousiasme, dont mon âme est remplie, en contemplant l'ensemble des vertus morales et politiques qui constituent l'Angleterre; – l'admiration d'un tel spectacle, le repos céleste qu'il me fesoit goûter; ces sentimens, si doux et si nécessaires après la tourmente de trois ans de révolution, s'unissent dans mon souvenir au délicieux séjour, aux respectables amis, près

desquels je les ai éprouvés. Je les remercie de quatre mois de bonheur échappés au naufrage de la vie; ...[23]

In this retreat [...] I found for a time a resting-place away from the crimes of France and the prejudices that are inspired by the horror that these crimes must cause, in all who have not the force to resist the opposing extremes. The respect, the enthusiasm which fill my heart when considering all the moral and political virtues of England; the admiration for such a prospect, the peaceful rest that it let me savour; these sentiments so gentle and so necessary after the torment of three years of revolution come together in my memory of this delicious stay, with that of the respectable friends who shared them with me. I thank them for four months of happiness stolen from the wreck of life.

Mme de Staël must be understood as an émigré writer because, had she not escaped on the technicality of being Swiss by birth and Swedish by marriage, she would have without doubt been proscribed on the émigré lists like so many of her friends.[24] Indeed when the republican armies overran Geneva in 1798 her possessions were seized.[25] During her exile, like so many other émigrés, she became more royalist and more religious than she had previously been. Yet, like Mme de Boigne, she was not so much a supporter of the Bourbons as an ardent anti-Bonapartiste.[26] She was also a great admirer of the British political system and her royalism although latterly ardent, was tinged with constitutional leanings which made her marvel that she was not a supporter of the opposition.[27]

Less famous as a writer than Mme de Staël, the comtesse de Flahaut avoided politics and wrote novels, not by vocation but of necessity. She arrived in London in 1792 with her infant son Charles, very little money and only a few jewels. Her first novel, which was to be the first of a dozen over the next twenty years, enabled her to live comfortably though quietly during her relatively short emigration. She returned to France in 1797 and through connections and intrigue obtained her removal from the émigré list. She nevertheless spent five long and lonely years in exile and during that time her solace was her writing which provided her with her only source of income.[28] In the preface of *Adèle de Senange* she wrote:

Cet essai a été commencé dans un temps qui semblait imposer à une femme, à une mère, le besoin de s'éloigner de tout ce qui était réel, de ne guère réfléchir, et même d'écarter la prévoyance.[29]

This essay was written at a time which seemed to impose on a woman, on a mother, the need to remove herself from everything that was real, not to think about the past and to avoid thinking about the future.

The comtesse de Flahaut used her creative instincts to combat the long days in exile but, more than that, because she was unable to afford a copy-editor, she edited and recopied her own manuscripts. She described how she functioned mechanically and she recommended the total absorption which the task required as the best tonic for the worries of emigration.[30]

The comtesse de Flahaut was a fairly typical late-eighteenth-century aristocratic woman. She had been married at 19 to the comte de Flahaut who was then 57, so her experience of marriage was a loveless respect for the ageing count, who treated her with respect and acknowledged her son Charles as his legitimate heir although the child was not his.[31] Her first lover Talleyrand, then the abbé de Périgord, shared her intellectual tastes and her wit. The comte de Flahaut was guillotined in 1794. He gave himself up to meet his fate when another was accused in his place. In a biography of his son Charles, the observation has been made that Charles may have regretted that this kind and honourable man of impeccable nobility was not his real father.[32] The comtesse de Flahaut later married the Marquis José-Maria de Souza Botelho, a Portuguese diplomat who retired into private life and remained in Paris when his official engagement ended in 1802. She devoted the rest of her life to her husband and to her son, whose career she followed with the possessive attention of a solo parent.

Eugénie et Mathilde, written in 1811, is Flahaut's émigré novel. It follows a family through the Emigration.[33] What the novel portrays with the skill of an Austen is how quickly *ancien régime* social conventions and practices were adapted during the Emigration. Corrupt practices were exposed and behaviour for which there was no longer any rationale was changed. It was a very clever piece of social history, and echoes of her own experiences create an authenticity.

> La nuit ne laissait rien voir autour de soi. Ils n'entendaient que le bruit qu'ils faisaient eux-mêmes; et leur imagination craintive leur persuadait qu'il devait parvenir aux environs et éveiller la malveillance. Ils tremblaient au plus léger cri du petit Victor.[34]

The pitch-darkness left nothing visible. They heard only the noises they made and their fearful imagination convinced them that they came from something other than themselves which left them uneasy. They trembled at the faintest cry from little Victor.

This experience struck a chord with many émigrés who had feared for their lives during their escape. Echoes of Madame de Staël's reaction to foreign places ring through this passage:[35]

> Quel que soit le pays où l'on arrive, quelle que soit la disposition que l'on y apporte, lorsqu'on se sent étranger à tout le monde la première personne qui vient vous prévoir, la première qui vous fait entendre des paroles bienveillantes vous devient chère.[36]
>
> Whatever country you arrive in, whatever disposition you take to it, when you feel you are a stranger to everybody, the first person who helps you or who shows you a kindness becomes very dear.

The helplessness, misery and humiliation of the circumstances people found themselves in is also expressed:

> Quel serrement de coeur en entrant dans cette auberge qui offrait l'aspect d'une extrême misère! [...] Monsieur de Revel regardait avec douleur sa femme et sa belle-mère qui se trouvaient si mal dans cette auberge qu'elles n'avaient voulu pouvoir repartir tout de suite. [...] On leur apportait des pommes de terre sur une assiette d'étain et quelques mets grossiers dont personne ne voulut, accoutumés qu'ils étaient à une éxcellente chère.[37]
>
> What a heart-rending sight upon entering this inn which offered an air of extreme misery .... M. de Revel looked at his wife and mother-in-law who were so uncomfortable in this lodging that they had wished to go on immediately. A servant brought them potatoes on a pewter plate and some coarse food which none of them wanted to taste, accustomed as they were to an excellent table.

Flahaut shows a compassion and an understanding devoid of judgemental criticism:

> Avec les habitudes d'une grande fortune, il suffit d'un caractère ferme, pour se soumettre aux privations, mais il faut bien du temps pour apprendre l'économie.[38]

When accustomed to an immense fortune, one only needs a firm character to submit to privations but it takes much longer to learn economy.

At another point she wrote:

Ceux qui n'ont jamais connu le malheur ignorent combien une seule circonstance imprévue peut jeter dans le désespoir.

Those who have never known misfortune are incapable of imagining how a single unexpected event can bring people to desperation-point.

Although she had been lucky enough to avoid complete destitution, Flahaut was highly aware of the toll it had taken on others who did not share her internal fortitude. Her comments are searching and she tackles the most complex issues at which other writers barely hint. Little wonder that Marie-Joseph Chénier, a republican and someone not likely to be sympathetic to this genre of royalist writing, wrote of her novels:

Ces jolis romans n'offrent pas, il est vrai, le developpement des grandes passions; on n'y doit pas chercher non plus l'étude approfondie des travers de l'espèce humaine; on est sûr au moins d'y trouver partout des aperçus très-fins sur la société, des tableaux vrais et bien terminés, un style orné avec mesure, la correction d'un bon livre et l'aisance d'une conversation fleurie, ... l'esprit qui ne dit rien de vulgaire, et le goût qui ne dit rien de trop.[39]

these delightful novels are not epic stories, neither do they offer in-depth studies of the human condition, but they present a very fine-tuned appreciation of society, very well-rounded accurate descriptions, elegant conversations and a tasteful style which omits anything vulgar or anything that suggests too much.

He was known for the integrity and ruthless criticism of his comments and he was rarely as generous as this towards contemporary writers. He wrote of Madame de Genlis, another prolific woman writer who also wrote an émigré novel in letter-form called *Les Petits Émigrés*, that

On n'écrit pas toujours bien quand on veut toujours écrire: l'esprit et l'imagination ne sont pas constamment aux ordres de ceux même qui en ont le plus.[40]

The desire to be constantly writing does not necessarily produce good writing: intellect and imagination are not necessarily at the command of those who possess the most.

An author whose importance did not survive the Emigration, but who for a short time enjoyed a giddy celebrity, was Cléry, the valet of Louis XVI, who escaped to Britain and published his *Journal de ce qui s'est passé à la Tour du Temple* (Diary of what happened in the Temple prison). It was a moving account of Louis XVI's martyrdom and its authenticity, particularly when read aloud by the author, made it a focus of public discussion and grieving in émigré circles.[41]

Burney described the reaction of the residents of Juniper Hall to this work in a letter to her father:

Indeed my dearest Father, M Cléry's book has half killed us; we have read it together, and the deepest tragedy we have yet met with is slight to it. The extreme plainness and simplicity of the style, the clearness of the detail, the unparading yet evident worth and feeling of the writer, make it a thousand times more affecting than it it had been drawn out with the most striking eloquence. What an angel – what a saint, yet breathing, was Louis XVI! – the last meeting with the venerable M de Malesherbes, and the information which, prostrate at his feet, he gives of the King's condemnation, makes the most soul-piercing scene, and stopped us from all reading a considerable time; frequently, indeed, we have been obliged to take many minutes' respite before we could command ourselves to go on. But the last scene with the royal Family is the most heartbreaking picture that ever was exibited.[42]

The émigrés' rejection of the new Republic had cost them very dearly in human terms. Émigré writing reflected this quality of sombre endurance and the need for great mental courage. The Président de Longueil, one of the principal characters in Senac de Meihan's novel said,

J'admis leur courage et je crois que cette facilité à se soumettre à son sort, à se conformer aux circonstances est un des attributs du caractère français.[43]

I admire their courage and I think that this ability to accept their fate and to adapt to circumstances is one of the attributes of the French character.

In contrast to the short-lived celebrity of Cléry, Jacques Delille figures among the most important literary figures not only of the emigration but of the late eighteenth century. When he came to London his reputation was established. He did not leave France until 1794 when, he was confronted with the dubious honour of being invited to write the lyrics of the 'Hymne à l'Être Suprême'; a task which he left to the unknown provincial, Théodore Desorgues.[44] By the time he came to London in 1798 he was the toast of émigré society in Europe.

Delille became the pride of the emigration for a poem he wrote in London entitled *Malheur et Pitié*. In it, he captured the nostalgia, the homesickness, the suffering and the anger of the London émigrés and his reproaches to the Napoleonic regime ensured that the poem was censored. The original and uncut version was finally published in London in 1803.[45] In France the poem was considered to contain 'subversive maxims for the social order'.[46] It did in fact contain some poisonous barbs:

> Par-tout la soif du meurtre et la faim du carnage
> Les arts jadis si doux, le sexe, le jeune âge,
> Tout prend un coeur d'airain; la farouche beauté
> Préfère à notre scène un cirque ensanglanté;
> Le jeune enfant sourit aux tourments des victimes;
> Les arts aident le meurtre, et célèbrent les crimes.[47]

'Thirst for murder' and 'hunger for carnage' is strong language. It refers to a 'bloody circus' and in another line 'the idol to whom France has confided its destiny'; all of which Napoleon could not have been expected to enjoy. Delille returned to France in 1802, the year of the publication of the censored *Malheur et Pitié*, and simultaneously published a translation of *Paradise Lost*, a translation of the *Aeneid* and a poem called *Imagination*. He relied upon his reputation and upon the fact that the members of the Institut National (the old Académie) had been trying to lure him back since 1795 to protect him from government officials. The line, 'les arts aident le meurtre et célèbrent les crimes' referred perhaps as far back as his own refusal to write the lyrics of the 'Hymne à l'Être Suprême'. There can be no doubt that he was perfectly aware of how provocative his writing was to the Consulat but was probably surprised by the ferocity of the reaction.

In London, Peltier's *Ambigu* reported:

> The publication of Mr. the Abbé Delille's poem 'La Malheur et la Pitié' has been suspended almost two months ago by order of the

police of Paris and the different editions have been seized at the printers just as they were about to go to print. It was made clear to the French publishers that they would be thrown into prison, them and their entire family, if a single copy or edition of this poem appeared outside France because they knew that foreign editions had been prepared at the same time as the Paris one. This threat worked perfecty but the first consul gave us another proof of his selective justice. One of the proprietors of the manuscript had just received a cathedral in compensation.[48]

The article goes on to note that the government was most scandalised by the verses which implied that the lowest classes were in possession of power. This was a particular humiliation to the Consulat which, like the Directory, felt that the class most suited to govern was the educated property-owning elite.

Malheur et Pitié is a complex mixture of literature and politics but the reason that the émigrés loved it so much was that Delille captured, with a perception that only personal experience could, the reality of emigration in London.

> Qu'il est dur de quitter de perdre sa patrie!
> Absents, elle est présente à notre âme attendrie:
> Alors on se souvient de tout ce qu'on aima,
> Des sites enchanteurs dont l'aspect nous charma,
> Des jeux de notre enfance, et même de ses peines.

He writes of the young, the orphans, the lonely and the old and the sentiment which unites them:

> Votre pitié, voilà leur unique partage!

He writes of their dreams of returning to France, of how

> Les maux de l'exil et de l'oppression
> Croissent au souvenir de sa chère Sion.

While Delille came to London having been a member of the Académie Française since 1772, Chateaubriand, who would later be admitted to its privileged ranks, was still a young man eager to further his own personal ambitions among London's émigré elite. Unpopular after his *Essai historique sur les révolutions anciennes et modernes*

(1796), which did not go far enough in condemning the Revolution, he wrote another work which won him the laurels he craved – *Le Génie du Christianisme*.

No other writer expressed as clearly as Chateaubriand the acute isolation imposed on a young émigré by the experience of emigration:

> Lorsque je quittai la France, j'étais jeune: quatre ans de malheur m'ont vieilli. Depuis quatre ans, retiré à la campagne, sans un ami à consulter, sans personne qui pût m'entendre, le jour travaillant pour vivre, la nuit écrivant ce que le chagrin et la pensée me dictait, je suis parvenu à crayonner cet Essai. Je n'en ignore pas les défauts: si le moi y revient souvent, c'est que cet ouvrage a d'abord été entrepris pour moi, et pour moi seul. On y voit presque partout un malheureux qui cause avec lui-même; dont l'esprit erre de sujets en sujets, de souvenirs en souvenirs; qui n'a point l'intention de faire un livre, mais tient une espèce de journal régulier de ses excursions mentales, un registre de ses sentiments, de ses idées. Le moi se fait remarquer chez tous les auteurs qui, persécutés des hommes, ont passé leur vie loin d'eux. Les solitaires vivent de leur coeur, comme ces sortes d'animaux qui, faute d'aliments extérieurs, se nourrissent de leur propre substance.[49]

> When I left France I was young. Four years of ill fortune have aged me. Four years buried in the country without a friend to consult and no one to listen, by day working to earn a living, by night writing down whatever my thoughts and grief dictated, have produced this essay. I am fully aware of its limitations. If its subjectivity often makes itself felt, it is because this work was undertaken for myself and for myself alone. One can see the trace of an unhappy man who talks to himself, his conversation errs from topic to topic and from memory to memory without any intention of writing a book but more of keeping a sort of regular account of his mental travels, a register of his feelings and his ideas. The first person is a characteristic of all authors who, persecuted by society, have lived withdrawn from the world. Solitary people live off their own heart rather like a sort of animal which, when it lacks all other form of food, reverts to its own body for sustenance.

The *Essai*, published in London in 1796, was an historical analysis of the French Revolution, comparing it with earlier revolutions. It did not appeal to the royalist émigrés, who criticised its findings because they were not sufficiently ultra. Chateaubriand freely acknowledged his disregard for social conventions and the fact that he was usually at odds with the opinions of those around him.[50]

The plea for justice he makes in the *Essai* brings him close to authors like Lally Tolendal and Montlosier with whom he was acquainted through Peltier (though they had little in common) and whose circumstances in London émigré society were very different from his own:

> Si l'on considère sans passion ce que les émigrés ont souffert en France, quel est l'homme, maintenant heureux, qui, mettant la main sur son coeur ose dire 'Je n'eusse pas fait comme eux.'[51]

> If one objectively considers what the émigrés have suffered in France there is no man now living comfortably, who, putting his hand on his heart, would dare to say 'I would not have done what they did'.

The Abbé Maury expressed similar feelings and, despite the fact that he was usually critical of the émigrés' behaviour, he challenged those who judged them severely to put themselves in the same situation and defied them to admit that they would not have done the same thing.[52]

Chateaubriand was highly aware of the complexity of the political issues involved in the Emigration which drew him intellectually towards the *constitutionnels*.[53] As time went on, however, he severed the link and became progressively ultra-royalist emphasising the moral force of religion in politics and developed a very acute sense of political correctness. He realised that opinions like those expressed in the *Essai* were not going to make him famous and he became very adept at saying and writing the right thing. Mme de Boigne described him as having a particular flair for catching the public mood and massaging it so skilfully that 'despite his political colours' he had managed to make himself popular.[54]

The *Génie du Christianisme,* from which he read extracts to an audience in London as early as 1799, set itself therefore to justify the role of the Church in French society and to win for its author the celebrity which had eluded him up to that point. The Revolution and subsequent dechristianisation which had ruined the prestige and power of the Catholic Church in France had also put it at the centre of the counter-revolutionary cause.[55] Anyone who promoted the importance of the Church would automatically receive the unanimous support of the exiled community as well as finding sympathy within France.

The *Génie du christianisme* made Chateaubriand simultaneously the champion of the Emigration and one of the early standard-bearers of the French romantic movement and earned him a place in the Académie.[56] The book, which has been described as 'one of the most brillant manifestos of emigration ideology', was a huge success.[57] It accused Voltaire (who was conveniently dead) of being responsible for the degradation of Christianity and of inciting atheism among the French people.

> Il eut l'art funeste, chez un peuple capricieux et aimable, de rendre l'incredulité à la mode. Il enrôla tous les amours-propres dans cette ligue insensée; la religion fut attaquée avec toutes les armes, depuis le pamphlet jusqu'à l'in-folio, l'epigramme jusqu'au sophisme.[58]

> He had the tragic art of making unbelief fashionable among a wayward and generous people. He employed all the vain arts in this insane league. Religion was attacked with every weapon from the pamphlet to the book, the epigram to sophistry.

The context in which the *Génie* appeared was responsible for a great deal of its influence and importance. Its central political message was that

> Quand les hommes perdent l'idée de Dieu, ils se précipitent dans tous les crimes en dépit des lois et des bourreaux.[59]

> When men lose the idea of God, they rush headlong into all sorts of crime in spite of laws and punishments.

It also justified everything that the émigrés held dear and implicitly acknowledged the enormous emotional cost of those convictions.

> La religion tire ses raisons de la sensibilité de l'âme, des plus doux attachements de la vie, de la piété filiale, de l'amour conjugal, de la tendresse maternelle.[60]

> Religion draws its reasons from the needs of the soul, from the close relationships which enrich our life, from filial devotion, from conjugal love, and from maternal tenderness.

It is a masterpiece of propaganda, which fulfilled the author's ambitions far beyond any expectations he might have had at the outset. But it also defined the author's character. Any accusations of scepticism or pragmatic writing for personal gain must be tempered by a consideration for the role of the *Génie* in Chateaubriand's own life. He not only convinced the entire Emigration but he also convinced himself of the human need for religion and the immortal mysticism of Christianity.

How much influence London had on the *Génie* is something we will never really know. Chateaubriand acknowledged that he had been profoundly affected by his experiences in the British capital and his contact with British culture. In 1822 he returned to London as Louis XVIII's ambassador and, like so many other émigrés, he found himself looking back on his dark London days with a certain nostalgia as time and wealth healed the wounds of poverty.

The émigré and the emigration not only produced literature but they inspired it. Take, for example, this extract from an obscure novel written in London in 1796 about an émigré, *Hubert de Sevrac*. It contains all the mystical fascination that an young English woman may have felt for these itinerant émigrés and their strange stories of adventure.

> The chateau which had always appeared gloomy to Mme de Sevrac now became insupportably lonesome. The vast extent of the building, many parts of which were marked by chasms, bound together with thick ivy; the deep moat which surrounded the outwalls with stagnant water, mantled over with dark shadowy green and so enclosed between lofty ramparts that the air would scarcely ruffle its surface; the gates surmounted by the strong portcullis which guarded the ponderous drawbridge; and the spacious courts overrun with weeds and long grass, were visible from the windows of every apartment.[61]

The gothic description of the chateau of Montnoir in northern Italy reinforces the foreboding nature of the circumstances of emigration for the Sevrac family in late 1792.

Rags-to-riches stories have always had a certain appeal and the émigrés provided the inverse scenario, which had a distinct charm for those who liked to imagine themselves in similar circumstances, particularly women. This case drawn from a mid-nineteenth-century two-act play is typical:

> Bertha is my companion: she was recommended to me by Mme Beaumonde, my modiste, a woman of high family but now an

Émigré and reduced to live by her skills; the poor girl, she said, was left destitute and unfitted by her high education for the toil of her business: my heart warmed to this friendly orphan and I engaged her as my companion. I have found her accomplishments and gentle manners far exceed Mme Beaumonde's eulogies.[62]

Bertha had been brought up in Paris by a Mme Dupont who died telling her nothing except that Dupont was not her real name. Her father was a French nobleman of high rank who had married an Englishwoman in Switzerland. He had kept his marriage a secret and, when Bertha's mother died, he married again. Her mother had entrusted the child to her brother but she also took the precaution of giving the child's papers to a trusted servant, Joseph. The brother lost his fortune gambling and put the child in a convent of Ursuline nuns. Bertha during the Revolution became an émigré and came to London where, in the house of friends of Lady Yelverton, Joseph, who was engaged as a servant, recognised his former charge. Bertha's fortune was recovered and she married her English cousin and lived happily ever after.

This was a very typical plot and can be found in varying degrees in other emigrant stories from *Lioncel or the Emigrant* to Fanny Burney's *Wanderer*.[63] These stories first began to be written by émigrés themselves as early as the mid-1790s and somewhat predictably the early ones overplay their gratitude to Britain:

> Thrice happy the country which produces such virtuous beings. Oh England how truly doth thou deserve the double title of parent and asylum of the unfortunate.[64]

There is also a very real émigré influence in British literature which can be traced from Fanny Burney whose long life spans almost the entire first half of the nineteenth century to Dickens and Conan Doyle. The Revolution itself held great fascination for the British public but the Emigration provided the author with an ideal mechanism for moving the novel from the internal revolutionary perspective to the external counter-revolutionary perspective. Dickens's *A Tale of Two Cities* is testimony to this and nowhere was the geographic and linguistic potential better exploited than by Conan Doyle. *Uncle Bernac* begins with a letter. Louis de Laval, a young émigré in exile in England, receives news that his uncle (a Republican) wishes him to return. His also informs Louis that he owns the family estate of

Grosbois which was seized after his father's emigration and sold as *bien nationaux* and that he is certain that his influence is enough to have Louis struck off the émigré list. The recent death of Louis's ultra-royalist father makes this option a possibility but the plot thickens almost immediately when he examines the outside of the letter.

> A seal of red wax had been affixed at either end, and my uncle had apparently used his thumb as a signet. One could see the little rippling edges of a coarse skin imprinted upon the wax. And then above one of the seals there was written in English the two words, 'Don't come'. It was hastily scrawled, and whether by a man or a woman it was impossible to say; but there it stared me in the face, that sinister addition to an invitation.[65]

This novel deteriorates from a rather promising intrigue into a romantic tale with Louis de Laval being reunited with his childhood sweetheart at the Napoleonic court. It is still a fine example of the enduring fascination of the British for the Counter-Revolution and particularly for their part in it, which was the *raison d'être* for novels like *Uncle Bernac* and, even more fantastically, in the twentieth century *The Scarlet Pimpernel*. The Baroness Orczy enshrined Franco-British counter-revolutionary culture in her story about Sir Percy Blakeney which, despite its flagrant historical inaccuracy, portrays the facade of indifference that the British upper class displayed toward the Revolution and its refugees, behind which there was real sympathy and understanding.

It is sometimes noted that Jane Austen makes no direct reference in her novels to the French Revolution yet she too had an important connection with the Emigration.[66] Her favourite cousin Eliza was married to the comte de Feuillide in 1781 and often spent time in England with the Austen family. Early in the Revolution Feuillide sent his wife to England and emigrated to Turin. He returned to France to save family possessions and was guillotined on 22 February 1794. Jane Austen's knowledge of these events and their impact on her cousin is absolutely certain. It is very likely that this contact with the turmoil of Revolution reinforced the social character of novels like *Emma* and *Mansfield Park* where the heroes are principled, socially responsible, publicly active members of society.[67]

British authors were not the only ones to recognise the importance of the émigré as a character or as a political metaphor. Balzac included many émigrés in the *Comédie Humaine* and showed how important the political stereotype of the émigré was and remained in Restoration France. Balzac demonstrated that, although he was no royalist, he had an acute appreciation of the importance of the émigré in French society and politics. His émigrés are metaphors infused with political significance and social innuendo. He was alert to the image of former émigrés in Restoration France and he plied his émigré characters with nuances and subtleties which disclosed the complexity of the French political system at a time when not all writers were so focused.

The émigrés in the *Comédie Humaine* are stereotypes and caricatures of whom Monsieur de Morsauf, 'la grande figure de l'Emigré' is the most derisory example.[68] He is prematurely aged and his health has suffered but he retains something of his former self:

> Quoique les dix années d'émigration et les dix années de l'agriculteur eussent influé sur son physique, il subsistait en lui les vestiges de noblesse.[69]
>
> Although ten years of emigration and ten years of farming had taken their toll on his appearance, the traces of nobility had not been extinguished.

Balzac also shows a compassion, albeit critical, for the circumstances of emigration which deprived many émigrés of a complete education. In the case of M. de Morsauf, his primary education was the same as that of most noble children, incomplete and superficial and his secondary education was forfeit to the Emigration.[70]

Yet even in the case of Morsauf, there remains an underlying potential energy and an intrigue which in Restoration France was inseparable from the notion of the émigré.[71] On the one hand, Morsauf is a wasted, pathetic and impotent figure; on the other, he is a despot in his own domains over his wife and his children.

Balzac describes the émigré as one of the most imposing characters of the period and makes the Emigration and its legacy a recurring theme in the *Comédie Humaine*. It is very possible that his characters are based on people he knew during his youth, including the duc de Fitz-James and the marquise de Castries from whom he gained much of his knowledge of emigration.[72]

He is one of the first social historians to indicate the importance of the émigré, which was in part due to the intense discussion of the Emigration around the time of the passing of the Indemnity Bill in 1825 and to the repercussions of this Bill which simultaneously scandalised and divided French society and politics. He was furthermore one of the first writers to acknowledge the lasting influence that the Emigration would have on politics.

The vast majority of Balzac's émigrés return to France during the Empire to take advantage of Napoleon's conciliatory policies and attitudes. The majority also recover in whole or in part their possessions and/or their fortune. This optimistic generalisation is carried over to the émigrés of the Restoration period, portraying the émigrés as individuals whose expectations were in large part met by the bounty of the royal purse. Balzac does not actually claim to be an historian and if his approach to the émigrés is subjective and rather fragmented, he does succeed in showing how strong the links were between the emigration, the aristocracy and the Counter-Revolution and how these links persisted long after the Restoration. He has been accused of making mistakes about the preponderant nature of the aristocracy in emigration and he also made exaggerated claims about their military achievements.[73] But if the focus of Balzac's work is not always borne out by the historical data his social analysis of the place of the émigré in society is extremely accurate.

In many ways Balzac could not make up his mind about the émigrés and there is an ambivalence in his approach which persists throughout the *Comédie Humaine*.[74] He reproaches their inflexibility and their inability to accept change yet he understands too the pace of change and the escalating political events which had produced these positions of staunch inflexibility. He also suggests that the presence of the émigré in French society represents the latent possibility for civil war. When he wrote about emigration as a 'sorry business' he was rallying to the nineteenth-century French political establishment; his own view he reserved for *Le Lys dans la Vallée*.

> Combien de maux a causés l'émigration, combien de belles existences perdues.[75]
>
> Such woes the emigration caused, how many great lives lost.

10 Franco-British Culture and Society

> Salut, salut, isle chérie!
> Mon coeur se voue à tes succès;
> Si par le sang, je suis Français,
> Avec toi je m'identifie
> Et je me sens un coeur anglais
> Quand ta vertueuse énergie
> Combat le règne des forfaits.[1]

Many of the émigrés of the Revolution were no strangers to Albion. From Voltaire in the middle of the eighteenth century to Rémusat in the nineteenth, the French came to study the peculiarities of the British state and to contrast them with their own political and social *moeurs*.[2] Yet the Emigration would prove this earlier relationship to be superficial and based on an appraisal of the country rather than its people.

> Ah! quand le ciel brûlant sèche nos paysages,
> Que ne puis-je, Albion, errer sur ces rivages
> Où la beauté foulant le tendre émail des fleurs,
> Promène en paix ses yeux innocemment rêveurs![3]

The French refugee priests provided the first and most confrontational meeting point for French and British culture. In other spheres, the confrontations were more muted and the consequences less easily measured. But there can be little doubt from comments made by the French about the British and vice versa that the years of the Emigration softened the animosity which had existed between the two populations and promoted lasting links between the two nations in the nineteenth century.[4]

The Test and Corporation Acts were not repealed until 1829. This alone points to the level of paranoia present in British society in the wake of the Gordon Riots and on the eve of the arrival of thousands of French priests after the September Massacres. The Catholic Relief Act (1778), which had repealed some of the oldest and most petty laws dating from the reign of Elizabeth, was complemented by a revision in 1791. Pitt was, however, unable to make any progress on the controversial issue of the Test and Corporation Acts, which were the main obstacles to Catholic participation in the public service.[5] The ban on the public practice of the Catholic faith as well as the interdiction on the building of Catholic chapels were lifted but only in return for an irrevocable personal declaration of loyalty to the Protestant succession from all Catholics. George III's inflexibility on the Test and Corporation Acts ensured that Catholics remained excluded from senior military and political careers.

In 1792 the threat posed by a Catholic population practising their religion was still an object of concern to many Britons. Catholics heard mass in secret behind closed doors, which perpetuated suspicions about the nature and content of these ceremonies. They were still excluded from the universities of Oxford and Cambridge and, until 1778, laws like the one forbidding a Catholic to own a horse worth more than £5 were in existence though they were not enforced. There was a double tax on land owned by Catholics and, in theory at least, Catholics were still prohibited from buying or inheriting land although these laws were easy to circumvent. There were, however, an increasing number of people who had no objections to Catholics practising their religion providing they did so with discretion in regard to politics. There were other complicating factors like the Marriage Act of 1753, which was not aimed at the Catholic population but at the prevention of secret marriages, bigamy and the subsequent problems in matters of inheritance. According to the terms of this act a marriage, in order to be legal, had to take place in an Anglican church observing the procedure of publishing the banns in advance.

There were also many inconsistencies between the existence and the enforcement of the laws regarding Catholics. While these laws had the potential to provide the government with a lucrative source of income, their enforcement had never really been attempted. This was in part due to problems of administration at the local level where many Catholics were respected and their contribution to the locality recognised and where many of the English Catholic families were well-established through several generations. By 1792 many individuals shared the opinions of the Reverend William Cole, who wrote in 1767:

> Why don't Bishops enquire after the Growth of Dissenters of multifarious Denominations? After Atheists, Deists and Libertines, surely these are more dangerous to our Constitution and Christianity in

General than the Papists, whose Tenets are Submisssion to Government and Order.[6]

So by the time the refugees, both lay and ecclesiastic, arrived in Britain, Catholics were free to practise their faith without persecution, yet even the bishops apostolic of the Catholic Church counselled their flock to be very cautious in their application of these liberties.[7] It was into this atmosphere of extreme caution that the French precipitated themselves, with little reason to be sensitive to the nuances of English Catholicism.

With the French clergy came almost subconsciously the ostentation of French Catholicism. This served to accentuate the separation of British and French Catholicism and inevitably there were conflicts of interest between the two strains of religion.

> It was the strangeness of the French clergy, the root of double allegiance, which created the greatest difficulties for their fellow Roman Catholics in England. The feeling against the French seemed as strong among the Catholics as among their Protestant countrymen. The anti-French feeling comes across in much of the Catholic records.[8]

This 'strangeness' was something that both British Catholics and non-Catholics had to confront, but for British Catholics, who in theory practised the same religion as the newly arrived French, the implications were more serious. Those who had worked to reintegrate Catholicism into the fabric of British society precisely by eliminating its strangeness felt quite rightly threatened by the intrusion of these mainstream European Catholics into a delicate national situation.

Nevertheless Catholic families were generous toward their persecuted brethren. Women particularly were tireless in their work to ensure that the needs of the women and of the priests were provided for and this was brought to the attention of the House.

> To the honour of the sex he must remark that the ladies of the first rank, character and respectability in this country had shewn their sympathy and liberality towards those of their own sex who in France had better days.[9]

Two women played an outstanding role in the relief of the clergy. One, Lady Abigail Sheffield, died on Good Friday (3 April)

1793 partly as a result of tending patients in the Middlesex hospital.[10] The other, the Marchioness of Buckingham, was remembered by women and clergy alike for her caring attention to their everyday needs. In 1793, the Marquis's regiment was stationed at Winchester, where a group of French priests had been settled in the King's House with funding provided by the government. While the government welcomed the opportunity to distance the priests from the capital, they provided only the building which had been a prison and was in bad repair. The relief committee was expected to make it habitable and furnish it for the priests. This was done with some difficulty but when the priests moved into the building it was only barely habitable and very sparingly furnished. When the Marchioness arrived in the district she saw to it that the priests had what they needed in the way of clothing but she was particularly loved for providing them with the tools and materials to keep themselves occupied. They made their own beer and kept a garden but with the help of the Marchioness they also made fine tapestries. She was a Catholic but had had to assume the Anglican faith upon her marriage and the link with the King's House meant she could hear mass daily. Verses were written to both her and the Marquis, praising their selfless generosity and their enormous contribution to the émigrés' well-being.[11]

> The goodness of her heart and her constant concern for the King's House are beyond words. She often came several times each day. She was especially attentive to the sick. She anticipated all their needs and took it upon herself to provide all the little extras to make them comfortable. Her presence, her sympathy for them, the consolation she provided, lessened the pain and even cured them.[12]

A little anecdote records that she gave to a priest a tapestry frame which had belonged to her mother-in-law. Edmund Burke dined out on this because even the thought of the reaction of Lady Temple to a Catholic sitting at her frame was deliciously amusing.[13] Yet times had changed and in the later years of emigration, groups of priests were among the many émigrés who received hospitality at Stowe.

Despite the traditions which might have made the British hostile toward the French Catholics, it was from the heart of the British establishment that a warm response came. The University of Oxford provided a special edition of 2000 copies of the Vulgate Bible printed for the use of the refugee clergy with an inscription *Ad usum Cleri Gallicani in Anglia exulantis*.[14] Delille did not omit to celebrate this:

Du vénérable Oxford l'antique académie
Multiplia pour vous ce volume divin
Que l'homme infortuné ne lit jamais en vain,[15]

Heads of colleges at Oxford, Cambridge and other universities were among the most generous contributors to the voluntary relief subscription along with prominent individuals from the provinces and senior members of the Anglican church.[16] The main subscription list is the best testimony to the extent of the impact that the émigrés had on the British population. It includes donors from all backgrounds, all ages and all echelons of society.[17] Schoolchildren, widows, poor people and servants are prominent in the lists, as are the profusion of anonymous givers – those who called themselves 'respecters of conscience' or who were responsible for money 'put into the pocket of the Bishop of St Pol de Léon'. The comparative generosity of the anonymous givers is particularly striking, some giving as much as £50 but many in the £5-5*s* category. Two guineas (£2-2*s*) was a very common modest contribution and five guineas (£5-5*s*) was the standard amount given by someone who placed Esq after his name. Many of the peers deemed ten guineas (£10-10*s*) quite sufficient as a contribution. Details of the donations including amounts were published in *The Times* as a way of both rewarding generosity and soliciting more.[18]

An analysis of the main list of subscribers reveals that, of the 2714 donors listed over the period from 1792 to early 1795 when the subscription finally closed, 7 per cent were drawn from the peerage, 17 per cent from the clergy, 25 per cent signed themselves Esq, a further 18 per cent called themselves simply Mr, Mrs or Miss, 18 per cent were anonymous givers who generally gave only initials or were inscribed as 'an unknown person'. Women accounted, perhaps surprisingly, for only 10 per cent of all subscribers.[19]

The most important period for British support for the émigrés was the year following September 1792. The flow of monies into the fund had dwindled to insignificance by the following September and, although the records cover a wider period, the real impact of the charitable relief was quite visibly focused in the early months (from September to November 1792) and was propped up with aggressive promotional activity on the part of the Committee and interested parties until the national church collection took place, which accounts for the second peak in March–April 1793.[20]

What is special about the main subscription list is the outpouring of compassion that it illustrates for the plight of the refugees. Even if they were not able to retain the same level of sympathy expressed in financial terms as they commanded in the initial period, it is nevertheless a concrete proof of the chord which they struck in British hearts.

Side by side with the most illustrious names in the country, the Duke of Northumberland, the Duke of Devonshire, the Duchess of Buccleugh were ones like: a common weaver 2/6, a poor person 1/-, an old maid's mite 6d, a young couple 2/- and servants whose donations varied. A protestant servant 2/6, a house maid 10/6, a chamber maid £1/1, or joint subscriptions – £4/7 came from a group of servants.[21]

Another feature of the list is the sustained contribution made by French priests who were able to return money which they had received from the Committee. As time went on and resources becme more limited, these return amounts became more and more substantial as the priests either found work or made greater personal sacrifice for the benefit of others. French contributions in general are extremely difficult to identify as only a few are entered as 'A French Gentleman' or have a readily identifiable French name. Many of the French had of course adopted anglicised versions of their names but in numbers of contributors, those that can be drawn out represent under 1 per cent and the sums contributed, with the exception of £50 from 'a French Lady', are minimal.

While members of the British aristocracy gave very generously, the bulk of the donors came from the London streets where the émigrés were more visible than anywhere else in Britain. Hence the profusion of small amounts of money ranging from a shilling or two to 10s-6d which was a significant contribution for an ordinary person in the 1790s. This is also reflected in the schoolchildren's efforts, which all came from the greater London area, and likewise in the number of servants who wished to help the refugees.

The enormous goodwill generated by the subscription and the fact that it was so representative of the entire British population was very important for the émigrés and it inspired a gratitude that reflected the depth of their feeling. The good behaviour of the clergy, although set out in official language by senior members of the French church, could never have otherwise been sustained or enforced. There were, as the necessity to elaborate a code of behaviour suggests, a few isolated cases of priests behaving inappropriately and visiting theatres, but there was no question at all about the sincerity of their gratitude:

The providence afforded to the French priests in England all the comforts which can be desired from humanity and the practice of their religion, and they were sensible of the whole extent of their obligation.[22]

and lay émigrés were equally sincere:

> Un asile donné si noblement, ces secours offerts comme étant dus à l'infortune avaient rempli nos coeurs d'admiration et de reconnaissance pour cette Angleterre, qui comparée aux pays où nous avions tant souffert, nous paraissait un port après le naufrage.[23]

> A refuge so nobly given, this help, offered as if it had been the rightful due of misfortune, filled our hearts with an admiration and a gratitude for this England which, compared to the countries where we had suffered so much, seemed like a port after the storm.

This rare point of agreement has not escaped the notice of historians:

> If there is a point about which the émigrés did all agree, in spite of their differences of opinion, it was that Britain was, of all the countries where they sought refuge, the one that offered them the most generous hospitality and the only one that accorded it to them in a constant way for nearly a quarter of a century.[24]

In the British case, the magnanimity of the Protestant nation welcoming the Catholic clergy, victims of the Revolution, added moral substance to the position of the British government as the principal party in the coalition against Republican France. Roman Catholicism as represented by the French Bishops in London (not by the Pope) created an image of alliance adding substance to the British crusade against Revolution.

There was more than a little political mileage to be gained from the association and Pitt's government was well aware of the fact. The rhetoric which surrounded émigré issues discussed in the House was charged with metaphors and allusions to other British victories over the French.

> Nothing cuts so severely into the feelings of the French rebels, as the noble and liberal manner in which the English have relieved those Loyalists whom they have expatriated. It convinces them that

their conduct and their new system of Government are detested in this country, as well as in all other civilized parts of the world; and that therefore it is an impossibility ever to maintain a Government to which all nations but that in which it is attempted, are inimical.[25]

And there was a certain amount of reflected glory in helping the émigrés:

> the highest honour upon the humanity and generosity of the English nation; this evidences true magnanimity and this is a triumph over avarice, self-interest and revenge which confers far greater and more lasting glory than the victories of fleets and armies. These also are the means by which we are taught to hope for the continuance of the favour of Providence, so abundant a share of which we have for a long time enjoyed.[26]

Whatever motives lay behind the relief effort, the desire to ease the suffering of the French exiles and a general horror at the distress of their circumstances and at the situation in France which 'exhibits a frightful spectacle of rapine and barbarity, which is not to be paralleled among the savages of New Zealand', characterised the British response.[27]

The fact was that many of the French fitted in well and even the Catholic clergy managed to provide a ready supply of Catholic priests to celebrate mass in areas where there were no British Catholic clergy available.[28] The lay population provided teachers, music-masters as well as straw hats and, long before the Revolution, there had been a thriving market for teaching skills in Britain. This was not something which the Emigration initiated but it certainly made access to spoken French language more available than it had ever previously been.

Domestic servants profited too. It was highly fashionable in the 1790s to engage a French *valet de chambre* in order to perfect the language. During the Emigration, the possession of a personal valet of French nationality became an affordable commodity and one which had considerable advantages and a certain prestige. British personal servants were aware of the discrimination in favour of the French and this was a source of animosity, the more so because the job of personal valet was one of the most sought-after positions in a household. Disgruntlement at this discrimination brought the matter of domestic servants before Parliament once in 1793 and again in 1795.[29] It resurfaced in 1802 when a tax on foreign domestic servants was proposed and rejected on the grounds that it discriminated so obviously against the members of one particular nation.[30]

Franco-British encounters are a recurrent source of reflection during the emigration years. Fanny Burney expresses perhaps better than any other example her own surprise at her choice of a French husband:

> As my partner is a Frenchman, I conclude the wonder raised by the connexion may spread beyond my own private circle; but no wonder upon earth can ever arrive near my own in having found such a character from that nation. This is a prejudice certainly, impertinent and very John Bullish, and very arrogant; but I only share it with all my countrymen, and therefore must needs forgive both them and myself.[31]

To her father she wrote:

> M. d'Arblay is one of the most singularly interesting characters than can ever have been formed. He has a sincerity, a frankness, an ingenuous openness of nature, that I had been unjust enough to think could not belong to a Frenchman.[32]

Burney and d'Arblay are only one of several examples of relationships where the barriers of language, religion and custom were quickly stripped away. Marc Brunel married Sophia Kingdom, who was British and of the Anglican faith.[33] Augustus Pugin married Catherine Welby, another Anglican, in London in 1802.[34] Walter Scott defied tradition from the other direction, marrying a Frenchwoman, but she was not an émigré.[35] She came to London around 1785 and was baptised into the Anglican Church in London on 13 May 1787.[36] She was the daughter of a wealthy member of the new nobility in Lyon and although they were not victims of the Terror there is evidence to suggest that he sent his family to London in order to avoid the coming political and economic storm.[37]

These connections alone underline how important the French legacy of the Emigration was to British culture. It is impossible to imagine nineteenth-century Britain without the engineering feats of Isambard Kingdom Brunel just as it is hard to imagine the London landscape without the churches and other buildings designed by Augustus Northmore Welby Pugin, despite the questions surrounding the true extent of his involvement in the refurbishment of the interior of the Palace of Westminster.[38]

The elder Pugin, like the elder Brunel, came to London at the height of his career. Born in 1762, he belonged to the generation of 1789 but his allegances were strictly royalist. Pugin's nobility dated back to 1477, and he

> witnessed many of the fearful scenes of the French Revolution and it is said that he fell fighting for the King and was thrown with some hundred bodies into a pit near the place de la Bastille whence he managed to escape by swimming across the Seine, flying to Rouen and embarking from that place to England. As a total stranger almost entirely ignorant of the English language his position was one of great difficulty. He now eagerly read all the advertisement columns of the newspapers and at last his attention was arrested by an advertisement in which the assistance of a draughtsman was required in the office of Mr. Nash, the celebrated architect with a further intimation that the services of a foreigner would be preferred. Pugin hastened to Mr. Nash's residence and when was shown into the waiting room was astonished to find a French nobleman whom he had known in Paris a candidate for the same appointment.[39]

Marc Brunel was even younger, born in 1769. His family had destined him for the Church and he was sent to a seminary in Rouen. There he determined to enter the navy and with the help of the maréchal de Castries obtained a commission aboard a ship named after Castries, then Minister of Marine, and went to the West Indies. This part of his career came to an end in 1792 when his ship was decommissioned. In 1793, after finding himself increasingly at risk because of his royalist sympathies, he departed for New York where he took the profession of civil engineer and architect. Between 1794 and 1799 he made his fortune in New York working on a number of projects including surveying huge tracts of land near Lake Ontario and was eventually appointed chief engineer of the city of New York. He returned to Britain in January 1799 where he hoped to find application for the labour-saving machinery he had designed for the manufacture of ships' blocks. His scheme was not adopted until 1803 and the machinery was not built until 1806 but he was fortunate in having good introductions to prominent individuals in the Admiralty and his career never really looked back. By the time the Emigration ended in 1814, he had no reason to return to France. He had a Biritsh wife and was setted in Cheyne Walk close to his own sawmills in Battersea where he was pioneering new milling machinery and working for the government. This relationship culminated in the building of the Rotherhithe tunnel under the Thames which was begun in 1825 and not finished until 1843. Brunel died in 1849 at the age of 81 and his son took over his business.[40]

Brunel is a perfect illustration of the émigré whose links with politics receded into insignificance when his commercial interests bound him more strongly to Britain than his blood-ties bound him to France. He had little interest in politics and his opinions of the restored monarchy are unknown. His commercial interests were certainly akin to those of the prosperous early-nineteenth-century British industrialists and the bankrupt economy of France offered very little opportunity for the public building works of the sort undertaken in Britain in the same period.

Few Londoners today would recognise that Isambard Kingdom Brunel was the son of a Frenchman, let alone the son of an émigré. Which rather invites the question: how important was the Frenchness of these émigrés and did they themselves assert their French nationality or downplay it in the interests of their other pursuits? Writing about the Abbé Morel, Bellenger concluded that his Frenchness had little impact beyond adding to his general eccentricity because he devoted himself to an English-speaking London congregation. Perhaps we should rather ask how willingly these French émigrés adopted British customs and culture. By posing the question in this way, it is relatively easy to see that the successful entrepreneurs among the émigrés were those who adopted British culture, including language and commercial practice, and used it for personal gain. Because only a small minority of émigrés chose to remain in Britain these cases are isolated and the successful ones like Brunel and Pugin spectacular. But there were nevertheless cases of lay and ecclesiastic individuals who preferred the life they had created in a foreign land to the uncertainty of post-Revolution France.

Moreover, why should the French prefer Britain to their own country when they were political exiles resident only because they were persecuted and proscribed in France? Windham made precisely this point when the Aliens Bill was first passed through the Commons.

> A common prejudice was entertained against them because they preferred France to this country and their ancient Constitution to our own; but this, in his opinion, was no objection to them. It would be indeed extraordinary if the case was otherwise, as well unreasonable, to require of them to sacrifice all their ancient opinions and

prejudices or to expect that a Frenchman for the allowance of a shilling a day would sacrifice what he considered his birth right.[41]

Between 1793 and 1832 no less than 102 French citizens made application for British naturalisation.[42] They include the grandson of the author of *De l'esprit des lois*, Charles de Montesquieu, who had married a rich Catholic British woman, Mary Ann MacGeoghegan,[43] and Marie-Gabriel-Noël Raymond de la Nougarède, who had been a wine merchant in Hart Street, Bloomsbury for nine years in 1807 and had served in the 1792 campaign and at Quiberon. Jean-Léonard Dutreuil applied for naturalisation in 1810; former professor of philosophy, he had come to London as tutor to the son of the Marquis de la Riandrie in 1794. Subsequently he had taken over the school started by M. Crawford and by 1810 was responsible for 110 pupils.[44] The owners of bookshops, Pierre Didier, based at 75 James Street and Laurent-Louis Deconchy, 100 New Bond Street also obtained naturalisation in this period as did Dominique de Saint Quentin, mentioned earlier as the head of the school attended by Mary Russell Mitford, in March 1798.

The list is not long and usually the names are unknown but their reasons for wanting permission to stay in Britain fitted into one of two categories – those who had married British women and those whose professional interests retained them in Britain. Often the two coincided.

In 1822, the little boy who had first come to London with his mother, the comtesse de Flahaut, in 1792 applied for naturalisation. In the meantime, he had had a dazzling career as one of Napoleon's most trusted aides-de-camp. He applied as Auguste-Charles-Joseph Mercer de Flahaut de la Billarderie. His wife was Miss Margaret Mercer, the only child of Admiral Lord Keith, who had been one of the most eligible women in Britain.[45] Lord Keith, despite the fact that he loathed all Frenchmen and particularly Bonapartists, was reluctantly won over by Flahaut's legendary charm and his daughter's headstrong preference. Charles de Flahaut had a profound and affectionate regard for the people and the landscape of Britain. He wrote:

> cette Angleterre m'est devenue ce qui était la province pour Mme de Sévigné, j'aimais jusqu'à l'accent anglais dans le français.[46]

> England has become for me what the provinces were for Mme de Sévigné, I love even an English accent in spoken French.

These feelings of great attachment for the British people were expressed time and time again by those who returned to France in 1802. For many émigrés, the strength of their affections for their country of exile was surprisingly nostalgic when they were no longer refugees. A priest in conversation with an Englishman travelling between Rouen and Paris put it nicely:

> If the English and my country are not friends, it will not be for want of my prayers. I fled from France without tears for the preservation of my life but when I left England, I confess it, I could not help shedding some.[47]

For those who said goodbye to Britain either in 1802 or later in 1814, parting was a surprisingly heartfelt wrench. The unexpected nature of their enforced stay in Britain, the longing to return to their beloved France ought to have made the émigrés ecstatic at the first opportunity to return. Yet their excitement was tinged with sadness and a profound respect for the British friends whom they were leaving behind.

The clergy and the laity were frequently in agreement about their indebtedness to the British nation. No other country had offered the refugees such sustained support even if the monetary sums involved were often only barely adequate for the needs of the sufferers. By the time they left, émigrés had formed attachments which made a nonsense of the political frontiers separating Britain from France.

The Abbé Carron wrote his adieux to John Wilmot with whom he had had a long and practical involvement:

> Monsieur et honorable et si généreux ami avec quelle profonde reconnaisance j'ai reçu le don que vous daignez faire à mes orphelins bien-aimés: je l'ai mis en dépôt pour le temps du départ dont l'époque n'est pas encore fixée, et où il me sera souverainement nécessaire: avant de quitter ce pays, et lorsque je serai sur le sol natal, Monsieur et vénérable ami, je ne manquerai pas l'occasion de vous renouveller l'homage constant de ma reconnaisance: ce sentiment si doux ne cède en moi qu'à celui d'un grand respect avec lequel je suis pour vous et pour votre honorable famille, Monsieur, Votre très humble et obéissant serviteur, l'Abbé Carron.[48]

> Monsieur, honorable and generous friend, with what profound gratitude I received the gift that you bestowed upon my well-loved

orphans. I have put it away against the time of departure which is not yet settled and when it will be extremely necessary. Before leaving this country and when I am at home in France, dear and venerable friend, I will not miss an occasion to renew the constant homage of my gratitude. This tender attachment is only equalled by the great respect with which I am, for you and all your family, your most humble and obedient servant, the Abbé Carron.

He wrote once more before their final parting[49] and he also left his adieux to the citizens of Great Britain. To them he wrote:

> Magnanimes Anglois, vous m'avez fait retrouver comme le doux sol qui me vit naître, sur votre terre hospitalière; mes parens d'adoption, vous m'avez prodigué, durant de longues années, les soins assidus de la mère. Comblé de vos bienfaits, je vais m'arracher de vos bras; la Providence me condamne à ce grand sacrifice, qui me devient comme une émigration nouvelle.[50]

> Generous Englishmen, you have welcomed me to your hospitable land as if it were my own, my adoptive family, you have, during many years, taken care of me like a mother. Filled with your goodness, I must tear myself from your arms. Providence condemns me to make this sacrifice which, for me, is like a new emigration.

No other émigré used the mataphor of a second emigration in relation to their return yet few had the experience of the Abbé Carron, who was an extraordinary organiser and administrator and knew many Britons like John Wilmot intimately. He knew that the France to which they were returning was going to pose as many organisational challenges as the Emigration had done and he saw his participation as a duty rather than a choice.

Writing about the return of the émigrés in 1802 John Carr, a British traveller, described his departure from Southampton and his fellow émigré travellers:

> During the whole of the second day after our arrival in the town Southampton was in a bustle, occasioned by the flocking in of a great number of french emigrants, who were returning to their own country, in consequence of a mild decree, which had been passed in their favour. The scene was truly interesting, and the sentiment which it excited, delightful to the heart. [...]

About noon they (the émigrés) had deposited their baggage upon the quay, which formed a pile of aged portmanteaus, and battered trunks. Parties remained to protect them, previous to their embarkation. The sun was intensely hot, they were seated under the shade of old umbrellas, which looked as if they had been the companions of their banishment.

Their countenance appeared strongly marked with the pious character of resignation, over which were to be seen a sweetness, and corrected animation, which seemed to depict at once the soul's delight, of returning to its native home, planted wherever it may be, and the regret of leaving a nation, which, in the hour of flight and misery, had nobly enrolled them in the list of her own children, and had covered them with protection.

To the eternal honour of these unhappy, but excellent people, be it said, that they have proved themselves worthy of being received in such a sanctuary. Our country has enjoyed the benefit of their unblemished morals, and their mild, polite, and unassuming manners, and wherever destiny has placed them, they have industriously relieved of the national burden of their support by diffusing the knowledge of a language, which good sense, and common interest, should long since have considered as a valuable branch of education.

To those of my friends who exercise the sacred functions of religion, as established in this country, I need not offer an apology, for paying an humble tribute of common justice to these good, and persecuted men; who, from habit, pursue a mode of worship, a little differing in form, but terminating in the same great and glorious centre. The enlightened liberality of the British clergy will unite, in paying homage to them, which they, in my presence, have often with enthusiasm, and rapture, offered up to the purity, and sanctity of their characters. Many of them informed me, that they had received the most serviceable favours from our clergy, administered with equal delicacy and munificence.[51]

There were Britons, too, who were sad to see the émigrés go. In country areas particularly, the initial hostility to the Catholic French, and especially the clergy, had been replaced by a much more amicable feeling of friendship and sympathy. In the villages of Britain where émigrés settled, which were mostly in the south, although members of the clergy did go to the north of England and to Scotland to make up for the lack of available British Catholic priests, they became much loved additions to the locality. Admiration for their fortitude, their courage and their hard work are the most commonly mentioned characteristics but above those rather Protestant ethics their individuality endeared them as quaint or curious or just good-natured members of the community.

The émigré women were also particularly reponsible for creating this image of stoic resignation drawing its strength from a strong Catholic faith, amiability and gratitude towards the British people. There were many widows among the émigrés or mothers with children whose husbands were serving with the British regiments. They often found their way out of London if they could afford to do so and lived quietly among country people.

Wordsworth, who had his own very personal reasons to sympathise with the plight of the émigré women, wrote a poem which expresses just how closely the émigrés touched the hearts of those they came into contact with. This little poem of no particular poetic quality is a very important indicator of the public image of the émigré woman. Wordsworth knew the personal agony of being parted from mother and child without any means of communication, because he had left France reluctantly in 1793 under threat of arrest, leaving Annette Vallon, whom he intended to marry, expecting their daughter.[52] His compassion for the emigrant mother who has left a young child in France is touching and profoundly sincere.

> Once in a lonely hamlet, I sojourned
> In which a Lady driven from France did dwell;
> The big and lesser griefs with which she mourned
> In friendship she to me would often tell.
>
> This Lady, dwelling upon British ground,
> Where she was childless, daily would repair
> To a poor neighbouring cottage; as I found,
> For the sake of a young Child whose home was there.
> Once having seen her clasp with fond embrace
> This Child, I chanted to myself a lay,
> Endeavouring, in our English tongue, to trace
> Such things as she unto the Babe might say:
> And thus from what I heard and knew, or guessed,
> My song the workings of her heart expressed.[53]

That the emigration represents a *'moment privilégié'* in the history of relations between Britain and France, and, more importantly, between the British and the French people, is certain. Prejudices which had divided the two nations were broken down by force of their own absurdity. In reality, the British found they had more in common with the French than they had ever imagined and the effect of being at war with Republican France made those ties closer still. Many anecdotes have survived about the years of emigration in Britain. Yet few of them relate as well as the following story the transformation which operated throughout British society in some degree or other, or provide a better metaphor for the enormously positive contribution that the émigrés made to Franco-British relations.

Betsy was

a short squat figure, somewhere about nine or ten years of age, awkward in her carriage, plain in her features, ill-dressed and over-dressed. She happened to arrive at the same time with the French dancing-master, a Marquis of the ancien régime, of whom I am sorry to say, that he seemed so at home in his Terpsichorean vocation, that one could hardly fancy him fit for any other.

She was

led into the room by her father: he did not stay five minutes; but that time was long enough to strike Monsicur with a horror evinced by a series of shrugs, which soon rendered the dislike reciprocal. I never saw such a contrast between two men. The Frenchman was slim, and long, and pale; and allowing always for the dancing-master air, which in my secret soul I thought never could be allowed for, he might be called elegant. The Englishman was the beau-ideal of John Bull – portentous in size, broad, and red of visage, loud of tongue, and heavy in step; he shook the room as he strode, and made the walls echo when he spoke. I rather liked the man; there was so much character about him, and in spite of the coarseness, so much that was bold and hearty. Monsieur shrugged, to be sure; but he seemed likely to run away especially when the stranger's first words conveyed an injunction to the lady of the house, 'to take care that no grinning Frenchmen had the ordering of Betsy's feet. If she must learn to dance let her be taught by an honest Englishman.' After which, kissing the little girl very tenderly, the astounding papa took his departure.

Betsy, who was shy and rather out of place in this elegant school, the daughter of a *parvenu*, a wealthy cheese merchant who sold Stilton, attached herself to Mademoiselle Rose, the granddaughter of two elderly Breton nobles, who despite her breeding, was

> a pallid drooping creature, whose dark eyes looked too large for her face, whose bones seemed starting through her skin and whose black hair contrasted even fearfully with the wan complexion from which every tinge of healthful colour had long flown.

She had supported her grandparents through tireless hat-making until she joined the school teaching French grammar when the elderly Count and Countess obtained a stipend from the Abbé de Calonne. The attraction between the older and the younger woman was somewhat of a mystery:

> probably the sweetness of her (Rose's) countenance, her sadness and her silence. Her speech could not have attracted Betsy, for in common with many of her exiled countryfolk, she had not, in nearly ten years' residence in England learned to speak five English words.

Betsy and Rose developed a silent complicity and Betsy became adept at plaiting straw. When she went home at the weekend she took a newly-finished hat for her Aunt to buy although it is not clear how she knew that they were for sale because that of course was never mentioned.

> Two hours after, Betsy and her father reappeared in the schoolroom. 'Ma'amselle', said he, bawling as loud as he could, with the view, as we afterwards conjectured, of making her understand him – 'Ma'amselle, I have no great love for the French, whom I take to be our natural enemies. But you're a good young woman; you've been kind to my Betsy, and have taught her how to make your fallals; and moreover you're a good daughter, and so's my Betsy. She says that she thinks you're fretting because you can't manage to take your grandfather and grandmother back to France again; so as you let her help you in that other handiwork, why you must let her help you in this.' Then throwing a heavy purse into her lap, catching his little daughter up in his arms, and hugging her to the honest breast where she hid her

tears and her blushes, he departed leaving poor Mdlle. Rose too much bewildered to speak, or to comprehend the happiness that had fallen upon her, and the whole school the better for the lesson.[54]

Another testimony pays a tribute to the memory of an unidentified émigré and his contribution to the local community. A contemporary wrote that she found this poem 'earnestly pathetic and above all, earnestly true'.[55]

THE EMIGRANT'S GRAVE[56]

Why mourn ye! Why strew ye those flowerets around
   On yon new-sodded grave, as ye slowly advance!
In yon new-sodded grave (ever dear be the ground!)
Lies the stranger we loved, the poor exile of France!

   And is the poor exile at rest from his woe,
     No longer the sport of misfortune and chance!
Mourn on, village mourners, my tears too shall flow,
For the stranger we loved, the poor exile of France!

   Oh! kind was his nature, though bitter his fate,
And gay was his converse, though broken his heart;
   No comfort, no hope, his own breast could elate,
   Though comfort and hope he to all could impart.

   Ever joyless himself, in the joys of the plain,
     The foremost was he mirth and pleasure to raise;
How sad was his woe, yet how blithe was his strain,
When he sang the glad song of more fortunate days!

   One pleasure he knew in his straw-covered shed
     The way-wearied traveller recruited to see;
One tear of delight he would drop o'er the bread
Which he shared with the poor, – the still poorer than he.

   And when round his death-bed profusely we cast
     Every gift, every solace our hamlet could bring,
He blest us with sighs which we thought were his last;
But he still breathed a prayer for his country and king.

Poor exile, adieu! undisturb'd be thy sleep!
From the feast, from the wake, from the village-green dance,
   How oft shall we wander at moon-light to weep
     O'er the stranger we loved, the poor exile of France!

To the church-bidden bride, shall thy memory impart
   One pang as her eyes on thy cold relics glance;
One flower from her garland, one tear from her heart,
     Shall drop on the heart of the exile of France!

Conclusion

The British society which absorbed the émigrés was that of *Evelina* and of *Pride and Prejudice*. The one they left was the complex politicised society of *The Wanderer* and *Mansfield Park*. The influence of the émigré years extended well beyond the first decade of the nineteenth century but, even during that time, progress was made which was to determine the relationship between Britain and France for many years to come. It is hardly surprising to find the heroines of *Corinne* and *The Wanderer* waging war against social convention. Michelet in his turn ridiculed the next generation of French women whom he described as daughters of the long peace, suggesting that their mothers weren't afraid to make sacrifices or to confront their destiny.[1]

The difficult question arising from this study is whether the émigrés left any indelible imprint on Britain, or on London in particular? There are a few buildings like the Chapel of the Annunciation which were not there previously and which were very identifiably French in character but in general the long-term answer has to be negaitve. Whether they changed Franco-British attitudes is a completely different matter. Chateaubriand, reflecting on his time in Britain, wrote:

> Je nourrissais toujours au fond de mon coeur les regrets et les souvenirs de l'Angleterre; j'avais vécu si longtemps dans ce pays que j'en avais pris les habitudes: je ne pouvais me faire à la saleté de nos maisons, de nos escaliers, de nos tables, à notre malpropreté, à notre bruit, à notre familiarité, à l'indiscrétion de notre bavardage: j'étais Anglais de manière, de goûts et, jusqu'à un certain point, de pensées; car si, comme on le prétend, lord Byron s'est inspiré quelquefois de René dans son Childe-Harold, il est vrai de dire aussi que huit années de résidence dans la Grande-Bretagne, précédées d'un voyage en Amérique, qu'une longue habitude de parler, d'écrire et même de penser en anglais, avaient nécessairement influé sur le tour et l'expression de mes idées.[2]

> At the bottom of my heart I always harboured the fondest memories of England. I lived for so long in this country that I had acquired its habits. I could not accustom myself to the dirtiness of our houses, of our stairways, of our dinner-tables or to our general

dirtiness, noisiness, familiarity and the indiscretion of our chatter. I became English in my mannerisms, my tastes and, up to a certain point, in my thoughts because, if, as has been suggested, Lord Byron took some inspiration from René in his Child Harold, it is also true to say that eight years of residence in Great Britain preceded by a trip to America, and a seasoned habit of speaking, writing and even thinking in English, has necessarily found an outlet in my turn of phrase and even in the expression of my ideas.

Certainly not all émigrés underwent such a transformation but many of the highly educated and literate émigrés who had mastered the language, including Louis XVIII, had an appreciation of British culture which they would not have otherwise acquired. The same is true, though perhaps to a lesser extent, of the British experience of the French during the Emigration. It is easy to draw on examples where the British attitude toward the French changed but it is impossible to guess at how representative these changes were of the British population at large. There is confusion too about the émigrés after the re-entry of Britain into the war in 1803 regarding the difference between émigrés and French prisoners of war who were also resident in Britain. What is certain is that there was a divergence between the tone of official diplomatic relations and personal links between the elites, and while the precise consequences of these close relations remain politically intangible, they are nevertheless socially very real, as the Chateaubriand quotation suggests.

Earlier this century, Donald Greer fought to overthrow the notion that all was 'black and white' in emigration – that émigrés were all aristocrats by arguing,

> The brilliant company of aristocrats obscures the presence of a dense throng of drab figures. But they too, were émigrés – the émigrés of the Third Estate.[3]

The importance of his work is pivotal but the analysis in as far as it is possible must be taken forward and taken further than the evidence, provided uniquely by the Émigré Lists in the police archives in Paris, will support. Country-specific studies of the emigration are imperative in order to develop the issues which the pioneering study of Greer brought into the historical arena nearly fifty years ago. The demographics of emigration tell us that there were significant proportions of women, children, priests, elderly people and domestic servants, many of whom would not have been active political players had they been in France. This only further serves to highlight the injustice of the traditional focus of attention on the political impotence of the Emigration rather than on the study of individuals who had the courage to be different.

This book I hope highlights the points which need to be considered and ones which are generally absent in the existing studies of the Emigration. Firstly, the need to juxtapose the chronological sequence and the social composition of the exodus. Secondly, the need to distinguish between the 'royal' emigration or the politics of the two French princes in exile and the other émigrés who had a very wide variety of motivations, both political and economic, for their presence in Britain and elsewhere. Thirdly, the tremendous importance of 1802 within the framework of the 1789–1814 period.

In France, the reigns of former émigrés Louis XVIII, Charles X and Louis Philippe, the last three French monarchs, ensured that the Emigration was not forgotten. In 1825, the Bill concerning the indemnification of the émigrés for properties sold as *bien nationaux* during the Revolution revived a controversy which raged throughout the 1820s and lingered under the July Monarchy.[4] Positions on emigration, the right or wrong of emigration and therefore the claim of former émigrés on compensation from the public purse were as sensitive, then, as issues of native land-rights in American or New Zealand society are today.

As late as 1873, conflict of interest between the Bourbon pretender, the comte de Chambord, and the Orléan candidate, the comte de Paris, ensured that a monarchy was not restored in France but it was primarily internal divisions which deprived the royalists of a serious chance. Issues which dated back to émigré days, and which carried a baggage of political grievances, divided royalists and ensured that neither of the two candidates gained enough support. Thus the monarchy renounced forever its place to the Republic.[5]

Britain, which was the only country to provide the mass of émigrés with financial support, is a very good example of the internal characteristics of the movement and the diversity of the people involved.[6] Émigré experiences in other countries were similar to those of the émigrés in Britain but the particular generosity of the British nation towards these Catholic refugees was recognised throughout Europe as something singular, voluntary and rather admirable.

If in this study I have highlighted the period 1789–1802, it is not to imply that the period 1802–1814 is any less interesting or less politically important but the numerical importance disappeared from the

Emigration in Britain and elsewhere. It subsequently became a crusade to restore the Bourbon monarchy, with an emphasis on espionage and political intrigue, rather than on the social intercourse and cultural exchange which makes the early years of the Emigration so rich and so interesting.

More than two-thirds of the émigré population resident in Britain returned to France in 1802, and the numbers receiving relief dwindled to insignificance.[7] The princes, the comte d'Artois, the prince de Condé, the duc d'Orléans and Louis XVIII all lived in Britain in this final phase. Yet, apart from their respective households, from the Bishops, who refused to recognise the Condordat, and from the political journalists who were still in exile, there were few émigrés, except those who had chosen to adopt British citizenship, who were prevented from returning. These remaining émigrés were known sneeringly as the *purs* for their unfailing loyalty, from the earliest days of emigration, to Louis XVIII. For the vast majority of other émigrés, the temptation to return, to assess the damage to their properties and the possibility of reaquiring them was too strong to ignore.

1802 therefore ends the emigration of the moderate royalists and constitutional monarchists. These members of the centre-right found little to object to in Napoleon's style of leadership. Parallels can indeed be drawn between the republicans and royalists at the Napoleonic court and the twentieth-century phenomenon of Left and Right cohabitation which characterises contemporary French politics. Only those who held with inflexible determination to the restoration of the absolute monarchy found it morally impossible to return. Therefore the venom with which all émigrés were accused of wishing to undermine the government would more fairly have been applied to this small minority than to the main body of refugees who were reacting against what they felt to be the unnecessary radicalisation of the Revolution.

Because Britain was at war, the interests of the British aristocracy and the French Bourbon exiles were drawn closer together and this can be seen in the fraternising that went on among the royal families. The Prince of Wales and the comte d'Artois were frequently in each other's company and the French princes were lavishly entertained in British society, as this account testifies.

> Her ladyship (Lady Charles Aynsley, Mrs. Mitford's cousin) has been in a very grand bustle, as the King of France, Monsieur, and the Duke d'Angoulême, Duke de Berry, Duke de Grammont and the Prince de Condé, with all the nobles that composed his

Majesty's suite at Gosfield, dined at the deanery last Thursday. Mr. and Mrs. Pepper [Lady Fitzgerald's daughter] were asked to meet him because she was brought up and educated at the French court in Louis XVI's reign. General and Mrs. Milner for the same reason, and Col., Mrs. and Miss, Burgogne – all the party quick at languages. [...] The bill of fare was in French top and bottom, and the King appeared well pleased with his entertainment. They were all dressed in stars and the insignia of different orders. They were three hours at dinner and at eight the dessert was placed on the table – claret, all kinds of French wine fruit etc., a beautiful cake at the top with 'Vive le Roi de France' baked around it.[8]

By 1808, shortly after Louis XVIII had arrived in Britain, there were frequent occasions of this kind involving a narrow francophile group of the British aristocracy which included the Buckinghams and their set. The tone was decidedly French and the chic of the company undeniable. It was almost as if the habits of the 1780s were being resumed in anticipation of a Bourbon restoration which would see just as many British peers at the French court as there were French nobles in the vicinity of London.

What is so often overlooked is that few émigrés returned to France unchanged by their experiences in exile. For the vast majority the years of hardship and isolation were formative and their political opinions evolved accordingly. Some émigrés, after their return, retired from the world and from politics to lead the life of a Monsieur de Morsauf withdrawing into their, by this time, familiar isolation and rejecting a society in which they had little or no sense of ownership. But, by contrast, former residents of Versailles or their children also held positions at the Napoleonic court.[9]

Power relationships and the constraints of revolutionary legislation disadvantaged the émigrés and hindered their relations with the European Powers while internal divisions, aggravated by geographic and financial problems, weakened their cause. But the circumstances of their failure to achieve 'success', which in the contemporary context meant military and political success, must not determine a blanket judgement on the worth of the individuals themselves. It must not be overlooked that

> The military emigration, so conspicuous from first to last, at Coblenz, at Valmy, at Quiberon, at Ghent, comprised only ten per cent of the total volume.[10]

Nor must it prejudice a consideration of the moral contribution to the alliance against the forces of Revolution which was strikingly visual and a potent propaganda weapon in itself.

Semantics contribute much to the confusion surrounding the make-up of the Emigration. History has rendered 'émigré' an interchangeable label for the royal princes, Provence and Artois, and by default has thrown all émigrés into the royalist camp. A meaningful definition of the three 'estates' which are the only categories we have to distinguish between the ranks of French men and women in eighteenth-century France is sadly lacking; Greer complained,

> As descriptive of the French social order it ('estates') had always been somewhat inaccurate; by the end of the eighteenth century it had lost all social validity, and was nothing more than a consecrated anachronism.[11]

There is a place for the Emigration in the historiography of the French Revolution – a place which has been quasi-vacant for too long. It is only now in the more open climate of post-revisionist French history that their position in French political culture can be recognised, not merely as the political antecedents of the French Right but as an important part of France's collective experience of Revolution.

But however long it takes for the émigrés to get their rightful share of the historian's ink, when politics recede into the background, the important lessons of the Emigration were social ones: lessons in tolerance, in patience, in political fortitude, in personal integrity and in survival which are still the lessons of major dislocations in society today. The Emigration in its turn was as universal as the Revolution – as universal as the right to resist.

> Even difficulties such as these are not insurmountable where mental courage, operating through patience, prudence and principle, supply physical force, combat disappointment, and keep the untamed spirits superior to failure, and ever alive to hope.[12]

In Britain, the Emigration was a meeting of two cultures with much in common and the emigration years served to demystify and whittle away prejudices which had shallow foundations. The mutual admiration which the two cultures developed for each other was a legacy to the nineteenth century of which the full extent is unknown. Certainly conjecture invites the researcher to question the demand for translated

English literature, the plays of Shakespeare, the novels of Scott, which poured into France in the early years of the new century beyond the development of the press. Where was this taste for British culture coming from? From the ties, connections and interests generated during the Emigration and taken with the émigrés back to France?

Moreover, in that dawn of human rights so epitomised and subsequently abused by the French Revolution, there was a growing awareness that Christianity was not a Catholic or a Protestant domain, just as compassion was classless. The Revolution opened the eyes of Europe to

> a species of equality more rational, because more feasible, than that of lands or of rank; an equality not alone of mental sufferings, but of manual exertions.[13]

The émigrés, who were among the best educated that the *ancien régime* had to offer, both male and female, old and young, were the carriers of this message to Europe. Through their actions and their integrity they won the respect and the support of their host nations and inspired admiration. It was this conviction that their cause was just which, together with their visible suffering, communicated so powerfully to Europe the injustice of the Revolution. This also perhaps explains an absence of bitterness or anger in the memoirs of the émigrés which might seem unusual when they suffered such a violent dislocation of their world. They felt that they were suffering for a higher cause and they felt that justice would eventually be done.

The Emigration was not the last time that French political exiles were to receive shoddy treatment from their own kind, nor was it the last time that the survival of the Republic would be linked to the victimisation of the innocent. Émigrés were no less patriots than the exiles of the 1848 Revolution, than the Dreyfusards who struggled to get their voices heard, or the members of the Free French who fought for the country they loved from exile in the Allied countries.

Exile is even an experience which has been hailed by many French intellectuals as the source of inspiration for that patriotism which gives the French nation such a strong identity in the twentieth century. Is it surprising that the experience of the Spanish Civil War inspired the novel *L'Espoir*?[14] In Spain in the thirties the problems were no clearer despite better communications than they were for the revolutionaries and the émigrés. 'The myths we live with are contradictory,' Garcia reasoned, 'pacifism and the need for defence, organisation and the christian belief, effectiveness and justice, and so on.'[15]

How well these sentiments could be applied to the 1790s where the republicans and émigrés alike were both trying to impose their myths and quash the contradictions. There are similarities that can be drawn between the Free French and the émigrés but there are also flagrant contrasts, particularly in the British case. Unlike the leaders of the Emigration and the British 150 years earlier, De Gaulle and Churchill did not speak the same language yet in other ways the experiences of the resistance fighters mirrored those of the émigrés.

> The unifying force of the refugees was the solidarity of misfortune, depression, illness and exile. I knew no one who was not affected by it and I knew several whom it killed.[16]

Descriptions of refugee life in the United States reveal how like émigré society these refugee societies must have been:

> the refugees as a group were volatile, vulnerable and constantly on the defensive. Nothing was forgotten or pardoned, political passions were as heated as before and the contacts with other French groups often drove these positions to extreme.[17]

In his memoirs Raymond Aron describes the generosity of his welcome in British society. Writing about this time in his life, he echoes the sentiments of Mme de Staël:

> Certes, j'aurai pu vivre dans un autre pays, en Grande Bretagne ou aux Etats Unis, et m'y conduire en bon citoyen. Mais sans y trouver une patrie de substitution. La langue, les symboles, les émotions, les souvenirs, tous les liens qui attachent un individu à une communauté se nouent dans les premières années de la vie; une fois ces liens déchirés, nous nous sentons amputés d'une partie irremplaçable de notre être.[19]

> Certainly, I could live in another country, in Britain or the United States and be a very good citizen. But without ever finding there a substitute for my own country. All the links, the language, the symbols, the emotions, the memories, that attach an individual to a community are created in the first years of life. Once these links are broken, we feel deprived of a irreplaceable part of our being.

Conclusion

'*Patrie*' is a concept more often associated with the revolutionaries or republicans in the French Revolution than with the émigrés. Yet, as much of the émigré poetry testifies, émigrés were no less firmly bound to their place of birth or to the people and places dear to them.

In 1795, Robert Southey wrote this poem which, at the time, he intended for the exiled patriots to the exclusion of the royalists. But just as there were no émigrés who did not love their country, its message extends to all émigrés and to political refugees everywhere who believe in the essential justice of their cause.

TO THE EXILED PATRIOTS[20]

Martyrs of Freedom – ye who firmly good
Stept forth the champions in her glorious cause
Ye who against Corruption nobly stood
For Justice, Liberty and equal Laws.

Ye who have urged the cause of man so well
Whilst proud Oppression's torrent swept along
Ye who so firmly stood, so nobly fell,
Accept one ardent Briton's grateful song.

For shall Oppression vainly think by Fear
To quench the fearless energy of mind?
And glorying in your fall, exult it here
As tho' no honest heart were left behind?

Thinks the proud tyrant by the pliant law
The timid jury and the judge unjust,
To strike the soul of Liberty with awe,
And scare the friends of Freedom from their trust?

As easy might the Despot's empty pride
The onward course of rushing ocean stay;
As easy might his jealous caution hide
From mortal eyes the orb of general day.

For like the general orb's eternal flame
Glows the mild force of Virtue's constant light;
Tho' clouded by Misfortune, still the same,
For ever constant and for ever bright.

Not till eternal chaos shall that light
Before Oppression's fury fade away;
Not till the sun himself be lost in night;
Not till the frame of Nature shall decay.

Go then secure, in steady virtue go,
Nor heed the peril of the stormy seas –
Nor heed the felon's name, the outcast's woe;
Contempt and pain, and sorrow and disease.

Tho' cankering cares corrode the sinking frame,
Tho' sickness rankle in the sallow breast;
Tho' Death were quenching fast the vital flame,
Think but for what ye suffer, and be blest.

So shall your great examples fire each soul
So in each free-born breast for ever dwell,
Till Man shall rise above the unjust controul –
Stand where ye stood, and triumph where ye fell.

Appendix 1: Chronology

1789
16–17 July 1789	The comte d'Artois departs Paris for emigration. With him go the prince de Condé, the prince de Conti, the Polignacs and others from the Versailles set.
late July	The Great Fear provides incentive for early emigration.
4–5 August 1789	The decrees of 10–11 August 1789 formalising the decisions taken on the night of 4–5 August increase the number of departures.
5–6 October 1789	The '*journées d'octobre*' reinforce emigration trends.

1790
13 February	Religious orders are disbanded.
12 July	The Civil Constitution of the Clergy voted by the Constituent Assembly.
22 December	Any émigré occupying a governmental position must return within a month or lose his salary.

1791
19 February	Departure of the King's aunts, Madames Adedaïde and Victoire to Turin. Emigration is discussed for the first time in the Assembly.
10 March	Pope officially condemns the Civil Constitution of the Clergy, and diplomatic relations with the papacy cease.
15 June	Émigré units are being organised under the leadership of the comte d'Artois at Coblenz.
21 June	The flight to Varennes prompts the closure of the frontiers and signals the King's lack of support for the Revolution.
23 June	The comte de Provence emigrates. He crosses the frontier to Mons and on the 27th meets the comte d'Artois in Brussels.
9 July	A triple tax is imposed on émigrés if they have not returned within a month.
27 August	Declaration of Pillnitz.
25 September	The death penalty is allocated for crimes involving persons taking arms against France.
30 September	Constitutional Assembly declares a political amnesty.
14 October	Declaration of Louis XVI calling for the return of his brothers from emigration.
20 October	Brissot demands military action to disperse the émigré forces.
31 October	Decree deprives the comte de Provence of his rights to regency (vetoed by the King on 11 November).

9 November	Law against the émigrés: death for conspirators and sequestration of their property (this is also vetoed by the King, 11 November 1791).
27 November	Oath of allegiance to the Civil Constitution of the Clergy is made obligatory for all clergy.
29 November	Legislative Assembly requests the King take diplomatic action to secure the disbanding of émigré military units.

1792

2 January	Decree of impeachment against the comte de Provence, the comte d'Artois, the prince de Condé, Calonne and other politically prominent émigrés.
14 January	Complicity with the émigrés is regarded as a crime of *lèse-nation*.
18 January	The comte de Provence is stripped of his rights to regency.
9 February	Sequestration of émigré land decreed.
25 March	French government requests that the Holy Roman Emperor disperse the émigrés on his territory.
8 April	Law codifying and extending existing émigré laws.
17 July	Émigré land to be sold off as *bien nationaux*.
15 August	Families of émigrés put under permanent surveillance.
26 August	Clergy who have not taken an oath of allegiance to the new government are to leave France within two weeks or be deported to Guiana.
30 August	Relatives of émigrés excluded from holding public office.
2–6 September	September Massacres.
20 September	Emigration is accepted as sufficient grounds for divorce.
23 October	All émigrés banished in perpetuity. Death as outlaws if they are caught in France.
24 October	Sequestration and sale of movable property of émigrés.
26 November	Returned émigrés to leave Paris within 24 hours, to leave France within a week.
4 December	Royalist press is outlawed.

1793

21 January	Execution of Louis XVI. His brothers Provence and Artois proclaim Louis XVII who is still imprisoned in the Temple. Provence proclaims himself Regent.
3 February	Britain enters the war against Revolutionary France.
14 February	A reward of 100 livres is decreed for capturing an émigré.
28 March–5 April	The most important codification of émigré legislation is enacted. It draws together and completes all the previous laws relating to the émigrés. Émigrés are henceforth considered to be legally dead and no longer citizens of France.
28 March	The death penalty is decreed for anyone seeking to re-establish the monarchy.

Appendix 1

17 September	Law of Suspects introduced a definition of suspect which implicated all relatives of émigrés.
7 December	The property of children whose parents have emigrated may be confiscated by the State.

1794

13 March	Ex-nobles are forbidden from living in Paris or in frontier towns and ports.
20 April	Refractory priests are legally qualified as émigrés.
June 1794	The Comte de Provence establishes himself in Verona.
15 November	The anti-emigration legislation is examined but retained by the Thermidorean government.

1795

11 January	An amnesty is issued to all peasants and workers from Alsace who emigrated in spring–summer 1794 to avoid the Terror.
8 June	Death of Louis XVII in the Temple prison.
24 June	Declaration of Verona.
21 July	Quiberon Bay expedition ends in victory for the Republican forces.
22 August	Constitution of Year III and the Law of Two Thirds voted. Two-thirds of the new legislature had to be made up of existing deputies.
19 September	Émigré laws discussed in the Assembly and retained in force.
5 October	13 Vendémiaire rising in Paris.
25 October	Law of 3 Brumaire is passed by which public office is denied to émigrés and their relatives. The anticlerical legislation of 1792 and 1793 which was not being strictly applied is re-implemented.
26 October	Convention dissolves itself, allowing for the new council of the Directory to be convened. A political amnesty is proclaimed but it pointedly excludes émigrés and those involved in the Vendémiaire rising.

1796

16–17 April	Councils decree the death penalty for persons advocating the restoration of the monarchy.
9 March	Oath of hatred to royalty imposed on all civil servants.
26 July	Louis XVIII moves to Blankenburg in the estates of the Duke of Brunswick and distances himself from the royalists in France who are in a strong position but who do not want absolute monarchy.
4 December	Law of 3 Brumaire is reaffirmed and former leaders of *chouans* and Vendéan rebels are excluded from public office.

1797

4 May	Law of 3 Brumaire is amended to allow émigrés with provisional radiation to vote in the Year V elections.
27 June	The Law of 3 Brumaire is withdrawn altogether.
5 September	Coup d'État of Fructidor purges the councils of royalists and the Law of 3 Brumaire is re-implemented. A short amnesty is allowed to permit returned émigrés to return to exile.
29 November	Ex-nobles are regarded as foreigners and excluded from public office.

1798

13 March	Louis XVIII, invited by Paul I, establishes himself at Mittau.

1799

12 July	Law of Hostages confers collective responsibility on relatives of émigrés for treasonable acts committed under civil war conditions.
November	Law of Hostage is repealed by Napoleon as First Consul and relatives of émigrés restored to full citizenship rights.
15 December	Revolution is declared at an end.

1800–02

15 July 1801	Concordat signed with Pope Pius VII allows the clergy to return to France.
25 March 1802	Peace of Amiens includes an amnesty for émigrés providing they swear allegiance to the Constitution which binds them to give up plotting to restore the monarchy.

Appendix 2: Figures and Table

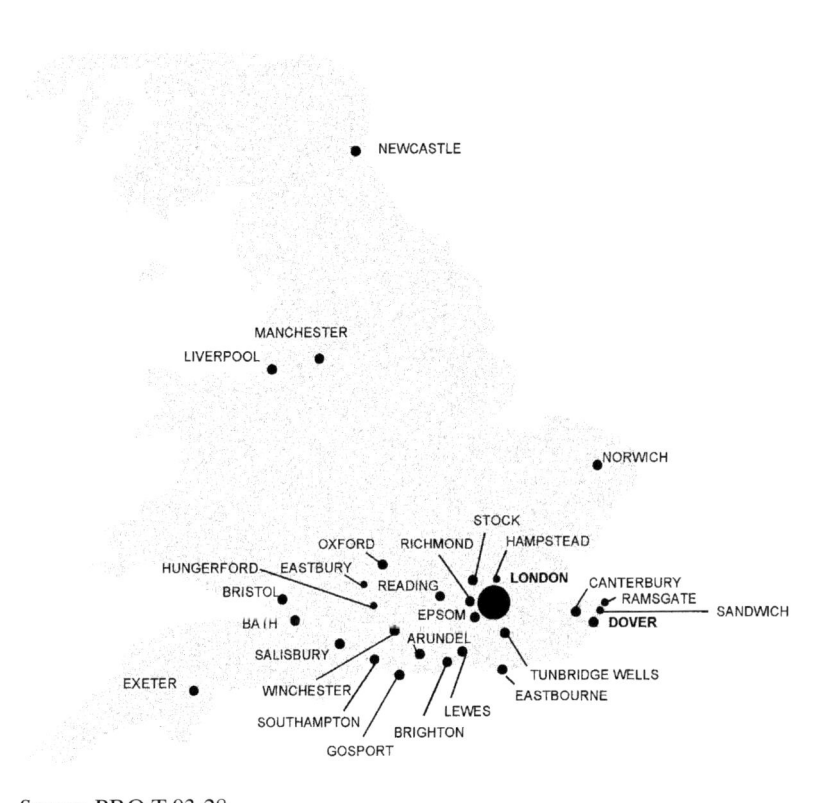

Source: PRO T.93-28.

Figure A.1 Towns listed as lay émigré centres in the British Relief Lists after the re-inscription of 1796

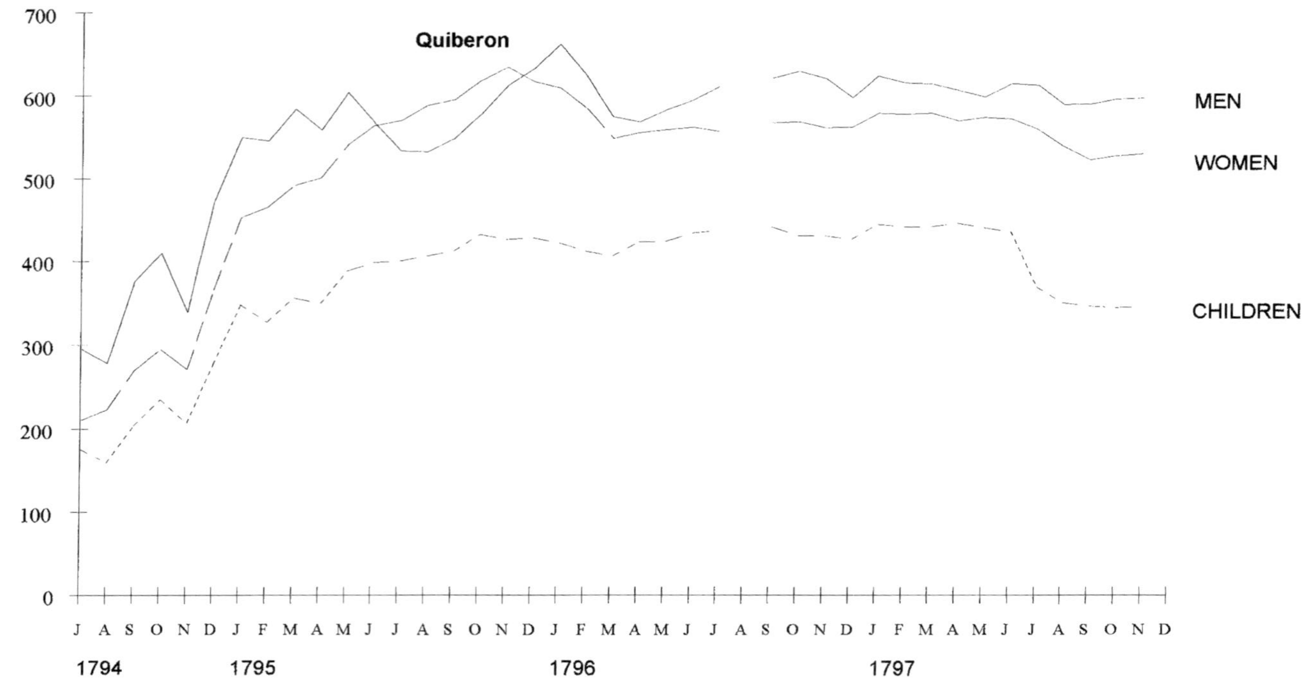

192

Source: Public Records Office T.93-29.

Figure A.2 Lay émigrés receiving relief from the British government, 1794–97

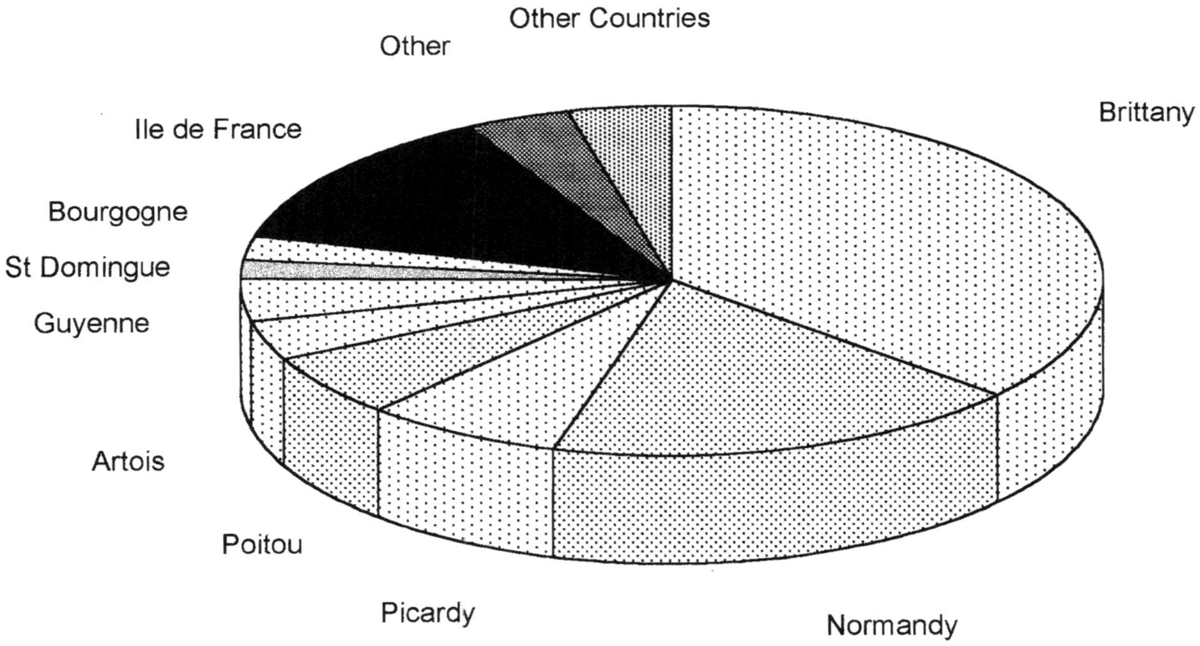

193

Source: This diagram comes from a mixture of sources and represents all those lay émigrés whose previous address is recorded in PRO T.93.

Figure A.3 Place of origin given by the refugees in London

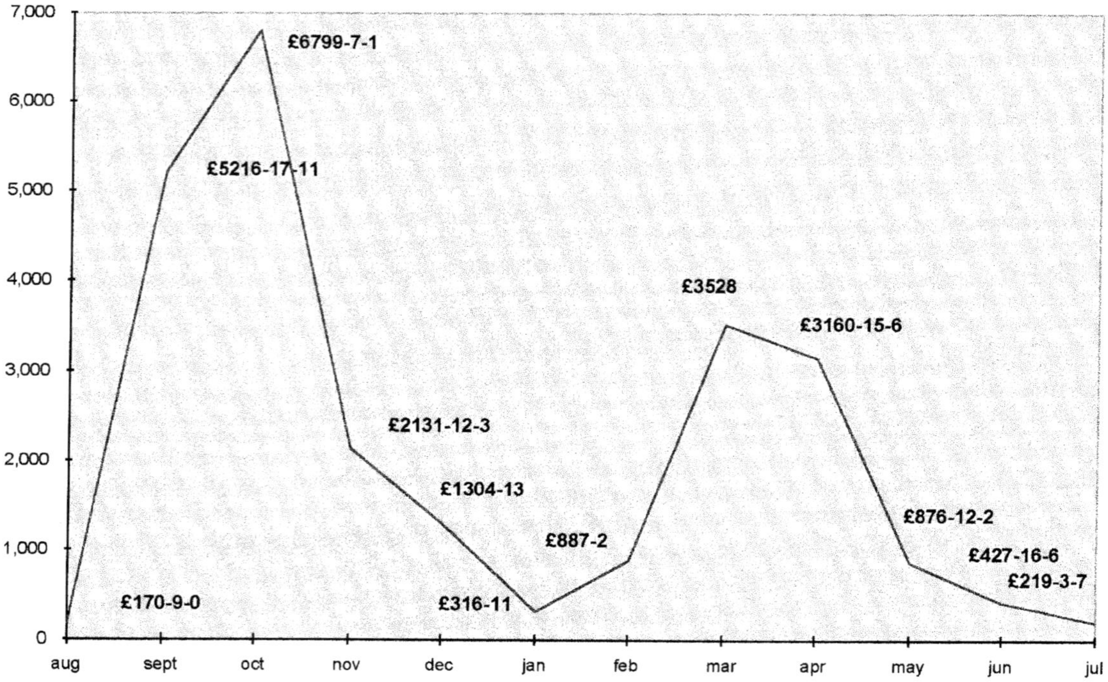

Source: Public Records Office T.93-8.

Figure A.4 Money-flow into the voluntary relief fund in its first year

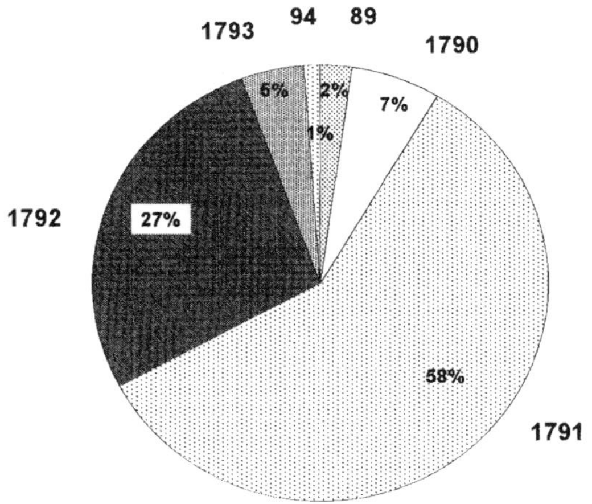

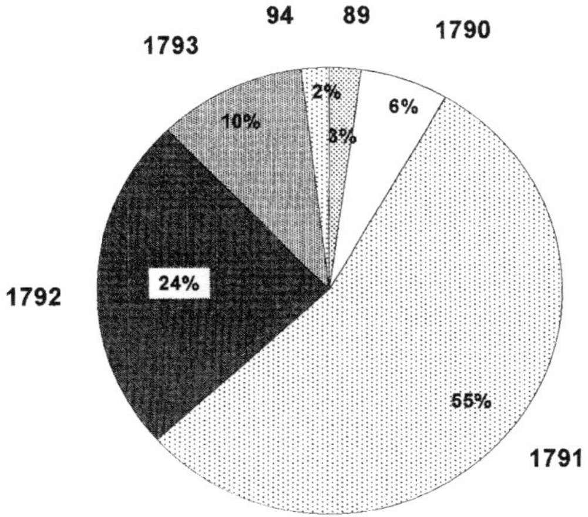

195

All Lay émigrés for whom dates are available

Figure A.5 Date of emigration from France
(*Note that this does not always correspond with arrival in Britain*)
Source: Public Records Office T. 93–57

These two diagrams serve to show how the lay emigres were more inclined to stay in the London area while the clergy dispersed further afield.

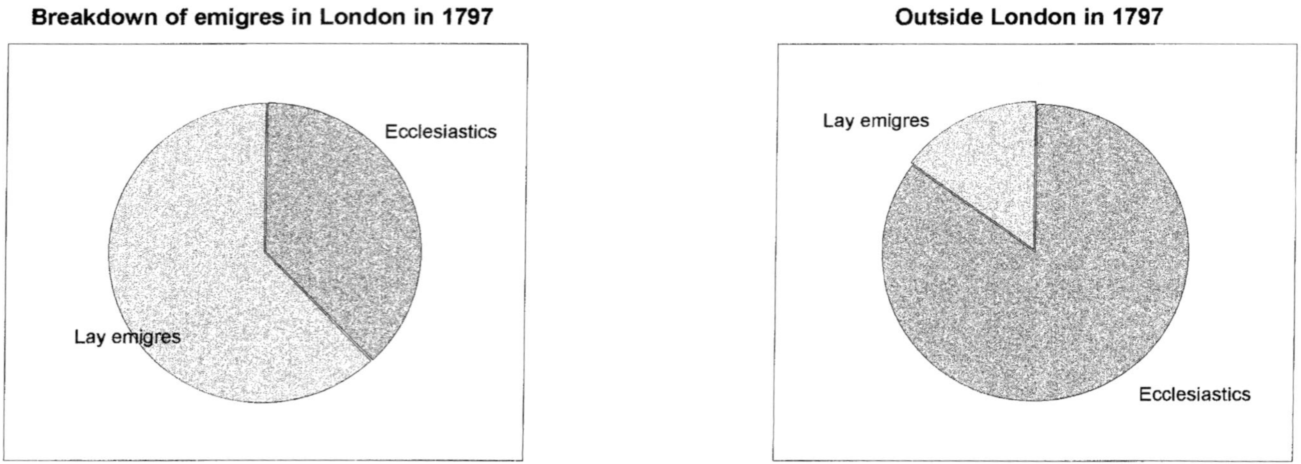

Breakdown of emigres in London in 1797

Outside London in 1797

Figure A.6　Émigrés in and outside London

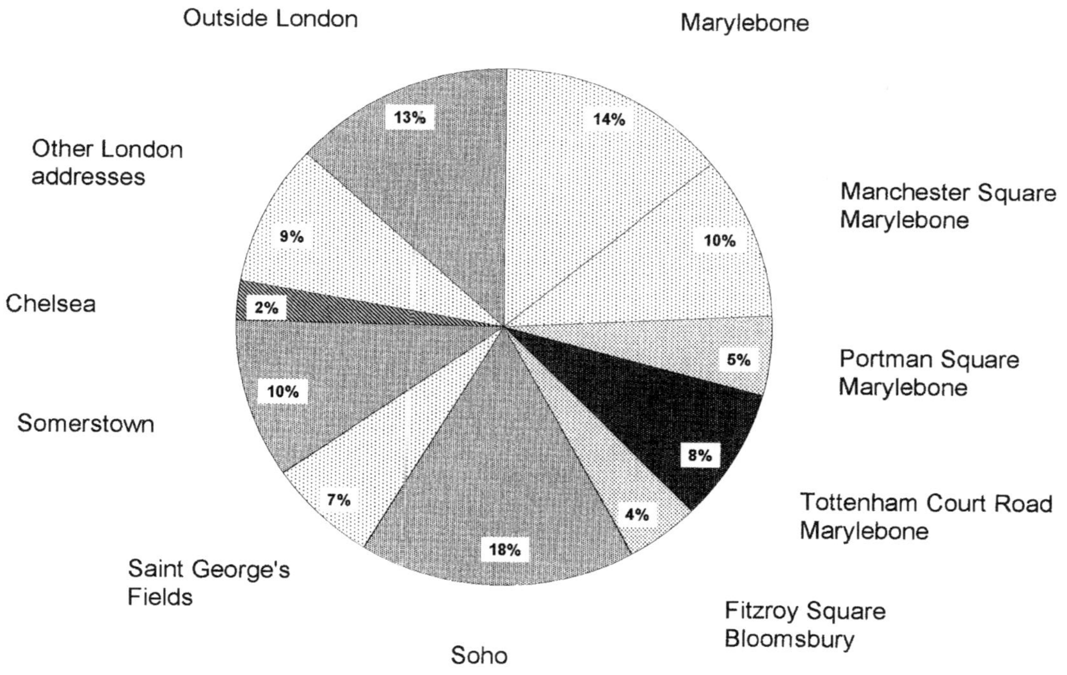

197

[Pie chart: Refugee addresses in London]

- Manchester Square Marylebone: 5%
- Portman Square Marylebone: 8%
- Tottenham Court Road Marylebone: 4%
- Fitzroy Square Bloomsbury: 18%
- Soho: 7%
- Saint George's Fields: 10%
- Somerstown: 2%
- Chelsea: 9%
- Other London addresses: 13%
- Outside London: 14%
- Marylebone: 10%

Source: Public Records Office T.93-28.

Figure A.7   Refugee addresses in London

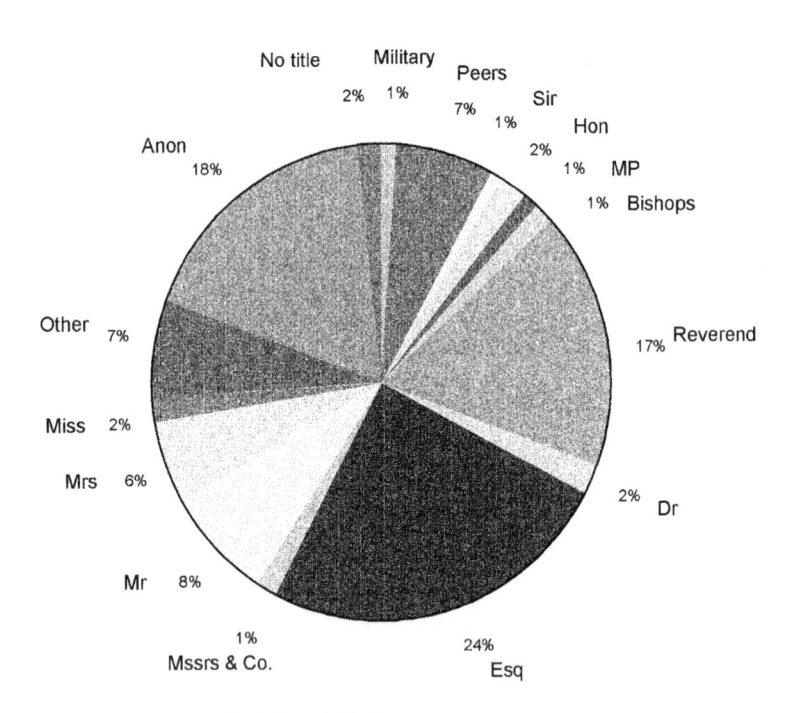

198   *Appendix 2*

Source: Public Records Office T.93-8.

Figure A.8   British subscribers to the voluntary relief fund

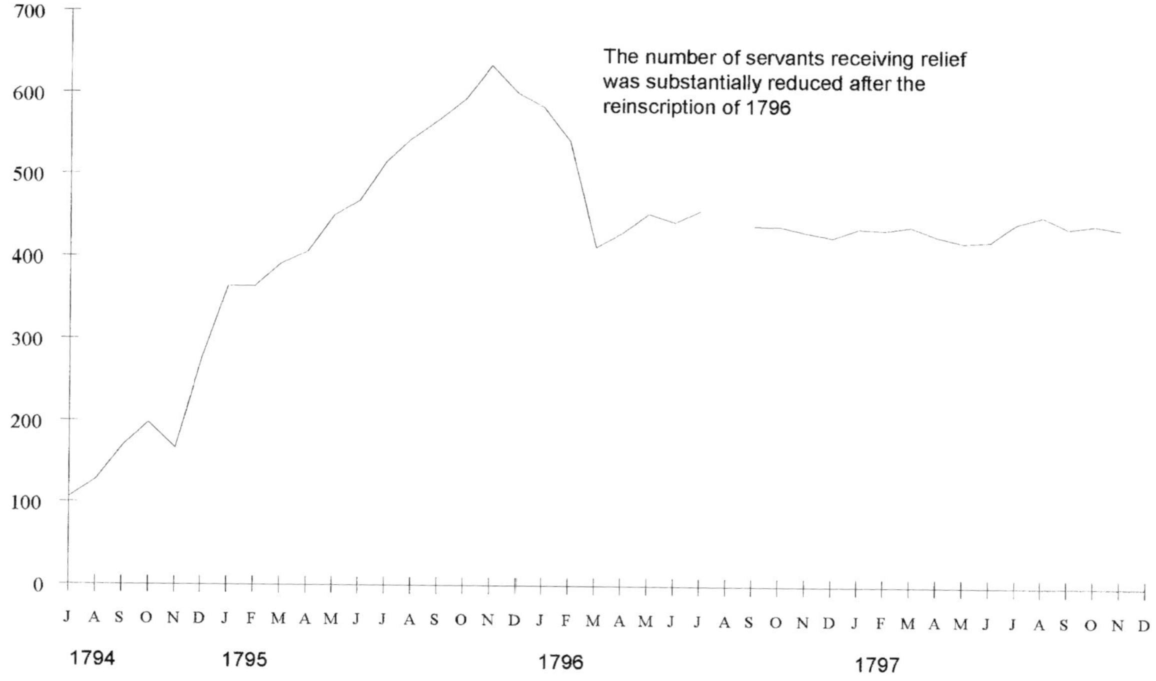

The number of servants receiving relief was substantially reduced after the reinscription of 1796

Source: Public Records Office T.93-29.

Figure A.9 Servants receiving relief, 1794–97

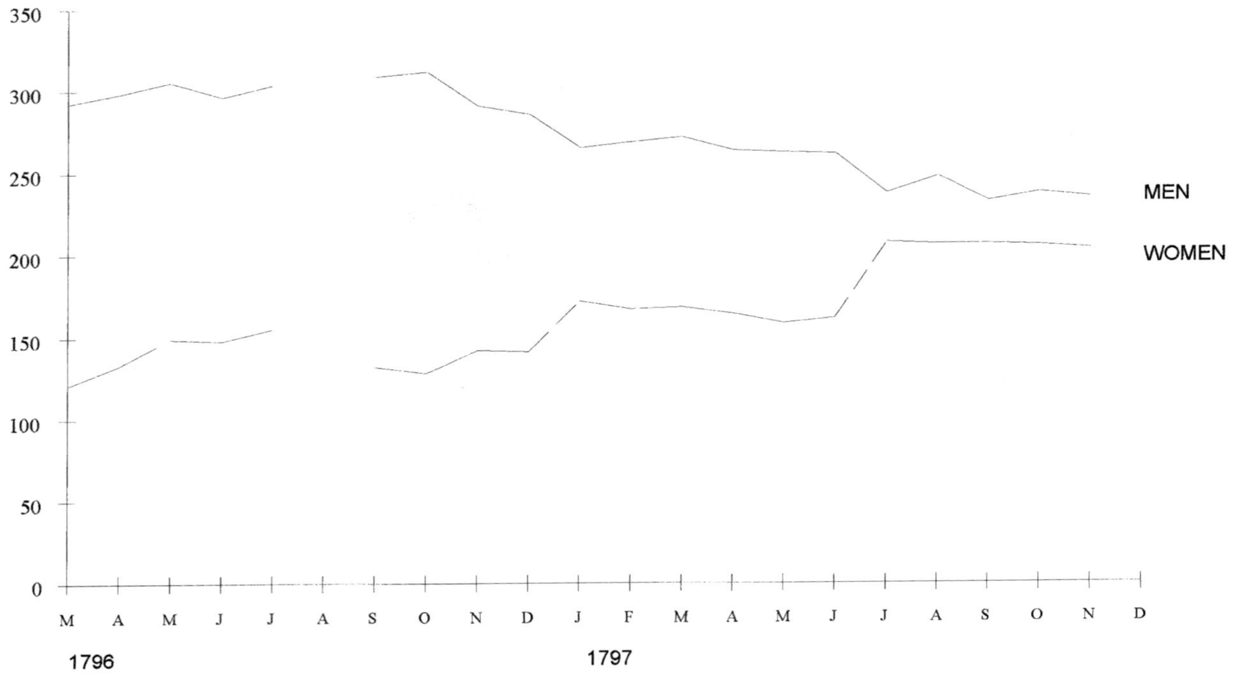

Source: Public Records Office T.93-29.

Figure A.10   Gender analysis of servants receiving relief after 1796

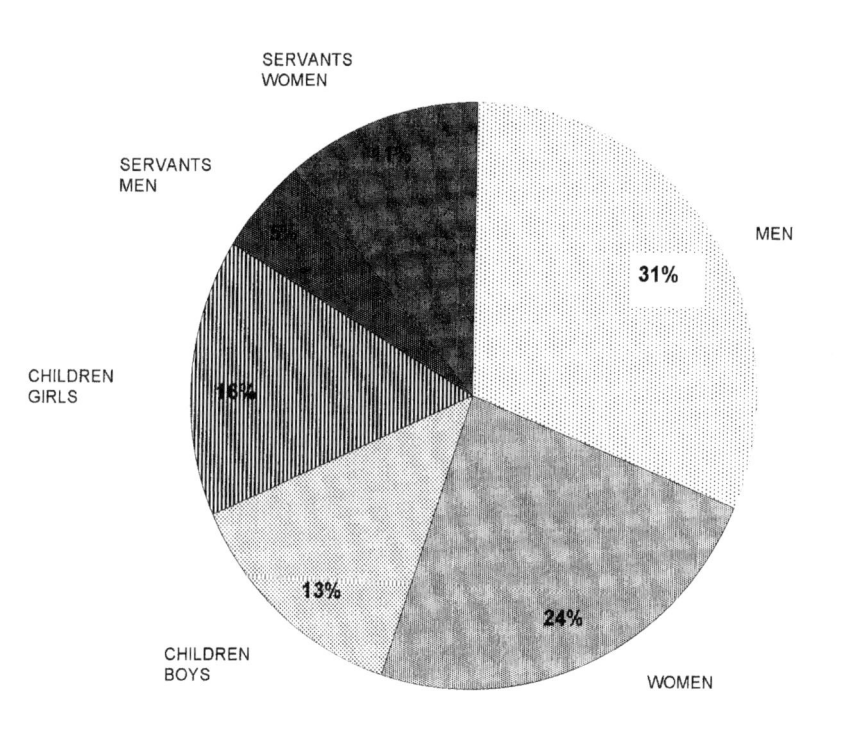

Source: Public Records Office T.93-57.

Figure A.11 Lay émigrés receiving relief in 1797

Source: Public Records Office T.93-16.

Figure A.12 Lay émigrés receiving relief in 1799

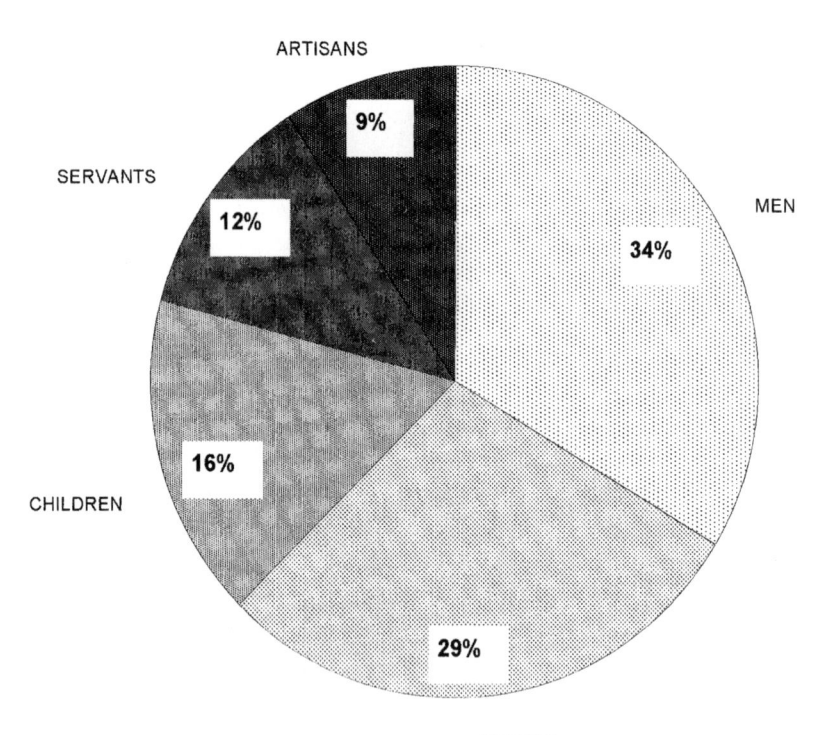

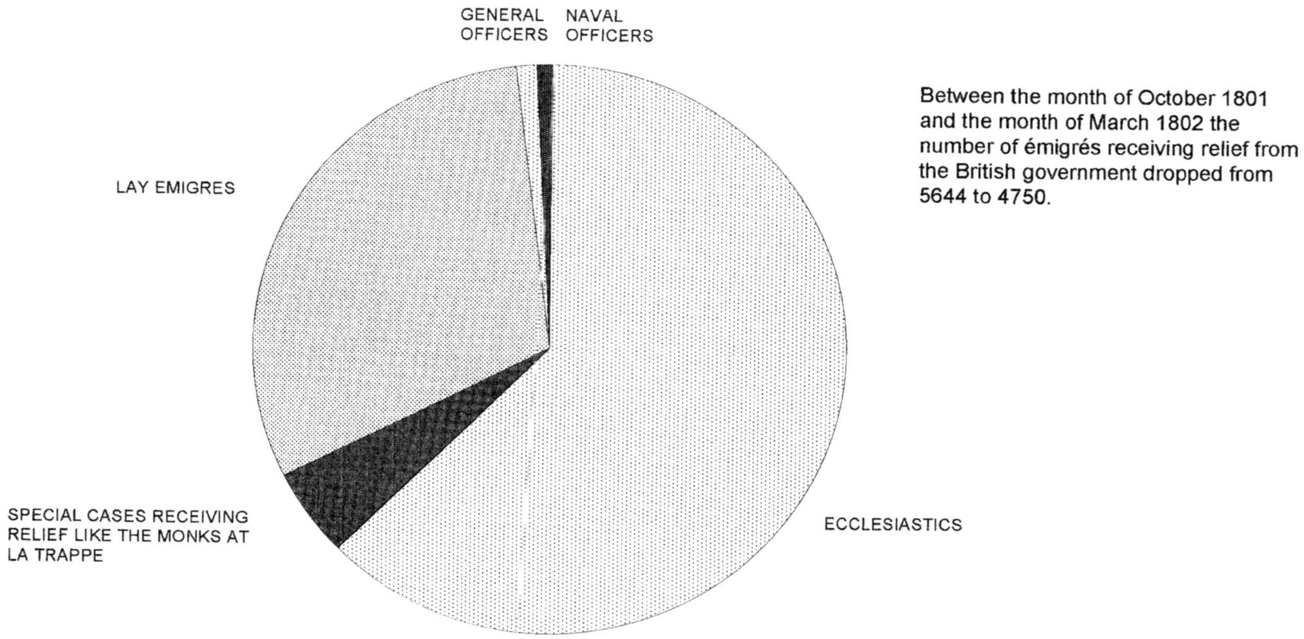

203

Between the month of October 1801 and the month of March 1802 the number of émigrés receiving relief from the British government dropped from 5644 to 4750.

ECCLESIASTICS

GENERAL OFFICERS

NAVAL OFFICERS

LAY EMIGRES

SPECIAL CASES RECEIVING RELIEF LIKE THE MONKS AT LA TRAPPE

Source: Public Records Office T.93-3.

Figure A.13   All émigrés receiving relief in October 1801

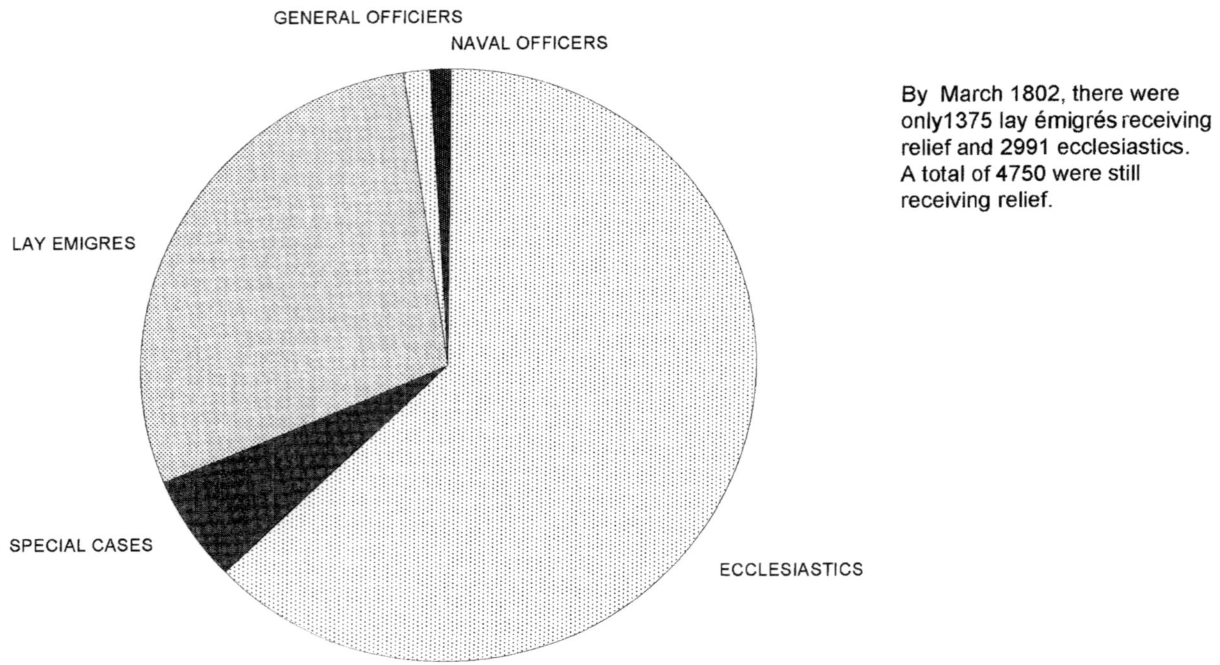

By March 1802, there were only 1375 lay émigrés receiving relief and 2991 ecclesiastics. A total of 4750 were still receiving relief.

Source: Public Records Office T.93-3.

Figure A.14 All émigrés receiving relief in March 1802

Table A.1 Statistical breakdown of lay émigrés receiving relief, 1794–97

	Men	Women	Children	Domestics Men	Domestics Women	Total
1794						
Jul.	296	210	176	106		788
Aug.	278	223	160	127		788
Sep.	376	269	204	169		1018
Oct.	410	295	235	198		1138
Nov.	339	271	207	167		984
Dec.	473	366	277	275		1391
1795						
Jan.	550	453	348	364		1715
Feb.	546	466	328	364		1704
Mar.	584	492	356	391		1823
Apr.	559	501	350	406		1816
May	604	541	388	451		1984
Jun.	568	564	398	468		1998
Jul.	533	570	400	516		2019
Aug.	532	588	406	545		2071
Sep.	548	595	412	568		2123
Oct.	577	618	432	593		2220
Nov.	612	634	426	635		2307
Dec.	632	617	428	601		2278
1796						
Jan.	661	609	422	584		2276
Feb.	623	585	412	542		2162
Mar.	574	548	406	292	121	1941
Apr.	586	555	423	298	133	1995
May	583	559	424	305	149	2020
Jun.	595	562	434	296	148	2035
Jul.	611	557	437	303	155	2063
Aug.						
Sep.	621	567	441	308	132	2069
Oct.	629	568	430	311	128	2066
Nov.	620	561	430	290	142	2043
Dec.	597	562	426	285	141	2011
1797						
Jan.	623	578	444	265	172	2011
Feb.	615	577	441	268	167	2068
Mar.	614	578	441	271	168	2072
Apr.	606	569	445	263	164	2047
May	598	573	440	262	158	2031
Jun	614	571	435	261	161	2042
Jul.	612	559	370	237	207	1985
Aug.	588	538	351	247	206	1930
Sep.	589	522	347	232	206	1896
Oct.	595	527	345	237	205	1909
Nov.	596	529	346	234	203	1908

Note There are no figures for August 1796.   *Source*: PRO.T.93-29/30

Notes

INTRODUCTION

1. This is stated in *Le cousin Pons* by Pons, himself a man (transparently Balzac) who cames from a long line of Frenchmen dominated by fads, by fashion and by the follies of Paris. *La Comédie Humaine*, Paris, Vol. V, p. 222.
2. See Jeremy Black, *America or Europe: British Foreign Policy 1739–1763*, London, 1998.
3. Helen Maria Williams, *Letters written in France in the summer of 1790 to a friend in England*, London, 1790, p. 216.
4. Rev. A. G. L'Estrange, *The Life of Mary Russell Mitford,* Vol. III, p. 85. In a letter to Miss Barrett dated 1 February 1838.
5. Archives of Chatsworth House, Correspondence of William Cavendish, the Fifth Duke of Devonshire.
6. The reciprocal was also true. In Paris English literature was admired in the salons of those like the ageing Baron d'Holbach where the plays of Shakespeare and the writing of Locke were daily read aloud.
7. Letter from Mme du Deffand, 23 February 1768, *Horace Walpole's Correspondence with Madame du Deffand*, edited by C. S. Lewis, New Haven and London, 1970, Vol. II, p. 30.
8. Sophie Wahnich, *La Notion de l'Étranger sous la Terreur*, unpublished mémoire de Maitrise, Université de Paris I, 1993: 'Il faut que les jeunes républicains sucent la haine du nom Anglais avec le lait des nourrices [...] Cette tradition de haine pour sauver la liberté en Europe et affermir la République en France doit devenir nationale.'
9. Ibid., p. 155. See also Norman Hampson, *The Perfidy of Albion: French Perceptions of England during the French Revolution*, London, 1998.
10. Translation of the death sentence AN W431, no 969. William J. Murry, *The Right Wing Press in the French Revolution: 1789–1792*, London, 1986, p. 195.
11. Ibid. Also see Jeremy Popkin, *Revolutionary News: the Press in France 1789–1799*, Durham, 1990 and by the same author, *The Right-Wing Press in France 1792–1800*, Chapel Hill, NC, 1980.
12. See Chapter 8, pp. 124–5.
13. See Chapter 9, pp. 147–55.
14. The work of Alison Patrick and Timothy Tackett deals with precisely these issues, e.g. Tackett, *Becoming a Revolutionary: The Deputies of the French National Assembly and the Emergence of Revolutionary Culture 1789–1790*, Princeton, NJ, 1996.
15. Pamela Pilbeam, *Republicanism in Nineteenth Century France*, London, 1995, p. 271.
16. The Constitution of Year III included a general provision in Title XIV no. 375 that 'None of the powers instituted by the constitution shall

have the right to change it in its entirety, or in any of its parts, except for reforms which may be effected by way of revision in conformity with the provisions of Title XIII.' Hall Stewart, *A Documentary Survey of the French Revolution*, p. 612.

17. Title XIV General Provisions, no. 373 & 374, Hall Stewart, op. cit., p. 612.
18. The Constitution of 1795 following those of 1791 and 1793 (which was suspended) made it impossible to change the constitution quickly and therefore impossible to implement the Terror as the law of 14 Frimaire had done.
19. Decree of 9 November 1791. Failure to comply by 1 January 1792 carried a penalty of being declared guilty of conspiracy, prosecuted and punished with death. Properties of the accused were to be acquired by the nation without prejudice to the rights of wives, children and legitimate creditors.
20. As the two brothers of Louis XVI were at this time in exile, any legislation pertaining to émigrés affected the members of his own family and hence his abject refusal to allow legislation which condemned them to death.
21. The laws concerning émigrés were examined in November of that year but they were maintained.
22. The successor to the Orléan line, Louis Philippe, was in exile in America at this point and was considered a more hopeful alternative by French royalists but the Year V elections and the coup of Fructidor pre-empted any further developments.
23. This error is essentially due to a lack of interest and therefore a lack of research on the Emigration and is covered in Chapter 8.
24. Theodore Zeldin, *A History of French Passions*, Oxford, 1993, p. 7.

1 LONDON: FIRST IMPRESSIONS

1. Abbé Tardy, *Manuel du voyageur à Londres: ou recueil de toutes les instructions nécessaires aux étrangers qui arrivent dans cette capitale précédé du grand Plan de Londres, par l'Abbé Tardy auteur du Dictionnaire de prononciation française à l'usage des Anglois*, London, 1800, p. 206.
2. See George Rudé, *Paris et Londres au XVIIIe siècle: société et conflits de classes*, in *Annales Historiques de la Révolution Française*, 1973, no. 4, pp. 481–502.
3. In Fanny Burney's *Wanderer*, Mr Tedman remarks, 'There's nothing the mode like coming from France. It makes any thing go down.' (p. 260).
4. La Marquise de La Tour du Pin, *Journal d'une femme de cinquante ans*, Paris, 1913, Vol. I, p. 165.
5. M. le Baron August de Staël, *Oeuvres Diverses*, Paris, 1829, Vol. 3, p. iii.
6. The comte de Provence, the younger brother of Louis XVI, later to reign as Louis XVIII (1814–24), was married to Marie-Josephine of Savoy; the youngest brother, the comte d'Artois, was married to her sister, Marie-Thérèse.

7. La Marquise de La Tour du Pin, op. cit., Vol. I, p. 286.
8. C. Butler, *Reminiscences*, London, 1822, p. 182: also mentioned by Plasse, *Le clergé français en Angleterre*, Paris, 1886, Vol. II, p. 51.
9. Hervé Vicomte de Broc, *Dix ans de la vie d'une femme pendant l'émigration: Adelaide de Kerjean, marquise de Falaiseau*, Paris, 1893, p. 142.
10. Hervé Vicomte de Broc, op. cit., p. 137.
11. La duchesse de Gontaut, *Mémoires 1773–1836 et Lettres inédites*, Paris, 1895, p. 22.
12. Abbé Tardy, op. cit., p. 206.
13. Helen M. Williams, *Letters from France in the summer of 1790 to a friend in England*, Dublin, 1892, p. 73.
14. M. l'Abbé Julien Loth and M. Ch. Verger, eds, *Mémoires de l'abbé Baston, chanoine de Rouen*, Paris, 1897, pp. 125–6.
15. This quote is taken from the introduction of a somewhat embittered political pamphlet written for the Consular government; Montlosier, *Le peuple anglais bouffi d'orgeuil, de bièrre et de thé*, Paris, 1803, p. iv.
16. Montlosier, *Souvenirs d'un émigré, 1791–1798*, Paris, 1951. The comment 'Quand vous verrez le soleil faites-lui mes compliments' was made in 1813 during a stay in Richmond. Ghislain de Diesbach, *Mme de Stael*, Paris, 1983, p. 505.
17. La comtesse de Boigne, *Mémoires*, London, 1907, Mercure de France, reprint 1986, vol. 1, p. 373.
18. Ibid., p. 373.
19. *L'Ambigu*, 20 March 1804, 'Anecdotes de Londres'.
20. Chateaubriand, *Mémoires d'Outre Tombe*, Flammarion reprint, Paris, 1982, p. 448.
21. *Diary and Letters of Madame d'Arblay*, edited by her niece, London, 1842, Vol. V, p. 353.
22. La duchesse de Gontaut, op. cit., p. 26.
23. M. l'Abbé Julien Loth and M. Ch. Verger, eds, op. cit., Vol. II, p. 12.
24. *Diary and Letters of Madame d'Arblay*, op. cit., Vol. 5, pp. 233–4.
25. Fernand Baldensperger, *Le mouvement des idées dans l'émigration française 1789–1815*, Paris, 1924, Vol. I, p. 225.
26. This is stated categorically by the painter Henry Pierre Danloux. R., baron de Portalis, *Henry Pierre Danloux peintre de portraits et son journal durant l'émirgation*, Paris, 1910, p. 50.
27. PRO T. 29-30.
28. PRO T. 57.
29. PRO T. 16.
30. The records relating to the relief of the French clergy can be found in PRO T.93-26.
31. See Bibliography section entitled 'Published Works' for books by Daudet, Forneron, Vidalenc, Lebon, Lubersac, Plasse and Bellenger, *The French Exiled Clergy in the British Isles after 1789*, Bath, 1986.
32. As above, see 'Published Works', e.g. Maurice Hutt, *Chouannerie and Counter-Revolution*, Cambridge, 1983, and Olivier Blanc, *Les hommes de Londres*, Paris, 1989.
33. Kirsty Carpenter and Philip Mansel, eds, *The French Émigrés in Europe and the Struggle against Revolution, 1789–1814*, London, 1999, is the first

Notes

34. J. Hall Stewart, *A Documentary Survey of the French Revolution*, New York, 1951, p. 115.
35. M. Ragon, *La legislation sur les émigrés 1789–1825*, unpublished law thesis, Paris I, 1904.
36. There were some exceptions. Children who were aged less than 14, provided they had not taken arms against the country, were ordered to return to France and to reside there within three months. For children less than 10 this order applied from their tenth birthday. Those who had been banished or deported were not subject to these laws. Nor were people whose absence predated 1 July 1789 provided they did not reside on enemy territory. Ambassadors and their families were exempt but the number of their domestic servants coming and going with them was strictly observed. Scholars studying abroad for specific purposes were also allowed to leave the country. Ragon, op. cit., p. 44.
37. Translation taken from J. Hall Stewart, *A Documentary Survey of the French Revolution*, New York, 1951, p. 415.
38. *Diary and Letters of Madame d'Arblay*, op. cit., Vol. 5, pp. 360 and 366.
39. La Rochefoucauld-Liancourt, *Journal de voyage en Amérique et d'un séjour à Philadelphie*, ed. Jean Marchand, Paris, [n.d.], p. 62.
40. Abbé Tardy, op. cit., pp. 248–51.
41. Jacques Delille, *Les Jardins*, Chant II, lines 699–722. *Oeuvres de J. Delille*, Paris, 1838, p. 19. (There are public places where the people gather, delighted to meet, to wander and to play together. So much sociable instinct in their noble desires, wishing like their work, to share their pleasures. There, our open glances meet with no obstacle. They seek only to embrace all this rich spectacle. These floating plumes, these pearls, these rubies. The pride of the hair styles and the chic of the costumes. These nets, these tissues, these stunning fabrics, with their changing shimmers and their subtle airs. Such that if in these gardens which in tales of old, hid heroes and beauties and Kings. Among the stems of lilies, carnations and roses, the Gods have put an end to their metamorphosis. Suddenly we saw by a contrary effect, come to life, the hyacinth, the carnation, the lily all in white, the golden daffodil and the roaming tulip in her gaily coloured dress. They please us so much these places: that in such Elysian fields Paris reunites her numerous citizens. At the return of springtime, they come to mingle in Kensington Gardens with the proud children of London. Vast and brilliant scene where each one is an actor; the amusing, the amused, the spectacle and the spectator.)
42. Portalis, *Danloux*, op. cit., p. 132.
43. Marquise de la Tour du Pin, op. cit., Vol. II, p. 154.
44. Vicomte de Broc, op. cit., p. 146.
45. Hannah More, *Village Politics*, Fourth Edition, London, 1793, reproduced in Gregory Claeys, ed., *Political Writings of the 1790s*, London, 1995, Vol. 8, p. 8.
46. Mary Russell Mitford, *Recollections of a Literary Life*, London, 1859, p. 235.

47. Helen Maria Williams, *Letters written in France in the summer of 1790 to a friend in England*, London, 1790, pp. 197–8.
48. Baldensperger, *Le mouvement des idées*, op. cit., Vol. II, p. 315.
49. Lord Auckland was among the critics. He wrote from the Hague, 'The levity and gaiety of the French in the midst of the calamities and the disgrace of their country, and in despite of the ruin of their own individual interests, are beyond all belief.' Lord Auckland, *Journal and Correspond-ence*, Lord Auckland to Mr. Burges, 31 July 1792, Vol. II, p. 424.

2 1789–92: A PROLONGED VACATION

1. E. M. Wilkinson, 'French Emigrés in England 1789–1802: Their Reception and Impact on English Life', unpublished B. Litt thesis, Lady Margaret Hall, Oxford, 1952, p. 8.
2. There are a few cases where émigrés who were later proscribed on the émigré lists left France before 1789 like the finance minister of Louis XVI, Calonne, but as these men (they invariably were men) did not become active political players in emigration until after the fall of the Bastille and the departure of the King's brothers from France so there is little need for analysis of 'emigration' prior to 1789.
3. Madame de Boufflers came to England via Valenciennes and Spa.
4. Madame de Souza, *Oeuvres Complètes*, Paris 1821, 'Eugénie et Mathilde', Vol. II, p. 79. He also receives a broken sword as a sign of cowardice.
5. Donald Greer, *Incidence of Emigration during the French Revolution*, Cambridge, Mass.,1951, pp. 44–5.
6. Greer, op. cit., p. 61.
7. *Gentlemen's Magazine*, Vol. LIX, part 2, July 1789, p. 658.
8. PRO T93-4 ff. 318–19.
9. G. Selwyn to Lady Carlisle, 6 November 1789, Friday morning, Richmond, Hist. MSS Comm. XV, Appendix Pt VI Manuscripts of the Earl of Carlisle, p. 674.
10. Ragon, op. cit., p. 10.
11. Living nobly was a precondition of obtaining noble status and nobles were therefore reliant on income from landed property or investment. Infringement of these rules or involvement in retail trade carried the risk of withdrawal of title. See. G. Chaussinand Nogaret, *The French Nobility in the Eighteenth Century*, London, 1985.
12. *The Journal and Correspondence of William Lord Auckland*, London, 1861, Letter from Mr A. Storer to Mr Eden, dated 21 August 1789, Vol. II, p. 350.
13. G. Selwyn to Lady Carlisle, 6 September 1789, Hist. MSS Comm. XV, Appendix Pt VI Manuscripts of the Earl of Carlisle, p. 671.
14. G. Selwyn to Lady Carlisle, July/August 1790, Hist. MSS Comm. XV, Appendix Pt VI Manuscripts of the Earl of Carlisle, p. 681.
15. *Horace Walpole's Correspondence with Madame du Deffand*, edited by C. S. Lewis London, 1970, Vol. VII, p. 87.

Notes

16. Archives of Coutts Bank. An account was opened for Madame de Boufflers on 21 November 1789 and for the duchesse de Biron on 1 December 1789.
17. G. Selwyn to Lady Carlisle, op. cit., p. 677, letter dated November 1789.
18. La comtesse de Boigne, op. cit., Vol. 1, pp. 59–61.
19. G. Selwyn to Lady Carlisle, 6 November 1789, op. cit., p. 674.
20. The mistress of the comte de Provence.
21. Raised to the rank of duke by Louis XVIII in 1809, he was a confidant of the future king until his death in Madeira in 1811.
22. Auckland, *Journal and Correspondence*, Vol. II, p. 370, A. M. Storer to Lord Auckland, 6 August 1790.
23. G. Selwyn to Lady Carlisle, 22 August 1790, op. cit., p. 685.
24. Portalis, op. cit., p. 68. He and his wife had no difficulty leaving France. He paid 100 louis each for themselves and 40 louis apiece for their two servants but six letters of credit were all he had been able to salvage (the largest worth 300 louis, the smallest worth 24) from a fortune in land to the value of three million louis.
25. G. Selwyn to Lady Carlisle, 19 November 1789, op. cit., p. 677.
26. 9 July 1791 and 1–6 August 1791, Ragon, op. cit., p. 21.
27. See: William Doyle, *The Oxford History of the French Revolution*, Oxford, 1989, chapter 6, pp. 151–8.
28. This can be demonstrated by the surge in newspaper space allocated to political affairs. A comparative study of the *Morning Chronicle* in the first six months of 1791 and 1793 revealed that the amount of space measured in print columns devoted to coverage of speeches in the House of Commons rose by 42 per cent and that of the French National Assembly rose by 66 per cent. J. M. Carver, *Editorial Liberty: Presenting the French Revolution to the British Public*, Massey University, unpublished B. A. Honours exercise, 1996. pp. 36–7.
29. Sir Lewis Namier and John Brooke, *The House of Commons 1754–1790*, The History of Parliament, Vol. 1, London, 1964, Vol. 1, pp. 2–3.
30. For examples of writing on these and other contemporary British political issues, see Gregory Claeys, ed., *Political Writings of the 1790s*, London, 1995.
31. A Royal Proclamation issued in September 1793 preceded the Act passed in 1795.
32. This was stated by H. T. Dickinson in 1989 (H. T. Dickinson, ed., *Britain and the French Revolution 1789–1815*, London, 1989, p. 103) and reiterated by David Eastwood in 1991, (Mark Philip, ed., *The French Revolution and British Popular Politics*, Cambridge, 1991, p. 147.)
33. S. T. Coleridge, *A Moral and Political Lecture*, Bristol, 1795, *Collected Works of Coleridge*, Lectures on Politics and Religion, Vol.1, p. 6.
34. A. Bardoux, *La duchesse de Duras*, Paris, 1898, p. 45.
35. Burke correspondence, Northampton Records Office, AXX.12, Richmond Green, Surrey, 28 September 1792. Mme de Cambis to Edmund Burke.
36. Burke correspondence, Northampton Records Office, AXX.10, 3 December 1791.

37. Among his correspondents one finds names like the Abbé Barruel, Cazalès, Champion de Cicé, the comte de Serent, the comte de Coigny, the duchesse de Choiseul, who is one of the few who writes from Paris in 1791, the others being already resident in Britain, and so on. The vast majority of his émigré correspondents give London addresses, Wigmore Street, Golden Square, Duke Street, Brewer Street, High Street Marylebone, Manchester Square, New Bond Street, and Oxford Street being typical of the range. Northampton Records Office, Burke Papers.
38. 19 February 1793, *The Journal and Correspondence of William Lord Auckland*, London, 1861, Vol. 2, p. 499.
39. *Gentleman's Magazine*, April 1792, Letter from Spa, 17 April 1792, Vol.LXII Pt. I, pp. 295–6. Another example can be taken from British newspaper, *The Morning Chronicle*, which also carried reports of irresponsible behaviour on the part of the Princes:
'The King of Sardinia has certainly intimated to the Count d'Artois that he ought forthwith to return to France, and not by his contumacy reduce himself and his family to ruin. Much disquiet has been excited among the fugitives at Turin by this intimation; and the result is, that his Majesty, in a conversation with the Prince de Condé, said that they behaved disrespectfully to him, and expected that they should quit his dominions. The burden of their maintenance has perhaps more than any other motive occasioned this resolution; and there is no doubt but they will make their submission and return'. Wednesday, 5 January 1791, Burney Collection, British Library.
40. For legislation of 9 November 1791, see J. Hall Stewart, *A Documentary Survey of the French Revolution*, New York, 1951, pp. 272–4.
41. For the Civil Constitution of the Clergy see: William Doyle, op. cit., chapter 6, pp. 139–46.
42. 20 January 1792, Société des amis de la constitution, séante aux Jacobins, à Paris. Troisième discours de J. P. Brissot, député, sur la nécessité de la guerre; Translation by P. H. Beik, *The French Revolution*, London, 1970, p. 188.
43. H.O. 1/1. A note dated 20 September 1792 informs the government that 'the Duchess d'Aiguillon with three of her children, Mr. Adrian Du Port and Mr. Charles Lameth reside at 24 Duke Street, St James.' Du Port is described as being 'short in stature, features that bespeak benevolence and an acute eye'. Charles Lameth is described as 'very tall, features very commanding, his shape well proportioned and never was in England before but talks English fluently. His enemies and the National Convention think he is dead, which has been circulated but his wife is at Paris to look after his property. The Duke d'Aiguillon is now in Switzerland but expected shortly to join his family in London.'
44. Lord Auckland, *Journal and Correspondence*, op. cit., Letter from Mr Storer to Lord Auckland, dated 27 July 1792, Vol. II, p. 421.
45. Hélène Maspero-clerc, *Un journalist contre-révolutionnaire: Jean Gabriel Peltier, 1760–1825*, Paris, 1973.
46. See. T. C. W. Blanning, 'The French Revolution and Europe', in Colin Lucas, ed., *Rewriting the French Revolution*, Oxford, 1991.
47. *Morning Chronicle*, Monday, 17 January 1791.

Notes 213

48. Ibid., Tuesday, 14 June 1791.
49. Ibid., Wednesday, 25 May 1791.
50. Bellenger, *The French Exiled Clergy*, Bath, 1986, p. 4.
51. *Public Advertiser*, 20 September 1792.
52. See L. Kerbiriou, *Jean-François de la Marche*, Quimper, 1924, pp. 285–347.

3 1792: THE INFLUX

1. Wordsworth, *Poetical Works*, Oxford, 1985, p. 353. Sonnet published in 1827.
2. J. D. Parry, *A Historical and Descriptive Account of the Coast of Sussex*, London, 1833, p. 65.
3. Issue of 11 September 1792.
4. The first use of the word 'refugee' was by E. Burke in his pamphlet *The Case of the suffering French Clergy, refugees in the British Dominions*, September 1792.
5. Letter from Dover dated 10 September 1792 printed in *The Public Advertiser*, 17 September 1792.
6. Lord Sheffield to Lord Auckland, 3 October 1792, Auckland papers, Add MS. 34445, piece 26.
7. PRO T.93-45, Abbé Dubrun to the Bishop of Saint Pol de Léon, 23 October 1792.
8. *The Public Advertiser*, 1 September 1792, reported that a coach had actually overturned because it was so heavily laden inside and out, but no one was hurt.
9. PRO T.93 40, J W. Brooksbank to J. Wilmot, 10 October 1792 f. 104.
10. *Public Advertiser*, 19 September 1792.
11. *Public Advertiser*, 4 October 1792.
12. Beaumarchais was caught between the Revolution and the Counter-Revolution over an arms deal which involved buying 60 000 muskets from a Dutch supplier for the French government. See *Le Courrier de l'Europe* for December 1792, AN ABXIX-3790 I90-91, also HO 1-1 unf, Le Cointe to Dundas, 1 July 1794, which is a letter seeking asylum for Beaumarchais, his wife and child who had remained in Paris up until that point. In another letter to his wife and daughter he affirms: 'Je n'ai jamais écrit au roi Louis XVI ni pour ni contre la révolution; et si je l'avais fait je serais glorieux de le publier hautement car nous ne sommes plus au temps où les hommes de courage avaient besoin de s'amoindrir lorsqu'ils écrivaient aux puissances.' ABXIX-3790 I/93.
13. *London Chronicle*, 22–5 September 1792.
14. This group is often represented as 39 including the two superiors as well as the 37 nuns.
15. *Public Advertiser*, 2 November 1792.
16. Abbé Barruel, Almoner to Her Serene Highness the Princess de Conti, *The History of the Clergy during the French Revolution, a work dedicated to the English Nation*, London, 1794, p. 233

On 2 September 1793 the nuns, who were housed near Diss in Norfolk, approached the Committee for financial assistance and were given 20 guineas but they were informed on the 5th that the committee had insufficient funds 'to answer the demands upon it' and it was suggested that the nuns take up offers from convents in the Netherlands. This would have meant their separation, going in small groups to a number of convents. On 7 November 1793 a letter was read from Madame Lévi de Mirepoix requesting the sum of £35 per month: 'it will be sufficient together with the profits arising from having the Education of young Ladies (of which they have only 4 at present) to enable them to support themselves until they have a great number of young ladies to educate'. This was voted by the Committee. BL Add Mss, 18591, Vol. I, p. 129.

17. Some émigrés were compensated for their mistreatment at the hands of unscrupulous boat-owners but this was rare. *The Public Advertiser* for 14 January 1793 records a case where 'the master of a fishing boat at Rotterdam engaged to convey from thence to London 40 French Emigrants at one guinea each; but he had no sooner cleared the coast of Holland that he confined the passengers to the hold and ran the vessel into Yarmouth refusing to carry them to London. The emigrants were advised to summon the master before the magistrate of that borough who adjudged that the whole of the money each the passengers had paid should be refunded and the expenses of the Emigrants during their detention in that town reimbursed.'

18. John Wilmot (1750–1815), later changed his name to Eardley Wilmot. He was educated at Westminster and University College, Oxford, and served as Master-in-Chancery in 1783. He served as MP for Tiverton, 1776–1784, and as MP for Coventry, 1784–96. See *Dictionary of National Biography*, London, 1908–9, xxi, pp. 540–1. In 1783, he was appointed commissioner and paymaster for the the Commission for Enquiring into the Losses, Services and Claims of the American Loyalists. This experience was central to his work with the French Émigrés. His political career was not spectacular but his highly developed administrative and organisational abilities gained him great respect from his peers.

19. E. Burke, *Case of the Suffering Clergy of France Refugees in the British Dominions*, 1792.

20. This private letter from one politican to another illustrates the high level of criticism both of the émigrés and of the efforts to relieve them: 'My dear Lord, – We get every day deeper and deeper into inaction, though possibly the hordes of vagabond French who are pouring in upon will give us something to do. Many thousands are arrived within this fortnight, and more are daily arriving. The fools here are opening subscriptions for their relief and support, which I understand our own poor take amiss, and, in my judgement, not without reason. I do not see under what pretence all this charity is set forward, for I cannot discover the merits of those who are its objects. Of those who are known, I am sure not one, except a few harmless old women, deserve anything; for the whole class were Jacobins and persecutors as long as they were in power, and would be so still, were they not supplanted by others of the

Notes

same stamp.' Correspondence of Lord Auckland, op. cit., p. 442, Whitehall, 14 September 1792, Mr Burges to Lord Auckland.
21. Lord Sheffield, John Baker Holroyd, 1735–1821. see Adeane, *The Girlhood of Maria Josepha Holroyd*, London, 1896.
22. Alexander Wedderburn, Baron Loughborough and first Earl of Rosslyn 1733–1805, *DNB*, Vol. LX, pp. 132–4.
23. Meteyard, *Life of Josiah Wedgwood* (London 1866), 2 vols, Vol. 2, p. 603.
24. *Public Advertiser*, 5, 9 October 1792.
25. Hankey's Bank, PRO T.93-50.
26. Kerbiriou, op. cit., p. 42.
27. The Bishop died in 1806.
28. BL Add Mss 18591, Vol. I, p. 93, dated 12 April 1793, records a motion of thanks to Hannah More for having given the profits of her '*Remarks on the speech of Mr. Dupont*' to the Committee for the use of the emigrant clergy and proposes that the following extract from her *Address to the Ladies of Great Britain* be published. 'Christian charity is of no party – We plead not for their faith but for their wants. And let the more scrupulous, who look for desert as well as distress in the objects of their bounty bear in mind, that if these men could have sacrificed their conscience to their convenience they had not now been in this Country. Let us shew them the purity of our religion by the beneficence of our Actions.'
29. William Frend, Fellow of Jesus College, Cambridge, *Peace and Union recommended to the associated bodies of Republicans and Anti-Republicans*, Cambridge, 1793. p. 51.
30. *Public Advertiser*, 17 September 1792.
31. *Conduit à tenir par M. M. les Ecclésiastiques françois réfugiés en Angleterre*, WDA, (pamphlet imprimé à l'imprimerie de J. P. Coghlan, London), 1794.
32. An oath of allegiance to the Civil Constitution of the Clergy was instituted on 29 November 1791.
33. The circular was sent on 1 December and asked for information on émigrés backdated to 30 August 1792.
34. For example, Southampton reported: 171 mainly priests. Shoreham, 58, including 37 nuns. Portsmouth, 1061, chiefly priests. Brighton, 346. Deal, 59, Dover 1670 predominantly clergy 540 from Flanders chiefly from the army. Harwich, 620, chiefly persons of distinction. Southwold, 18, soldiers. Yarmouth, 200, noblemen, priests, soldiers and their servants. Colchester, 7 soldiers. E. M. Wilkinson, 'French Émigrés in England 1789–1802', unpublished B. Litt. thesis, Oxford 1952, pp. 110–11.
35. PRO T93 30/8 the Collector at Harwich described the refugees as 'extremely quiet and orderly' (3 December 1792); the Collector at Dover described their behaviour as 'nothing improper' (2 December 1792).
36. *Public Advertiser*, 5 January 1793.
37. Introduced into Parliament on 19 December 1792, it was passed on 4 January 1793. See 33 George III, c. IV.
38. See Mary Thrale, 'London Debating Societies in the 1790s', *The Historical Journal*, 32, I, 1989, pp. 57–86. In the 1791–92 season, the

percentage of political topics debated rose 27 per cent to 61 per cent. On 21 May 1792 the king issued a proclamation 'for preventing seditious meetings and writings'.
39. *Parliamentary Register*, Vol. 34, Debates, pp. 253–270.
40. Fox reported in *Le Courrier de Londres*, 8 January 1793.
41. 'The National Convention declares in the name of the French nation, that it will grant fraternity and aid to all peoples who wish to recover their liberty; and it charges the executive power with giving the generals the orders necessary for bringing aid to such peoples and for defending citizens who have been, or who might be harassed for the cause of liberty'. Translation taken from Hall Stewart, op. cit. p. 381, based on the text published in the *Moniteur* on 20 November 1792.
42. William Wyndham Grenville, Baron Grenville (1759–1834), Foreign Secretary 1791–1801. He resigned with Pitt in 1801. He was Prime Minister in the ministry of 'All the Talents' in 1806–7. See *DNB* op. cit., viii, pp. 576–81.
43. See *Le Courrier de Londres*, 8 January 1793.
44. M. A. Taylor, ibid.
45. Wycombe, ibid.
46. *Public Advertiser*, 9 January 1793, AN ABXIX-3790.
47. K. Berryman, 'Great Britain and the French Refugees 1789–1802: the Administrative Response', ANU, unpublished PhD thesis, p.31 In 1608, 'alien' had in fact been given a legal defintion by Lord Chief Justice, Sir Edward Cooke in relation to the case of a Huguenot refugee as 'those born out of the allegiance of the King'. See Robin Gwynn, *The Ecclesiastical Organisation of French Protestants in England in the Later Seventeenth Century, with Special Reference to London*, unpublished PhD Thesis, University of London, 1976. See also Parry, *Nationality and Citizenship: Laws of the Commonwealth*, London, 1957.
48. H.O. 1/1 unf., 11 October 1793.
49. *Morning Chronicle*, 11 January 1792, Burney Collection.
50. H.O. 1/2, 28 March 1794.
51. The Aliens Office not only dealt with émigré issues inside Britain, its concerns made it the centre of British secret intelligence work. See Elizabeth Sparrow, 'The Alien Office, 1792–1806', in *The Historical Journal*, 33, 2 (1990), pp. 361–84 and by the same author, 'The Swiss and Swabian Agencies, 1795–1801', *The Historical Journal*, 35, 4 (1992), pp. 861–84.
52. Sparrow concludes that 'The alien office, for all its strength, led a somewhat ephemeral existence as the act which gave it a *raison d'être* had to be re-passed annually by parliament and re-enacted at five-yearly intervals.' 'The Alien Office, 1792–1806', op. cit., p. 375.
53. Berryman, 'The Administrative Response', op. cit., p. 147.
54. 42 Geo. III, cap. 92.
55. The most often quoted figure of 130 000 used by studies such as C. Jones, *The Longman Companion to the French Revolution*, London 1988, p. 201, is a rounded version of the 129 099 estimated by Greer. His analysis was based on 72 Départements where he counted a total of 109 720 émigrés. This excludes 15 Departements where documents pertaining to émigrés were damaged or non-existent. Greer obtains an

estimate of 129 099 using a mathematical formula to calculate the number for the missing Départements. The formula was derived and adapted from the work of André Gain, *La Restauration et les biens des émigrés*, which found that there were five émigrés for every indemnity granted in 1825. The biggest problem with the estimated figure is that the Départements for which information was unavailable or missing were Départements where emigration was heaviest. The 15 Départements are the Ain, the Eure-et-Loire, the Loiret, the Loire-Inférieure, the Charente-Inférieure, the Côtes du Nord, the Pas de Calais, the Lot-et-Garonne, the Vienne, the Haute-Vienne, the Calvados, the Jura, the Loire, the Puy-de-Dôme and the Sarthe. Without exception these are all areas of high incidence of emigration. See footnote 3, D. Greer, *The Incidence of Emigration during the French Revolution*, Harvard, 1951, p. 19. The figure of 150 000 comes from the total number of people on the official émigré lists in the police files in Paris.

56. W. Doyle, *The Oxford History of the French Revolution*, Oxford, 1989, p. 2.
57. Greer, op. cit., pp. 38–39 (see 'Cartogram of Emigration from France, 1789–1799').
58. Berryman proposes 'a maximum of 13 000 émigrés at any one time' but maintains that up to twice that many may have set foot there in the years 1789–1815. 'The Administrative Response', op. cit., p. 42.
59. *The Public Advertiser*, 1 October 1792, 'The number cannot possibly be less than 40,000. I believe if I were to say double that number I should be near the mark; the greater part of whom have not brought any property with them.'
60. *Public Advertiser*, 1 October 1792, also AN ABXIX-3790 I/72.
61. 40 000 also appears in the *St James's Chronicle*, 8–11 September 1792, 'upwards of 40,000 French men, women and children are at present in this country, two thirds of them of the lowest class, who taking advantage of the convulsed state of their native country, come over under the plausible title of Exiled Aristocrats'.
62. 23 October 1792.
63. *Le Courrier de Londres*, 9 July 1793. The fact that the émigrés brought considerable funds is also corroborated by the Auckland correspondence, op. cit., p. 459. Lord Sheffield writes on 21 October 1792: 'There is nothing more clear than that the émigrants have brought a good deal of money, and that the priests even are far from a disadvantage to us.'
64. Vicomte Walsh, *Souvenirs de cinquante ans*, Paris, 1862, p. 139.
65. *Correspondence of William, Lord Auckland*, p. 472.
66. Bishop Douglass papers, Westminster Diocesan Archives.
67. As Vicar Apostolic of the London District the Bishop Douglass was one of four Vicars Apostolic in England (the others being the Midlands, Northern and Western Districts). See Bellenger, op. cit., p. 49.
68. Bellenger, op. cit., p. 48.
69. Abbé Barruel, op. cit., p. 231.
70. État des émigrés français qui sont à présent en Angleterre, Jersey et Guernsey rédigé par le Baron de Nantiat, secrétaire du comité de secours, Windham Papers, BL Add Mss 37 863, f. 301.

71. Archives du ministère des affaires étrangères, Fonds Bourbons, 620, Liste d'émigrés établie par la police impériale avec une notice sur chaque personne.
72. Butler, C., *Historical Memoirs respecting the English, Irish and Scottish Catholics from the Reformation to the Present Time*, 4 vols, London, 1819–1821, iv, p. 375.
73. WDA, papers of Bishop Douglass.
74. PRO. 93–8.
75. Issue of 22 September 1792.
76. B.M. Add. Mss. 18,591, 5 October 1792, f. 19.
77. James Baillie, William Baker, Edmund Burke, Isaac Hawkins Browne, Robert Banks Jenkinson, Philip Metcalfe, William Moreton Pitt, Sir James Sanderson, Sir William Scott, Lord Sheffield, Henry Thornton, Brook Watson, William Wilberforce and John Eardley Wilmot.
78. For a list of the members of the Wilmot Committee BM Add Mss. 18,591.
79. *London Chronicle*, 11–13 September.
80. *St James Chronicle*, 27–29 September 1792.
81. BL Add, Ms. 18,591–593.
82. PRO T.93-1 dated 19 March 1794.
83. There were 20 shillings to the pound; 1-11*s*-6*d* could count as a shilling a day for a month.
84. ABXIX-3790 IV/28, Letter from the Bishop of St Pol de Léon to William Pitt, 26 July 1794 listing the designated people and the sums of money involved.
85. This sum included the lump sum of £600 contributed by the Ladies' Committee.
86. D'Arblay, *Doctor Burney*, iii, p. 185.
87. Minutes, 22 March 1793, BL. Add. Ms. 18,591 f.185.
88. Edmund Burke, *Reflections on the Revolution in France*, Penguin edition, London, 1987, pp. 202–3.
89. Minutes, 24 October 1793, ibid., f. 125.
90. Berryman, op. cit., p. 252. The Bishop of Saint Pol de Léon and the comte de Botherel, who distributed relief to the émigrés in Jersey, are particularly good examples of this. They had impeccable connections in British society.
91. Dundas to [?] 25 September 1792 H.O. 42/21 ff. 626–7, quoted by Berryman, op. cit., p. 248.

4 SOHO

1. Duchesse de Gontaut, op. cit., p. 23.
2. Dulau and De Boffe, see p. 54.
3. In the 1790s Oxford Street alone according to one visitor, Sophie von la Roche, 'contained as many lamps as the whole of Paris'. Cited by Mackenzie, op. cit., p. 77.

Notes

4. This hotel occupied a house which formerly belonged to Hogarth. Leigh Hunt, *The Town, Its Memorable Characteristics and Events, St Paul's to St James's*, London, 1906, p. 479.
5. Gueudon, Leicester Square and Saulieu, corner of Gerrard Street and Nassau Street, Soho. Tardy, op. cit., p. 17.
6. Ibid., pp. 17–18.
7. These eating-houses were given very indifferent ratings by the *European Magazine*, see Bellenger, op. cit., p. 67.
8. M. Goldsmith, *Soho Square*, London, 1948, p. 12.
9. In 1711, 612 French inhabitants (Huguenot refugees or their descendants) were listed in the parish of St Anne. Douglas Newton, *Catholic London*, London, 1950, p. 278.
10. C. L. Kingsford, *The Early History of Piccadilly, Leicester Square, Soho, and their Neighbourhood*, Cambridge, 1925 p. 116.
11. V. Pierre, 'Un Curé de Normandie', *Revue des Questions Historiques*, Vol. LXVIII, 1900, p. 484.
12. Judith Summers, *Soho: a History of London's Most Colourful Neighbourhood*, London, 1989.
13. Among the most recent, Evelyn Farr, *The World of Fanny Burney*, London, 1993 and Kate Chisholm, *Fanny Burney: Her Life 1752–1840*, London, 1998.
14. See p. 197.
15. Particuarly, T.93-28.
16. Portalis, op. cit., p. 50. He left Paris on 11 January 1792 electing not to take his wife until he could support her. She came one year later in February 1793.
17. 'Un des premiers soins de Danloux, en arrivant à Londres, avait été d'organiser son atelier et d'y créer, à l'instar des anglais, une sorte d'exposition permanente. Aidé de John Greenwood, il en disposa l'éclairage afin d'y concentrer la lumière se munit d'un fauteuil de pose chez le tapissier Stevens, et couvrit ses murs de serge verte, nuance avantageuse aux tableaux.' Portalis, op. cit., p. 106.
18. Ibid., pp. 106–8.
19. Talleyrand, who had been made the Bishop of Autun in his twenties, created something of a scandal by wearing a pigtail which was the style later adopted by the Jacobin revolutionaries like Collot d'Herbois. Many of the émigrés who arrived in London still wore their hair powdered, which had been the fashion under the *ancien régime*, and this did not disappear in France until well into the Revolution. Robespierre, for instance, wore his hair powdered, a hangover perhaps of his days as a lawyer, but many of the other members of the Committee of Public Safety had abandoned the custom in favour of the natural style of the *sans-culottes* who could not, of course, afford to wear powdered hair. In Britain, where the fashion of wearing powdered hair was in abeyance, Pitt imposed a tax on hair powder in 1794 which caused much resentment among the émigrés.
20. Talleyrand was probably the father of the comtesse de Flahaut's only son Charles.
21. Portalis, op. cit., p. 160.
22. Ibid., p. 300.

23. Ibid., p. 169.
24. Elsewhere he makes remarks like, 'On sent que la misère le gagne'. (Misery is getting the better of him) writing of the vicomte de La Tour du Pin La Charce, Portalis, op. cit., p. 64.
25. Ibid., p. 351.
26. *Diary and Letters of Mme d'Arblay*, op. cit., Vol. VI, p. 145.
27. Charvin, *Les religieux de la Congrégation de Saint Maur pendant la Révolution*, Revue Mabillon, LVI, 1996, pp. 101–66 and LVII, 1967, pp. 157–219.
28. 75 Great Queen Street, Lincoln's Inn Fields.
29. These are among works listed in the book catologue dating from 1812, preserved in the British Library.
30. Dulau and Deboffe were certainly not alone among the French bookshops. At least two other Frenchmen sought naturalisation in Britain in order to continue in the book trade. Pierre Didier, born in Venezey in 1773, jointly owned a bookshop at 75 St James Street; and Laurant-Louis Deconchy, born in Paris in 1755, arrived Britain in 1793, established a business at 100 New Bond Street, and married an Englishwoman. ABXIX-3973 Parrel papers.
31. Le comte de Lally-Tolendal, *Le comte de Strafford, tragédie en cinq actes et en vers*, Londres de l'imprimerie de T. Spilsbury et fils: Et se vend chez MM Elmsley, *Strand*, Edwards *Pall-Mall*, White, *Piccadilly*; De Boffe, Gerard Street, *Soho*, 1795.
32. Fanny Burney described how the first edition of the novel *Cecilia* at 2000 copies was thought to be ridiculously high but *Evelina* had sold 800 then 500 then 1000 copies in its third edition. Op. cit., Vol. IV, p. 76. In 1830 the first edition of Stendhal's *Le Rouge et le Noir* was only 1500 copies.
33. Her address in Soho was No. 27 Half Moon Street. See Baron de Maricourt, *Madame de Souza et sa famille, les Marigny, les Flahaut, Auguste de Morney, 1761–1836*, Paris, 1907, p. 175.
34. Chateaubriand, *Mémoires d'Outre Tombe*, Édition du Centenaire, Flammarion, Paris, 1982, p. 444.
35. The argument continues forcefully: 'Cela rappelle le portrait des Chinois et des Nègres: tout bons, ou tout méchants. Si l'on convient qu'un grand seigneur peut être un fripon, qu'un royaliste peut être un malhonnête homme, cela ne suffit pas actuellement: un ci-devant gentilhomme est de nécessité un scélérat. Et pourquoi? Parce qu'un de ses ancêtres, qui vivoit du temps du roi Dagobert, pouvoit obliger ses vassaux à faire taire les grenouilles de l'étang voisin, lorsque sa femme étoit en couche.'
36. 16 Wardour Street. PRO T.93-28.
37. 52 Poland Street, ibid.
38. 58 Dean Street, ibid.
39. George Rudé, *Hanoverian London, 1714–1808*, London, 1971, pp. 235–6.
40. *Two Centuries of Soho* by the Clergy of St Anne's, Soho, London, 1898, p. 43.
41. Ibid.

Notes

42. Plasse, op. cit., p. 122.
43. Newton, *Catholic London*, op. cit., p. 278.
44. Plasse, op. cit., p. 118.
45. For the King's House, Winchester, see Bellenger, D. A., 'The French Priests at the King's House, Winchester, 1792–1796', *Proceedings of the Hampshire Field Club and Archaeological Society*, XL, (1984), pp. 99–105, Bellenger, D. A., 'The King's House, Winchester: Religious Life in Community', *Downside Review* C (1982) pp. 101–9, and Wilkinson, thesis, op. cit., pp. 188–236.
46. These are logged as extraordinary payments in the Bishop of Léon's accounts for 1792.
47. Dominic Bellenger, 'Dorothy Silburn (1753–1820) Mother of the French Exiled Clergy', *Northern Catholic History*, XVII (1983) pp. 14–16. and 'Dorothy Silburn: a Further Note', *Northern Catholic History*, XX (1984), pp. 18–20.
48. Two wards in the west wing of the Middlesex Hospital were offered at a cost of 8s per week for each patient which was to include maintenance, medicines, washing and other necessary articles like bedding. BM Add Mss, 18, 591, 6 May 1793.
49. Records of Middlesex Hospital, 1794–96. Soeur Masson received a salary of one guinea per month and was responsible to the Committee for the expenditure incurred in regard to the Hospital.
50. Baston, op. cit., Vol. II, p. 62.
51. PRO T.93-51 f. 328.
52. D Ball, Surgeon, 4 Warwick Street, Charing Cross, 26 January 1793, Add Ms 18,591.
53. PRO T.93-52, S. Wegener to the Committee, 19 October 1792.
54. PRO T.93-4, 8 January 1802, Records of the Committee.
55. PRO T.93-52, 16 May 1793.
56. K. Carpenter, *Les émigrés à Londres 1792–1797*, unpublished Doctorat de l'Université thesis, Université de Paris I, 1993, p. 162, based on 88 consultations of which only 85 list the cause of illness, AN ABXIX-3791, dos 3.
57. Add Ms. 18,591 f-16, 6 February 1794. She was paid £50 to cover her previous costs and paid 2 guineas per month from January 1794 for 'extraordinary expenses incurred at her house'.
58. See Chapter 6.
59. B.M. Add Ms. 18,592, Minutes 19 December 1793, (clergy). T.93-29&30 (laity).
60. Ibid., 23 January 1794.
61. Ibid., 27 February 1794.
62. PRO T.93-8, 2 March 1794.
63. PRO T.93-1, 23 July & 3 September 1794.
64. Ibid.
65. The uprisings in Saint Domingue and other French dependencies like Martinique and Guadeloupe were a direct result of the Revolution in France. They originated with plantation-workers demanding their rights as French citizens and freedom from oppression. The debate and minor uprisings began as early as 1790; the British became involved, supporting

222 *Notes*

the royalist planters, in the spring and summer of 1793 and this involvement forced the French to ally with the slaves. Fighting went on until 1801 when the slave-leader Toussaint l'Ouverture gained control but the economy of the once-wealthy colony had been decimated, much property had been destroyed and from mid- to late 1794 émigrés with property in Saint Domingue were cut off from their funds and subsequently denied credit in London.

66. See p. 192.
67. PRO T.93-1, 5 March 1795.
68. B.M. Add Ms. 18,592, 9 November & 16 December 1795.
69. B.M. Add Ms. 18,592, Minutes of Committee Meeting, f 76. He details the most pressing cases: those very recently arrived in Britain, military men particularly the aged and infirm, volunteers who had escaped from Quiberon, and pregnant women faced with giving birth in squalid conditions.
70. Ibid., 16 December 1795.
71. B.M. Add Ms.18,592, 28 January 1796.

5 MARYLEBONE, RICHMOND, HAMPSTEAD – THE HIGH LIFE

1. Gordon Mackenzie, *Marylebone, Great City North of Oxford Street*, London 1972, p. 229.
2. Lysons, op. cit., Vol. III, p. 242.
3. Le Colonel de Guilhermy, *Papiers d'un émigré, 1789–1829: Lettres et notes extraitées du portefeuille du baron de Guilhermy*, Plon, Paris, 1886. pp. 116–17. Jean-François César de Guilhermy took refuge in Britain in 1801.
4. *Journal d'une femme de cinquante ans*, op. cit., Vol. II, p. 165.
5. La duchesse de Gontaut, op. cit., p. 30.
6. Mallet du Pan, *Mémoires et correspondance*, Paris, 1951, Vol. II, p. 369.
7. Mme de Boigne, op. cit., Vol. I, p. 105.
8. Portalis, op. cit., p. 305.
9. A. Bardoux, *La duchesse de Duras*, Paris, 1898, pp. 57–8.
10. Margery Weiner, *The French Exiles, 1789–1815*, London, 1960, p. 100.
11. See p. 197.
12. Vicomte Walsh, op. cit., p. 151.
13. Manchee, W. H., *Marylebone and Its Huguenot Associations*, in *Proceedings of the Huguenot Society of Great Britain*, 1915, Vol. 11, no. 1.
14. Harting, *Catholic London Missions from the Reformation to the Year 1850*, London, 1903, pp. 231–3, cited by Wilkinson, op. cit., p. 484.
15. Walsh, op. cit., p. 151.
16. Margery Weiner wrote in 1960: 'The curious can still see the Chapel of the Annunciation although it has long since ceased to be called by that name. From the mews in Carton Street one steps into what is scarcely more than a large room, whitewashed and lit by a skylight in the roof. Above the entrance passage a gallery is supported on slender pillars.

On one side of the gallery a corkscrew staircase leads up three flights, each with a small room where lived the ministering clergy.' *The French Exiles 1789–1815*, p. 123.
17. FB, *Mémoires et Documents*, p. 620 provides a list of those present at the funeral.
18. Mackenzie, op. cit., p. 231.
19. Walsh, op. cit., p. 153.
20. La fille d'une victime de la Revolution Française, Mme de Ménerville née Fougeret, *Souvenirs d'Emigration 1791–1797*, Paris 1934. p. 158.
21. Duchesse de Gontaut, op. cit., p. 24.
22. Menerville, op. cit., p. 169.
23. Walsh, op. cit., p. 153.
24. Ibid.
25. Walsh, op. cit., p. 154.
26. Add Ms 18,591, Vol. I, p. 130.
27. Menerville, op. cit., p. 171.
28. Ibid.
29. M. Kelly, *Reminiscences*, 2 vols, London, 1826, Vol. II, pp. 86–7.
30. Duchesse de Gontaut, op. cit., p. 31.
31. Duc de Bourbon à la Comtesse de Vaudreuil, 20 juillet 1798. *Correspondance*, ed. E. de Bathélemy, Paris 1886, p. 22.
32. Daudet, *Histoire de l'émigration*, Vol. I, p. 131. This comment is quoted from the letters of a lawyer, Christin, in the diary of Princess Tourkestanow, held in the Russian Archives.
33. *Courrier de Londres*, 17 May 1793, Monsieur Brillaud de Lonjac, 103 High Street Marylebone.
34. Portalis, op. cit., p. 117.
35. Vicomte Walsh, op. cit., p. 267.
36. A. Grangier, *A Genius of France: a Short Sketch of the Famous French Inventor, Sebastien Érard and the Firm He Founded in Paris 1780*, translated by Jean Fougueville. (Third Edition, Paris, 1924); Pierre Érard, *The Harp, In its Present Improved State Compared with the Original Pedal Harp*, London, 1821; and F. Fétis, *Notice biographique sur Sebastien Érard, Chevalier de la Légion d'Honneur*, Paris, 1831.
37. Which later moved from Marylebone High Street to 18 Great Marlborough Street.
38. The description of the forthcoming auction by H. R. Woudhuysen in *The Times Literary Supplement*, 25 November 1994, decribed the Érard records. 'It consists of four volumes covering the years from 1798 to 1917 in which the firm founded at London by Sebastien Érard recorded details of sales and the renovation of some 7,000 harps.' The previous owners of these records, the firm of Morley Bros, informed me that the information on the early period was very limited and listed no likely émigrés.
39. Montlosier, *Souvenirs d''un émigré*, p. 221 quoted by, H Maspero-Clerc, *Un journaliste Contre-révolutionnaire J-G Peltier*, p. 70.
40. The expression is used by Mme de Menerville.
41. These were advertised in the French and British papers. The *Courrier de Londres* and *The Morning Chronicle* between 1793 and 1795 both published venues, prices and programmes.

42. *Promenade autour de la Grande Bretagne précédé de quelques détails sur la campagne du Duc de Brunswick,* par un officier français émigré, p. 103.
43. Walsh, op. cit., 220.
44. Marquise de la Tour du Pin, op. cit., Vol. 2, p. 182.
45. Gordon MacKenzie, op. cit., pp. 228–9.
46. Duc de Castries, *La vie quotidienne des émigrés,* Hachette, 1966, p. 145. This account claims that he made a fortune of 80 000 francs.
47. Walsh, op. cit., p. 220.
48. A. G. L'Estrange, ed., *The Life of Mary Russell Mitford, Authoress of our Village. Related in a Selection of her Letters to her Friends,* London, 1870, Vol. 2, p. 102. Letter dated 5 July 1820, to Sir William Elford.
49. She lived in a house on the corner of the Green once known as Cedar Grove and now as the Virginals but rebuilt in 1813. Filson, J., 'French Emigrés in Richmond, 1785–1815', *Richmond History,* No. 7, 1986, p. 7.
50. Daniel Lysons, Chaplain to the Right Hon. the Earl of Orford, *The Environs of London,* London, 1792, Vol. I, p. 436.
51. H. Walpole à Miss Berry, 3 August 1791., Lady T. Lewis Ed., *Extracts from the Journal and Correspondence of Miss Berry,* 3 vols, London, 1865, Vol. 1, p. 322.
52. Burke Correspondance, Northampton Public Records Office, AXX.12, Mme de Cambis to Burke, 28 September 1792.
53. The princesse d'Hénin rented a house called the Rosary in Ormond Row (now Road) in 1793 for an annual rent of £6-40*s*. Filson, op. cit., p. 4.
54. Marquise de la Tour du Pin, op. cit., Vol. 2, p. 182.
55. Sellwyn to Lady Carlisle, op. cit., p. 692, September 1790.
56. Lewis and Wallace, eds, *Correspondence of H. Walpole with Mary and Agnes Berry,* Vol. I, p. 148, 27 November 1790.
57. Marquis de Valous, *Sur les routes de l'Emigration, Mémoires de la Duchesse de Saulx-Tavannes, 1791–1806,* Paris, 1834, p. 46.
58. Marquise de la Tour du Pin, op. cit., p. 164.
59. D'Arblay, *Diary and Letters,* op. cit., Vol. VI, p. 15, Alexandre d'Arblay and Fanny Burney lived in a cottage which was 'about a mile and a half from Norbury Park and two miles from Michelham'.
60. Sellwyn to Lady Carlisle, op. cit., p. 689, 7 September 1790.
61. Walsh, op. cit., pp. 260–1.
62. Marquise de la Tour du Pin, op. cit., Vol. 2, p. 175.
63. Filsen, op. cit., p. 7.
64. 'There are now only 130 acres of pasture and meadow, and about 170 of arable, the greater part of which is occupied by market gardeners; this deficiency is to be attributed to the prodigious increase of buildings since the above mentioned survey.' Ibid. Lysons quotes a survey of 1664 which puts the pasture and meadow at 164 acres and the arable land at 300 acres.
65. Chateaubriand, *Mémoires d'Outre Tombe,* op. cit., Vol. I, p. 486.
66. Abbé Tardy, *Manuel d'un Voyageur à Londres,* op. cit., pp. 248–50 contains an extended description of Ranelagh where its delights are

expounded in detail. He describes the rotunda as 'as majestic on the inside as it is on the outside'. He gives the dimensions (150 feet in diameter) to emphasise the immense size and the number of lodges where tea and coffee were taken. The rest of the gardens and the superb lighting arrangements are rapturously praised.

67. E.g. 29 March 1793, 'Bal masqué à Ranelagh', *Courrier de Londres*.
68. See Dominic Bellenger, *The French Exiled Clergy in the London District: Voyaux de Franous*, London Recusant, VII, 1977, pp. 32–5.
69. Lysons, op. cit., Vol. 2, p. 527.
70. Marquis de Valous, *Sur les routes de l'Émigration, Mémoires de la Duchesse de Saulx-Tavannes (1791–1806)*, Paris, 1834, p. 46.
71. Mme de Menerville, op. cit., p. 173.
72. The present purpose-built chapel in Holly Place was opened in 1816 once the congregation had grown sufficiently large to justify it. The new chapel therefore appeared only after the last of the émigrés had returned to France.
73. Dominic Bellenger, *The Exiled French Clergy in the London District: the Abbé Morel*, London Recusant, V (1975) pp. 97–8.
74. Walsh, op. cit., p. 288.
75. Ibid. At the beginning of the nineteenth century a French-American, Louis Simond, wrote: 'On winter days in London ... the smoke of fossil coal forms an atmosphere perceivable for many miles, like a great round cloud attached to the earth'. Louis Simond, *Journal of a Tour 1810–1811*, Christopher Hibbert, ed., London, 1968.
76. T.H.R., Cashmore, *The Orleans Family in Twickenham, 1800–1932*, Twickenham Local Historical Society, 1982.
77. The duc d'Orléans and Miss Forbes were very fond of each other but the relationship of course had no possible future.
78. Richmond Local Studies Collection, The Paton Collection; Le Chevalier de Broval to Mrs Forbes, 25 February 1808.
79. Ibid., 7 April 1808. 'En partant, il m'a racommandé de vous écrire, je l'eusse toujours fait, mais vous aimerez à savoir qu'il a pensé à vous dans ce moment. S'il a du tems a Portsmouth ou le tems les retient, il vous écrira sans-doute lui-même'.
80. Ibid., 21 November 1807.
81. See Reiset, vicomte de, *Les enfants du Duc de Berri*, Paris, 1905, and André Castelot, *Le Duc de Berri et son Double Mariage*, Paris, 1951.
82. Rev. A. G. L'Estrange, *The Life of Mary Russell Mitford*, op. cit., Vol. I, p. 190. In a letter to Sir William Elford dated 22 April 1812.
83. Marqise de la Tour du Pin, op. cit., Vol. I, p. 386. 'Je trouvai mes cheveux que j'avais très longs, tellement mêlés que désespérant de les remettre en ordre et prévoyant apparemment la coiffure à la Titus, je pris des ciseaux et je les coupai tout à fait courts ce dont mon mari fut fort en colère. Puis je les jetai à la mer et avec eux toutes les idées frivoles que mes belles boucles blondes avaient pu faire naitre en moi'.
84. Burney, *The Wanderer*, p. 220.
85. La comtesse de Boigne, op. cit., p. 373.

6 ST PANCRAS, SOMERSTOWN, SAINT GEORGE'S FIELDS – THE LOW LIFE

1. Walsh, op. cit., p. 155.
2. See pp. 90–2.
3. Lysons, op. cit., Vol. III, pp. 342–3.
4. La duchesse de Gontaut, op. cit., 1891, p. 39.
5. Diary of Bishop Douglass, entry for 27 November 1806.
6. Lee, C., *St Pancras Church and Parish*, London, 1955.
7. Lysons, op. cit., Vol. II, p. 619. The cemetery already contained members of old Catholic families: Howards, Arundels, Cliffords, Blounts, Tichbornes, Doughtys, Constables and many Jacobites.
8. Dr Johnson recorded that Catholics chose St Pancras for their burying place because some Catholics in Queen Elizabeth's time had been burnt there.
9. Lysons, op. cit., Vol. III, p. 351.
10. Douglas Newton, *Catholic London*, op. cit., p. 278. The chapel in Saint George's Fields is mentioned in the diary of Bishop Douglass in relation to a retreat in Lent given after Easter in 1793 to the French clergy resident in London. Similar retreats were organised in St Patrick's Soho. Douglas papers, WDA. The Abbé Tardy lists seven London chapels in his guide to London. Holly Place, Hampstead is missing from this list because it was a mixed ministry and services were in the English language. They are Chapellle de la Croix, Dudley Court, Crown Street, Soho, Chapelle de Ste Agnès, London Street, Fitzroy Square, Chapelle de St Marie, Somerstown Chapelle de l'Annonciation, King Street, Portman Square, Chapelle de St Louis, Prospect Place, St George's Fields, Chapelle de Chelsea and Chapelle de Paddington Green. Op. cit., p. 221.
11. Plasse, op. cit., Vol. II, pp. 150–1. When it opened in 1796 the French chapel was situated at 44 Pitt Street but this chapel was not big enough to accommodate the émigrés, so in 1798 it was relocated to a more spacious building, 21 Prospect Place.
12. Walsh, op. cit., p. 170.
13. In all, some 6000 men were taken prisoner by Hoche's troops including 3600 *chouans* and 1000 émigrés a significant number of whom (748, made up of 600 émigrés and the rest *chouans*, p. 322) were later executed. Maurice Hutt, *Chouannerie and Counter Revolution: Puisaye, the Princes and the British Government in the 1790s*, Cambridge, 1983, Vol. II, p. 325.
14. Maurice Hutt, ibid., Vol. II, chaps 8 and 9.
15. *Chouan* was originally the nickname given to Jean Cottereau's men but it came to refer to all royalist resistance fighters in West France. *Chouans* were local men who knew forest paths and smugglers' routes and were well-informed about local people, places and happenings. Importantly therefore, *chouannerie* as a movement came to embody many different strains of resistance, combining local tensions with royalist politics. See M. Hutt, *Chouannerie and Counter-Revolution,* op. cit., chap 1.

Notes

16. Patrick Huchet, *1795, Quiberon ou le destin de la France*, Rennes, 1995, p. 196.
17. Walsh, op. cit., p. 162.
18. Lubersac, op. cit., p. 83.
19. The clergy were themselves facing great hardship. On 4 June 1794 Wilmot submitted a proposal to the Committee 'for making an Extra Allowance to the French Clergy for the present month of June on account of the very great Distress many and indeed most of them, are in, for the want of either shoes, hats, stockings or some other of the smaller articles of Dress which have not been furnished by the Committeee and which they find the greatest difficulty to supply themselves.' BL Add Mss 15592, f. 27.
20. Walsh, op. cit., p. 198.
21. Mme de Menerville, op. cit., p. 181.
22. Ibid., p. 183.
23. PRO T.93-54, Letter from the Abbé Duheron to the Committee, quoted by Wilkinson, op. cit., p. 265.
24. This was the subject of a letter to *Le Courrier de Londres*, 29 April 1794.
25. PRO T.93-73.
26. PRO T.93-2.
27. PRO T.93-50 & PC 1/115A.
28. The members of the Ladies' Committee were: Marchioness of Buckingham, Lady Mary Bentinck, Marchioness Townsend, Lady Mary Grenville, Lady Mary Coke, Lady Julie Howard, Lady Charlotte Greville, Lady Anne North, Countess of Cardigan, Hon. Mrs Soulhowel, Countess of Carlisle, Hon. Miss Walpole, Countess of Harcourt, Hon. Miss Fox, Countess of Mount-Edgecumbe, Hon. Miss Dutton, Viscountess Newark, Hon. Miss Chetwyne, Lady Mary Churchill, Miss Ogilvie, Lady Malmesbury, Miss Mackenzie, Lady Muncaster, Miss Vernon, Hon. Mrs Robinson, Miss Francis, Mrs Moore Lameth, Miss Macnamara, Mrs Lock, Miss Canning, Mrs Crewe, Miss Wilmot, Mrs Berners, Miss Lukin, Mrs Leigh, Miss Percival, Mrs Robert Thornton, Miss Johnson, Mrs Angerstein, Miss Saladin, Lady Georgina Cavendish. Abbé Lubersac, *Journal Historique et religieux de l'émigration et déportation du clergé de France en Angleterre*, op. cit., p. 86.
29. Lubersac, op. cit., pp. 79–82
30. Ibid., p. 85.
31. Add Ms. 18,591, Vol. I, p. 118.
32. WDA, papers of Bishop Douglass, Diary.
33. Berryman, op. cit., p. 315.
34. Ibid., p. 318.
35. P.C. 1/118 n 73, Mémoire, Londres, le 23 juin 1797, le comte de Botherel.
36. Ibid., p. 2.
37. A.N. ABXIX 3797.
38. Bellenger, *French Exiled Clergy*, op. cit., p. 106.
39. Lubersac, op. cit., p. 108.
40. Ibid., p. 106.

41. Delille, *Malheur et Pitié*, Chant II, lines 217–220. *Oeuvres de J. Delille*, ed. August Desrez, Paris, 1838.

7 EDUCATIONAL PURSUITS

1. Delille, *Malheur et Pitié*, chant IV, lines 545–6. (The dashing marquess is content at the counter, and more than one young warrier holds Emile's pointer.)
2. Suzanne Blum, *Vivre sans la patrie*, Paris, 1975, p. 216.
3. *St James Chronicle*, 22 September 1792.
4. Senac de Meilhan, *L'émigré*, roman, 4 tomes, Brunswick 1797, tome II, pp. 11–12.
5. Mme de Menerville, op. cit., p. 169.
6. Preface to *Adèle de Senange*. *Oeuvres Complètes de Madame de Souza, comtesse puis marquise de Flahant*, Paris, 1821.
7. Mme de Boigne, *Mémoires*, op. cit., Vol. I, pp. 99–100.
8. See *La Comédie Humaine*, Tome II, Scènes de la vie privée, *Beatrix*, p. 97. 'Sabine, trouvée heureuse par sa mère et sa soeur qui virent dans la froideur de Calyste un effet de son éducation anglaise, abandonna ses idées noires; .....'
9. *Le Courrier de Londres*, 19 July 1793. (In Rugby in the county of Warwick we take as boarders a small number of young men for the purpose of instructing them in the French, German and Italian languages. The price of Boarding which includes washing, mending and ironing as well as the use of a horse, is 100 guineas per year. Young foreigners who may need instruction in the English language are also accepted on the same conditions. Address correspondence to etc. NB: If the use of a horse is not required the price is 80 guineas.)
10. Walsh, op. cit., pp. 52–4.
11. A. Martin, 'Le clergé normand au temps de la Révolution', *Revue Catholique de Normandie*, July 1892, p. 65.
12. AN 565 AP dos 1, 13 September 1815, letter from Madame de Souza to her son.
13. Letter from the Abbé Devoye to the Wilmot Committee in 1794, PRO. T.93-52.
14. Abbé Couespel, ibid.
15. Walsh, op. cit., p. 231.
16. Add Ms 18,592, f.98. On 17 March 1796, the minutes of the Wilmot Committee, it was resolved that: 'The plans of the French School from the Committee of Ladies being presented by the Rev. Dr. King. They were approved and the Rev. Dr. King desired to present to them the thanks of the Committee.'
17. Lubersac, op. cit., p. 87.
18. WDA, Diary of Bishop Douglass, 26 March 1801, reads: 'The School for French young Ladies at Blyth House being broken up and the few young Ladies which remained being removed to M. Carron's Somerstown.'

19. Lysons, op. cit., Vol. II, p. 71.
20. Mary Russell Mitford, *Recollections of a Literary Life*, op. cit., p. 235.
21. L'Estrange, *The Life of Mary Russel Mitford*, London, 1870, Vol. II, p. 11.
22. *Bath Journal*, 5 September 1796 – an observation signed 'Civis'.
23. Mme de Ménerville, op. cit., p. 183.
24. Fitzwilliam and Bourke, eds, *E. Burke, Correspondence*, op. cit., Vol. IV, pp. 338–9.
25. Lubersac, op. cit., pp. 157–9.
26. Edmund Burke to Rev. Thomas Hussey, 25 May 1796, *Correspondence of Edmund Burke*, Cambridge, 1970, Vol. IX, p. 21. The full correspondence can be read in the Northampton Public Records Office, AXX.14 Correspondence with the French Committee relating to the Penn School.
27. PC1-115, pièce 85, François-Louis du Bahuno, *comte* then *marquis de Liscoët*.
28. A list of these names can be found in the Burke correspondence relating to the Penn school.
29. Plasse, op. cit., Vol. II, p. 59, Jean Marin Maraine, born in Gerville near Havre in the department of the Seine Inférieure. Died in Rouen in 1830 aged 84.
30. Ibid., pp. 64–5.
31. Add Ms. 37824 f-213, a codicil from EB's will reads: 'I have now only to recommend to the kindness of My Lord Chancellor Lord Loughborough, to his Grace the Duke of Portland, the Most Honorable Marquis of Buckingham, to the Right Honorable William Windham to Doctor Lawrence of the Commons and Member of Parliament, that they will after my death continue their protection and favour to the Emigrant School at Penn, and will entreat with a weight on which I dare not presume the Right Honorable William Pitt to continue the monetary allowance which he has so generously and charitably provided for these unhappy children of Meritorious parents and that they will superintend the same which I wish to be under the immediate care and direction of Dr Lawrence and Dr Walter King; and that they will be pleased to assert their influence to place the said young persons in some military corps or other service as may best suit their disposition and capacities praying God to bless their endeavours.'
32. He was paid £31 per annum, the teachers, £25-4s-0d, the Housekeeper, £21. Add Ms. 37867 f. 132.
33. Add Ms 45723, f-24, 10 January 1800, Maraine to King.
34. The boys in theory received a clothing allowance of £10-10s-0d. Add Ms 37867 f. 132.
35. Ibid., f-43, 1 March 1801.
36. Ibid., f-51, 3 July 1801.
37. Ibid., f-54.
38. Ibid., f-59.
39. PRO T.93-10 p. 220, letter from the Treasury to the Committee, dated 25 March 1808, instructing them to pay the Abbé Maraine's extraordinary expenses at the French school at Penn to the order of £74-18s-5d.
40. Family papers of the Marquis de Genouillac, letter from Gustave, vicomte de Rocquefeuil to Casmir de Genouillac, 15 February 1820.

41. L'Abbé Levasseur, PRO. T.93-52.
42. PRO T.93-52, Abbé Toussaint to the Committee, 21 July 1803.
43. Lubersac, op. cit., p. 149.
44. ABXIX-3973, The school had 110 pupils in 1810.
45. P. Langlois, *Essai historique sur le Chapitre de Rouen pendant la Révolution, 1789–1802*, Rouen, 1856, p. 54.
46. PRO PC1 1/118A, letter from the abbé de Cernay to the Prince de Bouillon, 4 July 1797.
47. PRO T.93-52, letter from Abbé Brémont to the Committee, 22 July 1803.
48. PRO T.93-52, letter from Abbé Doublet to the Committee, 2 August 1803.
49. PRO T.93-52, letter from the Abbé Dourlen to the Committee, 22 July 1803.
50. PRO PC1 1/115A, letter from M. l'Ainé to the Prince de Bouillon, 2 July 1795. This reveals that M. l'Ainé, who had been appointed to teach the daughters of the Mayor of London, wrote that the numerous acquaintances he had made in the city assured him plenty of pupils.
51. PRO PC1 1/117A, letter from M. de Sepmanville to the Prince de Bouillon, 27 November 1797. In these cases it was necessary to investigate the political and religious views of the accompanying tutor and Lord Glenbervie narrowly escaped appointing a tutor for his son whose principles were 'by no means orthodox'. F. Bickley, ed., *Diaries of Sylvester Douglas, Lord Glenbervie*, London, 2 vols, 1928, I, p. 32.
52. Walsh, op. cit., p. 165.
53. Ibid.
54. Ibid., p. 263.
55. Ibid., p. 109.
56. Plasse, op. cit., Vol. II, p. 137.
57. WDA, Diary of Bishop Douglass, 22 June 1805.
58. This letter is quoted in its entirety by Lubersac, op. cit., pp. 114–15.

8 POLITICS – THEIR OWN WORST ENEMIES?

1. AN 419AP1, pièce 18, Letter from the Cardinal Maury to the Comte d'Antraigues, dated 17 November 1798.
2. Calonne, *Tableau de l'Europe en novembre 1795 et pensée sur ...*, London, 1795.
3. Boissy d'Anglas was a deputy in the Convention who, in a famous speech on 23 June 1795, 5 Messidor Year III, spelt out why the property-owning elite should govern France. 'We must be ruled by the best citizens [....] The best are the most learned and the most concerned in the keeping of the laws. Now with very few exceptions you will find such men only amongst those who own some property, and are thus attached to the land in which it lies, to the laws which protect it and to the public order which maintains it; men who owe to their property and to the affluence that it affords, the education which has fitted them to discuss

widely and equitably the advantages and disadvantages of the laws which determine the fate of their country. [...] A country governed by landowners is in the social order; a land where non-landowners govern is in the state of nature.'

4. Calonne, *Tableau d'Europe*, op. cit., pp. 134–5.
5. Norman Hampson, 'The Heavenly City of the French Revolutionaries', in Colin Lucas, ed., *Rewriting the French Revolution*, Oxford, 1991, p. 46.
6. Ghislain de Diesbach emphasisied this point when we wrote: 'London, still the Mecca of liberal thinking, became the capital of the most intransigent royalism, the last bastion of the *ancien régime* which counted more partisans now (1797) than three years previously. Those who, like d'Antraigues, came over after having agitated for the opposition were eager to show themselves more zealous in order to make up for their past attitudes, loudly denounced those émigrés (the *constitutionnels*) who persevered in their error. See *Histoire de l'Émigration 1789–1814*, Paris, 1975, p. 291.
7. The translation is quite literal. Sabatier de Cabre recorded by Danloux on the 23 November 1792. See Portalis, op. cit., p. 182. On the basis of information in these documents arrests were issued for people like the baron de Breteuil, the abbé Courvoisier and the comte de Moustier.
8. The comte d'Antraigues wrote of her: 'Elle introduisit a Colbentz un luxe effréné auquel d'ailleurs les princes n'avoient que trop de penchant et après avoir décrié leur politique, énervé leur discipline militaire. Madame de Balbi achèva la ruine de l'émigration en les excitant à en consommer les dernières ressources par le faste le plus déplacé.' AN 419AP/1, Emanuel-Henri-Louis-Alexandre de Launay, Comte d'Antraigues, *Mes mémoires pendant les années 1789 jusques en 1799*, Fragment, pp. 97–8.
9. Le Marquis de Beauregard, *Souvenirs tirés des papiers du Comte A. de la Ferronnays, 1777–1814*, Paris, 1900, p. 231.
10. *Mémoirs de l'Abbé Baston chanoine de Rouen*, par l'M. l'abbé Julien Loth et M. Ch. Verger, réimpression de l'édition de Paris 1897–99, Paris, 1977, p. 89.
11. See Robert Griffiths, *Le Centre Perdu, Malouet et les 'monarchiens' dans la Révolution française*, Grenoble, 1988.
12. On 5 April 1797 Mme Danloux writes that she read the work 'plein de sens, de raison, et d'éloquence' to her husband while he painted. Portalis, op. cit., p. 364.
13. *Defence of the French Emigrants addressed to the People of France*, translated by John Gifford Esq, London, 1797, p.38.
14. Ibid., p. 39. See Chapter 1, p. 12.
15. Ibid., p. 42.
16. Ibid., p. 42.
17. Ibid., p. 45.
18. Ibid., p. 170.
19. Ibid., p. 195.
20. Ibid., p. 196.
21. Ibid., p. 370.
22. Ibid., p. 371.

23. Ibid., p. 290.
24. Mme d'Arblay, op. cit., Vol. VI, p. 31, Bookham, 1794, Mme d'Arblay to Mrs Philips.
25. Mme de Boigne, *Mémoires*, Vol. II, p. 16.
26. The formation of the Second Coalition (April–December 1798) was Europe's response to the expansionist policies of the Directory. See Albert Soboul, *The French Revolution 1787–1799*, Paris, 1962, in translation, London, 1974, p. 529.
27. Valmy (20 September 1792), and Jemappes, (6 November 1792). At Valmy, the Republican army routed the Prussian army, the most efficient, well-trained force in Europe, and stopped the advance towards Paris. At Jemappes, the Republican forces pushed the Austrians back and this victory allowed them to take Brussels on 16 November. These two victories marked the turning-point of the fortunes of the Republican army, which had had to recover from the disorganisation caused by the defection of most of its officer corps into emigration.
28. See Philip. Mansel, *Louis XVIII*, London, 1981, Chapters IV–VI.
29. See Guy Antoinetti, *Louis Philippe*, Paris, 1994.
30. The Marquis de La Fayette, who was a veteran of the American War of Independence, the Revolutionary and Napoleonic conflicts, and the one who had brought King Louis XVI and Marie Antoinette back to Paris avoiding a revolt in October 1789, brokered the deal between the liberals (quickly to become conservatives) and Louis-Philippe in 1830. See, P. Pilbeam, *The French Revolution of 1830*, London, 1991. pp. 67 and 85.
31. Translation: P. Beik, *The French Revolution*, London, 1990, pp. 325–9.
32. '*Constitutionnels*' and '*monarchiens*' for the purposes of this book refer to essentially the same group. of people. The distinction is a matter of nuance but in the case of the *monarchiens*, it reinforces the importance of the monarch to their philosophy. Mallet du Pan, Mounier and Malouet are examples of men who considered themselves to be *monarchiens*, whilst Lally Tollendal and Montlosier were *constitutionnels*. It is a very slim distinction.
33. AN 419AP-1, Letters from the Cardinal Maury to the Comte d'Antraigues, no. 2.
34. Griffiths, Robert Howell, *Le Centre Perdu*, Grenoble, 1988, p. 177.
35. Simon Burrows, *The French Exile Press in London, 1789–1814*, unpublished D. Phil. thesis, Oxford, 1992.
36. Simon Burrows, 'The Struggle for European Opinion in the Napoleonic Wars: British Francophone Propaganda, 1803–1814', *French History*, Vol. 11, No. 1, pp. 29–53.
37. Maspero-Clerc, *Un journaliste contre-révolutionnaire, J-G Peltier*, op. cit., p. 92.
38. Maspero-clerc, op. cit., p. 92, The *Journal de France et Angleterre*, entirely owned and edited by Montlosier, first appeared 6 January 1797. The Bodleian Library holds a complete collection of the 28 issues. It appeared weekly until July but was in financial difficulty when it merged with the *Courrier de Londres* and Montlosier took over the editorship from the abbé de Calonne on 1 August 1797.

Notes

39. This was published in London in 1796.
40. Montlosier, *Vues sommaires sur les moyens de Paix pour la France, pour L'Europe, pour les Émigrés*, Londres, 1796, p. 11.
41. Montlosier, op. cit., p. 62.
42. By 1800 Montlosier wrote in disgust, 'Je n'ai rien à faire avec la France, ce n'est plus mon pays. Mes habitudes, mes dispositions ne me permettraient pas d'y vivre heureux'. (I want nothing to do with France, it is no longer my country. My tastes and habits no longer permit me to be happy there.) Baldensperger, op. cit., Vol. II, p. 281.
43. This refers to the King's Speech at the royal session in the Assembly in 1789 where the King made some very limited concessions to the progress of the Revolution to that point. He agreed for instance to the principle of fiscal equality but he insisted that the feudal system should be retained. He conceded that that the Assembly had the right to vote taxes but obliged the orders to meet separately instead of in one body. He acknowledged the Assembly's jurisdiction over matters of individual liberties and most importantly over freedom of the press. In concluding, he threatened to dissolve the Assembly if its members did not heed his warning, and their response was of course defiant. The following day the majority of the members of the two first orders, the Clergy and the Nobility, joined the Third Estate in the National Assembly to deliberate as one body. For the King, 23 June was a political defeat.
44. Doyle, *The Oxford History of the French Revolution*, Oxford 1989, pp. 197–8.
45. Philip Mansel, *Louis XVIII*, Paris, 1982, pp. 95–6.
46. See Martin Lyons, *France under the Directory*, Cambridge, 1975.
47. Strophe 35 of an ode entitled 'Le 18 Brumaire an VIII' attributed to Chénier and quoted in its entirety in the first issue of *l'Ambigu*, pp. 7–8, is as follows:

    C'est par les lois que l'Angleterre
    Affermit sa prosperité;
    Là, sous leur abri tutélaire
    On peut braver la royauté;
    Là, devant leur toute puissance,
    Et le pouvoir et la naissance
    Baissent un front religieux;
    Là, l'homme pense sans contrainte,
    Et, satisfait, jouit sans crainte
    Des mêmes droits que ses ayeux.

    From 1802 until it went out of existence in 1818, *l'Ambigu* exploited its advantage and alienated almost everybody, including the British government.
48. Furet and Ozouf, *A Critical Dictionary of the French Revolution*, Harvard, 1989, translation Goldhammer, p. 328.
49. Donald Sutherland, *France 1789–1814, Revolution and Counterrevolution*, London, 1985, p. 108.
50. Doyle, *The Oxford History of the French Revolution*, Oxford 1989, p. 316.
51. Vovelle, *The Fall of the French Monarchy*, Paris, 1972, translation Cambridge, 1984, p. 140.

234 Notes

52. ABXIX-3973 3/66, Windham's remarks noted in a Report from a Committee of the House of Commons considering the Aliens Bill, 1797.
53. See Philip Mansel, *The Court of France, 1789–1830*, Cambridge, 1988.
54. The Concordat of 1801 was Napoleon's way of destroying the propaganda power of the French bishops, most of whom were in exile in Britain. By signing the Concordat, Pope Pius VII confirmed his authority, which was imminently threatened by Murat's troops (as well as by the Bishops' independence) and he achieved a reconciliation with France. Most importantly, the treaty between Napoleon and the Pope signed on 15 July 1801 enabled the exiled clergy to return home. See McManners, *The French Revolution and the Church*, London, 1969, Chapter 15.
55. Fonds Bourbon, Mémoires et Documents 620, lists the persons under surveillance in 1807 and is the best indication of those still resident in Britain.
56. Archévêque d'Aix, Jean de Dieu, Raimond de Boisgelin, un des quarantes de l'Academie française, *Discours pour le première communion à King-street*, London, 1799.
57. *Memoirs*, Vol. I, p. 219.
58. *L'Ambigu*, 'Les Loisirs d'un émigré, ouvrage posthume, dédié aux honnêtes Gens, Ma profession de Foi, by the Cardinal de Bérulle', p. 71. It continues:
    > Vous allez courir plus d'un bord;
    > Pauvres émigrés, bon courage,
    > Partez ... Moi, je reste, et du port
    > Je vous souhaite bon voyage
    > Je l'aimerais votre vaisseau!
    > Il fut bon, il est encor beau;
    > Mais la bouline le balotte,
    > Son pavillon me fait horreur,
    > Sa manoeuvre glace mon coeur,
    > Et je ne veux pas de pilote
59. Arthur Young, Esq, *The Example of France a Warning to Britain*, Fourth Edition, London, 1794. Claeys, op. cit., Vol. 8, pp. 72–3.

9 ÉMIGRÉ WRITERS AND WRITING ABOUT ÉMIGRÉS

1. The most recent book in English is Linda Kelly, *Juniper Hall*, London, 1989.
2. Her arrival was originally planned for 20 November 1792.
3. For a full account of Burney's personal connection of the emigration with her writing see Margaret A. Doody, *Frances Burney: the Life in Works*, Cambridge, 1988 and Kate Chisholm, *Fanny Burney: Her Life*, London, 1998.
4. *Diary and Letters of Mme d'Arblay*, op. cit., Vol. VI, p. 170.
5. Vol. V, p. 427.
6. Ibid., p. 341.

7. Ibid., p. 341.
8. Ibid., p. 339.
9. Ibid.
10. Ibid., p. 398.
11. Ibid., p. 409.
12. The relationship became strained when they were all in Paris in 1802 because the link with Mme de Staël proved socially embarrassing for the d'Arblays. Yet, although they did not see each other, the friendship remained intact. See R.J. Forsberg, *Madame de Staël and the English*, New York, 1967, p. 28. Burney wrote, 'How truly sorry I am to find her now in Paris! for nothing is so painful as repressing kindness, and nothing seems so odious as to return condescension by contempt.'
13. Mme de Staël wrote: 'Il arrivera, je le crois, une époque quelconque, dans laquelle des législateurs philosophes donneront une attention sérieuse à l'éducation que les femmes doivent recevoir, aux lois civiles qui les protègent, aux devoirs qu'il faut leur imposer, au bonheur qui peut leur être garanti.' (I believe that there will come a time when enlightened politicians will give serious thought to the education that women must receive, to the civil laws which protect them, to the duties imposed on them by society and to their happiness which could be guaranteed.) (*De la Literature*, Paris, 1991, p. 332.) Burney questioned: 'Why for so many centuries, has man alone been supposed to possess, not only force and power for action and defence, but even all the rights of taste; all the fine sensibilities which impel our happiest sympathies, in the choice of our life's partners? Why, not alone, is woman to be excluded from the exertions of courage, the field of glory, the immortal death of honour; – not alone to be denied deliberating upon the safety of the state of which she is a member, and the utility of the laws by which she must be governed?' (*The Wanderer*, p. 177.)
14. Mme de Staël, *Corinne*, Paris, reprint, 1985, p. 38.
15. Ibid., p. 38.
16. Ibid., p. 34.
17. Ibid., p. 48.
18. Ibid., p. 378.
19. Ibid., p. 447.
20. Ibid., p. 448. Contrast this interpretation with the scathing criticism expressed by Montlosier: 'L'Anglais n'a point de gestes, et le moins qu'il peut de paroles. Si vous avez besoin de lui, il pourra vous obliger, il n'y mettra certainement ni grâce ni compliment, il aima mieux vous donner son argent que sa pensée, il va ouvrira sa bourse plutôt que son âme ... (An Englishman has no expression and a strict economy of words. He can be obliging if approached, but his action lacks all grace or compliment. He would rather give you his money than his thoughts, rather open his purse than his soul.) *Souvenirs*, op. cit., p. 184.
21. Ibid., p. 339.
22. *Diary and Letters of Mme d' Arblay*, Mme de Staël to Mme d'Arblay Copet, 9 August 1793, op. cit., Vol. V, pp. 432–3.
23. *Diary and Letters of Mme d'Arblay*, op. cit., pp. 433–4, August 1793.

24. Georges Audrey, *Mme de Staël et l'émigration essai d'inventaire des problèmes*, Le groupe de Coppet et de la Révolution fran&caise, Coppet, 1988.
25. Ghislain de Diesbach, *Mme de Staël*, Paris, 1983, pp. 207–9.
26. Mme de Boigne, *Mémoires*, Vol. I, p. 219.
27. Ibid., p. 271.
28. Her husband, the comte de Flahaut, was guillotined in 1794.
29. *Oeuvres Complètes de Madame de Souza, comtesse puis marquise de Flahaut*, Paris 1821, *Adèle de Sénage*.
30. Baldensperger, *Le mouvement des idées*, op. cit., Vol. II, p. 40.
31. A question mark lingers over the identity of the father of Charles de Flahaut. It was generally assumed to be Talleyrand and this certainly seems most likely but there is also a possibility that it was Lord High Wycombe and it was the subject of an article written in 1986, 'Un Amour Secret de la comtesse de Flahaut', in the *Revue des Deux Mondes*, 15 November 1966.
32. Françoise Bernardy, *Son of Talleyrand, the life of the comte Charles de Flahaut, 1785–1870*, London, 1956, translation Lucy Norton, p. 26.
33. There is much of Souza's own experience of childhood in this novel. The family has three daughters: the eldest, Ernestine, is raised by her grandmother; Mathilde is kept by her parents; and Eugenie is put with a paternal aunt in a convent which it was not ever intended she would leave. The estate of the father is entailed to the male line but through the marriage of Mathilde and her cousin Edmond it stayed in the family. Practices of inheritance and dowry dictate the lives of the children.
34. Mme de Souza, *Eugénie et Mathilde*, Oeuvres complètes, Vol. II, p. 169.
35. In *Corinne* Mme de Staël wrote: 'Voyager est, quoi qu'on en puisse dire, un des plus tristes plaisirs de la vie. Lorsque vous vous trouvez bien dans quelque ville étrangère, c'est que vous commencez à vous y faire une patrie; mais traverser des pays inconnus, entendre parler un langage que vous comprenez à peine, voir des visages humains sans relation avec votre passé ni avec votre avenir, c'est de la solitude et de l'isolement sans repos et sans dignité; car cet empressement, cette hâte pour arriver là où personne ne vous attend, cette agitation dont la curiosité est la seule cause, vous inspire peu d'estime pour vous-même, jusqu'au moment où les objets nouveaux deviennent un peu anciens, et créent autour de vous quelques doux liens de sentiment et d'habitude.' op. cit., p. 32.
36. Mme de Souza, *Eugénie et Mathilde*, op. cit., Vol. III, p. 7.
37. Ibid., Vol. II, p. 300.
38. Ibid., Vol. II, p. 302.
39. *Oeuvres posthumes de Marie-Joseph Chénier*, Paris, 1824, *Tableau historique de la littérature française*, Vol. III, chap. VI, p. 226.
40. Ibid., p. 217. Mme de Genlis, *Les petits émigrés ouvrage a l'usage de la jeunesse*, Paris, 1797.
41. Peltier wrote an article in *Paris Pendant l'Année*, Vol. XVII, 30 January 1793, describing the morbid fascination the émigrés derived from Clery's book and the intensity of the personal reactions to the sight of the author torn by emotion reading extracts from his work.

Notes 237

42. *Diary and Letters of Mme d'Arblay*, op. cit., Vol. VI, p. 192, dated 7 June 1798.
43. Senac de Meihan, *L'émigré*, Brunswick, 1797, Vol. II, p. 248.
44. See Michel Vovelle, *Théodore Desorgues ou la désorganisation*, Paris, 1985.
45. *La Malheur et la Pitié* poème en quatre chants publié par M. de Mervé. A Londres, chez A. Dulau et Co., Soho Square, et Prosper et Co. Wardour St, 1803.
46. P. Gallet, *Commentaire politique du Poème de la Pitié suivi de l'Analyse morale et littéraire de l'Exposition du Poème*, Paris, 1803, p. 3.
47. *Malheur et Pitié*, chant III, lines 119–124 from the de Mervé edition.
48. *L'Ambigu*, No 3, p. 65. 'M. Dubois, préfet de la police de Paris, en eut, dit-on, la tête toute renversée.'
49. Chateaubriand, *Essai historique, politique et moral sur les Révolutions anciennes et modernes*, Oeuvres Complètes, Bruxelles 1835, tome I, p. 7.
50. Chateaubriand, *Mémoires d'Outre Tombe*, op. cit., pp. 101–2.
51. Chateaubriand, *L'Essai historique*, p. 109.
52. AN 419AP1, pièce 18, Letter from the Cardinal Maury to the Comte d'Antraigues, 17 November 1798. 'Si nous revoyons un jour la France, je les plains après pour les excuser et même pour les aimer toujours – que ceux qui les jugent avec une si commode sévérité de principes, se mettent à leur place, et qu'ils nous disent, s'ils s'osent qu'ils vaudroient mieux qu'eux tous, avec leurs défauts sans aucun vice, comme vous en convener vous même.'
53. Fernand Baldensperger, 'Chateaubriand et l'Emigration française à Londres', in the *Revue d'Histoire littéraire de la France*, 14, 1907, p. 595.
54. Mme de Boigne, op. cit., Vol. I, p. 200.
55. For dechristianisation, see Michel Vovelle, *La Révolution contre l'Église de la Raison à L'Être Suprême*, Paris, 1988, translated as *The Revolution against the Church*, Oxford, 1992.
56. It is not possible to analyse the *Génie* in the context of this book but it is a work of central importance to the Emigration and to the nineteenth century.
57. Fernand Baldensperger, *Chateaubriand et l'émigration à Londres*, op. cit., p. 626.
58. Chateaubriand, *Le Génie du Christianisme*, Paris, 1966, p. 55.
59. Chateaubriand, *Génie*, op. cit., I, VI, iii, p. 203.
60. Ibid., p. 214.
61. Mary Robinson, *Hubert de Sevrac*, A Romance, London 1796, 3 vols, Vol. 1, p. 42.
62. Katharine Colquhoun, *The Emigrée: a Drama in Two Acts*, London, 1858.
63. Louis de Bruno, *Lioncel or the Emigrant*, London, 1803.
64. *The Emigrant in London: a Drama in Five Acts*, by an Emigrant, London, 1795, Act V, final scene, p. 117, the Count Valincourt alone.
65. Conan Doyle, *Uncle Bernac*, London, 1897.
66. Warren Roberts, *Jane Austen and the French Revolution*, London, 1979, p. 5.
67. Ibid., p. 208.
68. *Le Lys dans la Vallée*. Honoré de Balzac, *La Comédie humaine*, Text intégral, Paris, 1966, Vol. VI, p. 391: 'il achèva de me dessiner complètement

la grande figure de l'Émigré, l'un des types les plus imposants de notre époque. Il était en apparence faible et cassé, mais la vie semblait devoir persister en lui, précisément à cause de ses moeurs sobres et ses occupations champêtres. Au moment où j'écris il vit encore.'
69. Ibid., p. 310.
70. Ibid., p. 312.
71. Natalie Basset, 'Le type de l'émigré dans "La Comédie Humaine": un type sans histoire?' *Années Balzaciennes*, 1990, p. 99.
72. Ronnie Butler, 'Les émigrés dans la Comédie Humaine, données historiques', *Années Balzaciennes*, 1991 p. 189.
73. Bulter cites Greer's statistics which put the combined percentage of nobles and clergy in emigration at less than 50 per cent. The figure for the nobility is 17 per cent, therefore Bulter concludes that Balzac's émigrés are not reflective or representative of the entire émigré population. This analysis is too simplistic and must be tempered by a full knowledge of the Greer statistics and their weaknesses and the purpose to which Balzac was applying his émigré figures in the *Comédie Humaine*.
74. Butler, op. cit., p. 224.
75. Balzac, *Le Lys dans la Vallée*, op. cit., Vol. IV, p. 312.

10 FRANCO-BRITISH CULTURE AND SOCIETY

1. ABXIX 3790 X p. 47, Verses sent in a letter from de Malherbe to William Windham, 4 May 1798.
2. Leigh Hunt, *London: the town, its memorable characters and events*, op. cit., p. 475.
3. Jacques Delille, *Les Jardins*, Chant III, lines 51–5 *Oeuvres de J. Delille*, Paris, 1838.
4. Bellenger quotes this letter from John Bullock (a Dominican) in Kent to Richard Huddleston (a member of an old Catholic family) at Sawston Hill, dated 13 March 1793: 'What a change has taken place in the general opinion in this Country with regard to Catholics especially Priests since the arrival of the emigrant Clergy, their Conduct has been so exemplary – people who had been taught to consider them as the worst of characters begin now to be persuaded they are good Christians and many own they had been much imposed on by their teachers with respect to the morals of Catholics – I doubt not many conversations will be wrought in consequence – at a little town we have many of these unfortunate people, if I may so style them, who suffer in so good a cause, whose sole defence is on providence – yet they are in want of nothing so abundant are the charities they receive in all parts – in which I cannot but admire the goodness of God who abandons not those who quit all for his sake.' 'The French Ecclesiastical Exiles in England 1789–1815', a dissertation presented for the degree of PhD of the University of Cambridge, 30 June 1977, Chapter 3, p. 75.
5. The Catholic Relief Act of 1778 removed the penal restrictions on the activities of priests and ended other Catholic disabilities such as

the prohibition on owning land. The futher Act of 1791 granted full religious toleration though not political rights. With this situation the Catholic community remained content for the next 16 years. Ian Christie, *Wars and Revolutions, Britain 1760–1815*, London, 1989, p. 40.
6. Stokes, ed., *Rev. William Bletchley Cole, Diary*, London, 1931, p. 253.
7. Pastoral letters of the Bishops Douglass, Gibson, Walmesley and Talbot for June and July 1791.
8. Dominic Bellenger, *French Exiled Clergy*, op. cit., p. 51.
9. AXIX-3973 3/66, Remark by Windham in a Parliamentary subcommittee report on the Aliens Bill in 1797. The same report opened with a warning against the 'vulgar prejudices against which gentlemen ought to guard on a subject of this nature.' That 'there was a sort of prevalent error concerning every foreigner that he must be a Frenchman, and concerning every Frenchman that he must be an Emigrant.'
10. J. H. Adeane, ed., *The Girlhood of Maria Josepha Holroyd (Lady Stanley of Alderley) Recorded in Letters of a Hundred Years Ago from 1776 to 1796*, London, 1896, pp. 218–19, Maria Josepha to Miss Ann Firth, 1 April 1793. (There is no trace of this obituary in the paper of this date but it is recorded in full in a letter cited by Adeane and recorded in ABXIX-3790 III/6).
11. Lubersac, op. cit., p. 231.
12. Baston, *Mémoires*, op. cit., pp. 122–3.
13. 15 August 1793, correspondence of E. Burke.
14. In 1796, 2000 copies were printed and sent to the Bishop for distribution to the priests in London.
15. *Malheur et Pitié*, op. cit., p. 92.
16. The individual contributions are listed by name in PRO T93-8. They include £500 from the Vice-Chancellor of Oxford on behalf of the university with further contributions from Magdalen, Oriel, New College, Convocation and All Souls colleges. Similarly from Cambridge, where Emmanuel, King's, Clare Hall, Trinity, Bennet Hall, Queen's and St Peter's all augmented the sum of £200 voted by the Senate. Senior members of the clergy include the Bishop of Durham, the Archbishop of Canterbury, and the Archbishop of York, who all gave substantial sums and whose example was followed in a more modest way by other bishops, deans, chapters, archdeacons and canons.
17. PRO T93-8 contains the records of the *Subscriptions for the Relief of the Distressed French Clergy Refugees in the British Dominions* from 8 August 1792 until 29 July 1794 a total of £26 901-6s-8d.
18. The academy in Soho Square gave £10-10s, from their pocket-money, the children at Wardour Castle gave 12s6d, a St Paul's schoolboy 2s6d, a schoolgirl 2s6d. Eton gave £21, Harrow and Rugby followed suit. See: PRO T93-8.
19. PRO T93-8, see p. 198
20. See p. 194
21. Wilkinson, 'French Emigrés in England', op. cit., pp. 147–8.
22. Abbé Barruel, *Histoire du clergé pendant la révolution*, op. cit., p. 231.
23. La duchesse de Gontaut, op. cit., p. 23.

24. Ghislain de Diesbach, *Histoire de l'Émigration 1789–1814*, Paris, 1975 p. 264.
25. *The Times*, 10 October 1792.
26. *Public Advertiser*, 8 October 1792.
27. Ibid.
28. Bellenger, *The French Exiled Clergy*, op. cit., p. 53.
29. In 1793, following an article in *The True Briton* which pointed to the dangers to national security presented by domestic servants in positions of confidence in Brittish households, a petition was sent to the King. This petition warned of the danger of servants rallying to support an invasion by Republican forces, but it gained no support. In 1795, the matter surfaced again and a second time a petition to Parliament gained no support from the politicans. *Parliamentary Register*, Vol. 41, p. 210.
30. Ibid., 14 April 1802, Vol. 18, p. 71.
31. *Diary and Letters of Mme d'Arblay*, Vol. VI, p. 16.
32. Ibid., Vol. V, p. 399.
33. See *Dictionary of National Biography*, Vol. VII, 1886, pp. 144–7, entry: Marc Isambard Brunel.
34. See *Nouvelle Biographie Universelle*, Paris, 1862, Vol. 41, p. 179: Augustus Pugin.
35. There are references in literary sources to Charlotte Carpenter being the daughter of a French refugee but these are quite unfounded. It is, however, true that her origin was a mystery even to close friends. See, Fiona Robertson, ed., *Lives of the Great Romantics* II, Vol. 3, Scott, London, 1997, p. 72.
36. Charlotte Carpenter, wife of Walter Scott, was christened Marguerite Charlotte Charpentier (b. Lyon, 16 December 1770). At the time of their marriage, she was a ward of Lord Downshire. When she married Scott she had been resident in Britain since 1785. She and her brother had anglicised their name for convenience when Charles (né Jean David) entered the service of the East India Company. Her father had invested money in Britain prior to the Revolution so she had income from these investments and from her brother in India. Her mother died in 1788 and her father died sometime around 1789. Charlotte and her brother Charles are recorded as living in Hanover Square in London in 1785, possibly in 1784 and definitely in 1787. Her mother returned to France in 1786 and died in 1788. She married Walter Scott on 24 December 1797. Edgar Johnson, *Sir Walter Scott: the Great Unknown, 1771–1821*, London, 1970, Vol. I, part iii, II, pp. 138–55.
37. Her father was Jean François Charpentier, écuyer du Roi de l'Académie de Lyons, ibid., p. 144.
38. Pugin has been attributed with the architectural design of the interior of the Palace of Westminster which was refurbished after the fire, but this is contested.
39. Pugin, Augustus, *Recollections of A.N. Welby Pugin and his Father*, London, 1861, p. 1.
40. There are no full-length biographies of Marc Isambard Brunel. Most of the available information concerning his life is appended to biographies and work relating to his son.

41. ABXIX-3973 3/66, Windham's remarks noted in a Report from a Committee of the House of Commons considering the Aliens Bill, 1797.
42. ABXIX- 3793 liste des Français ayant demandé la naturalisation de 1793 à 1832. Parrel papers.
43. Ibid., October 1795.
44. Ibid., May 1810.
45. Françoise de Bernardy, *Son of Talleyrand*, London, 1956, p. 158.
46. AN AP 565, 14 February 1816, C. de Flahaut to his mother.
47. John Carr, *The Stranger in France*, London, 1803, p. 34.
48. Add Ms 9828, f. 197 Wilmot Papers, London, 13 March 1814.
49. 'J'ai l'honneur de vous addresser les deux seuls adieux qui me restent: partons et jusqu'à mon dernier soupir je ne souviendrai d'un ami si noble et si délicat dans ses procédés; je ne cesserai de le bénir ainsi que ses généreux et admirables compatriotes: de France je manderai ma direction à mon honorable ami; bien jaloux de conserver avec lui les relations les plus tendres: je suis avec un respectueux attachement, votre humble et obéissant serviteur, abbé Carron.' Add Ms 9828, f. 198 Wilmot Papers, London, 8 July 1814.
50. Add Ms 9828, f. 200, extract from *Les Adieux de L'abbé Carron de Somerstown à ses bienfaisans amis, les citoyens de la Grande Bretagne*, Somerstown, le 29 juillet 1814.
51. John Carr, op. cit., pp. 6–8.
52. For Wordsworth's connection with the Revolution, see John Williams, *Wordsworth: Romantic Poetry and Revolution Politics*, Manchester University Press, 1989. This study makes no mention of 'The Emigrant Mother' or Wordsworth's personal opinion or awareness of the émigrés.
53. Thomas Hutchinson, ed., *Wordsworth: Poetical Works*, Oxford reprint, 1985, p. 95. 'The Emigrant Mother' was written in 1802 but not published until 1807.
54. Mary Russel Mitford, *Recollections*, op. cit., abridged from pp. 236–40.
55. Ibid., p. 233.
56. Mary Russell Mitford, *Recollections of a Literary Life*, London, 1859, pp. 233–4, poem by William Robert Spencer.

CONCLUSION

1. Michelet, *Oeuvres Complètes*, Paris, 1980, Vol. XVI, p. 485.
2. Chateaubriand, *Mémoires d'Outre Tombe*, op. cit., Vol. II, p. 15.
3. Donald Greer, *Incidence of the Emigration*, op. cit., 1951, p. 63.
4. Boloiseau, M., 'Etude de l'émigration et de la vent des biens des émigrés 1792–1830', *Bulletin d'Histoire économique et sociale de la Révolution Française*, 1961, pp. 25–89. Also, Almut Franke 'Le Milliard des Émigrés: the Impact of the Indemnity Bill of 1825 on French Society' in Kirsty Carpenter and Philip Mansel, eds, *The Émigrés in Europe and the Struggle against Revolution, 1789–1814*, London, 1999, Chapter 8.
5. The ageing Bourbon pretender, the comte de Chambord (b. 1820), grandson of Charles X, returned to Paris in July 1871 from an exile

which had begun on the eve of the July Days (1830). In stark contrast, the comte de Paris, who had been only 9 years old when his grandfather Louis Philippe abdicated in his favour in 1848, was a much more attractive candidate. A very logical solution would have been to make the childless comte de Chambord king with the comte de Paris his heir. The latter was willing but the comte de Chambord was only prepared to reign as Henry V on his own terms and under the *fleur de lys* flag of the Bourbons. After an unsuccessful attempt to have himself proclaimed King before the Assembly he went back into exile.

6. Donald Greer, *Incidence of the Emigration*, op. cit., p. 69, emphasised that 'French society, from its crest to its base, participated in the movement. Every class, every condition, and every profession, trade, and craft contributed its quota. And the prototype émigré was not Talleyrand, the priest-noble, but a composite figure, priest-noble-bourgeois-artisan-peasant.'
7. 4750 refugees were still receiving relief see p. 204.
8. Rev. A. G. L'Estrange, ed., *The Friendships and Letters of Mary Russell Mitford as Recorded in Letters from her Literary Correspondents,* London, 1882, Vol. I, p. 15. In a letter from Mrs Mitford to Dr Mitford, dated 26 February 1808.
9. Philip Mansel, *The Court of France, 1789–1830*, London, 1988, p. 60.
10. Donald Greer, *Incidence of Emigration*, op. cit., p. 90 (the total being 130 000).
11. Ibid., p. 65.
12. Burney, *The Wanderer*, op. cit., p. 873.
13. Burney, *The Wanderer*, p. 639.
14. André Malraux, *L'Espoir*, Paris, 1937.
15. Garcia, p. 249 folio edition. 'Les mythes sur les quels nous vivons sont contradictoires: pacifisme et nécéssité de défense, organisation et mythes chrétiens, efficacité et justice, et ainsi de suite.'
16. Suzanne Blum, *Vivre sans la patrie*, Paris, 1975, p. 222.
17. Ibid., p. 221. How like the opinion of the baron Guilhermy on p. 63.
18. Ibid., p. 216.
19. Raymond Aron, *Mémoirs*, Paris, 1983, p. 191.
20. Poem by Robert Southey written, according to David B. Comer III, in the spring of 1794 for publication in Daniel Isaac Eaton's *Politics for the People*.

Bibliography

MANUSCRIPT SOURCES

The Public Records Office

Emigré relief records are kept under PRO T.93. This series includes ecclesiastic and lay relief and covers the period 1792 to 1814. The material includes letters, reports, receipts, applications and references as well as other written testimonies to the work and dedication of the Committee members on the émigrés' behalf. *Refugees of the French Revolution* draws extensively on T.93:1-99.

Aliens Office Records
H.O. 1/1   Emigré correspondence 1789–93
H.O. 1/2   Emigré correspondence 1794
H.O. 1/3   Emigré correspondence 1795–97
H.O. 1/4   Emigré correspondence 1798–1811

Bouillon Papers
P.C. 1/115A   Emigré correspondence 1795
P.C. 1/117A   Correspondence in French 1796–97
P.C. 1/117B   Letters to Henry Dundas 1795–96
P.C. 1/118A   Emigré correspondence 1796–97

Calonne Papers, 1791–94
P.C. 1 1/128–130

Historical Manuscripts Commission

15th Report, Appendix, Part VI, The manuscripts of the Earl of Carlisle preserved at Castle Howard, London, 1897. *Letters of George Selwyn to Lady Carlisle*, Papers of the Frederick Howard fifth Earl of Carlisle.

British Library

Auckland Papers
Add Ms. 34444-34455 1792–1802

Relief Committee Papers
Add Ms. 18591-3 Wilmot Committee

Penn School Papers
Add Ms. 45723

Huskisson Papers
Add Ms. 38734

Windham Papers
Add Ms. 37843, 37844, 38845, 37855, 37858-865
37905 (Correspondence of Lally Tollendal and Mallet du Pan, 1793-98)

Archives Nationales

The papers of Christian de Parrel
Of particular interest:

ABXIX-2032
Documents concerning Calonne and his papers.

ABXIX-3784-3795
Documents concerning émigrés in Britain: letters, lists, reports from the Relief Committees, press clippings and biographical notes.

ABXIX-3854-3857
Supplements to the above.

ABXIX-196 other; emigration

The Police archives for the French Revolution contained in the F7 series hold a great deal of information on émigrés. Among these are official émigré lists, removals from the émigré lists, amnesties and other matters. BB1 also holds useful information, particularly removals from the émigré lists for the period 1790-1807. The fichier of Mlle Robinet is a useful starting point for anyone tracing émigrés in Britain to their department of origin.

Archives du Ministère des Affaires Etrangères

The collection known as the Fonds Bourbon is indispensable to any study of the émigrés (documents like Mémoires et Documents 620, which contains a detailed list of those émigrés still under surveillance in 1807) and the repatriated records of the French Catholic chapels in London are held in the provincial Foreign Affairs Archival Centre in Nantes.

Université de Paris I

M. Ragon, *La legislation sur les émigrés 1789–1825*, Thèse de Droit, unpublished, Paris I, 1904.

Bodleian Library Oxford

E. M. Wilkinson, *French Émigrés in England 1789–1802: Their Reception and Impact on English Life.* Unpublished Oxford B. Litt dissertation, 1952.

Australian National University

K. Berryman, *Great Britain and the French Refugees, 1789–1802: the Administrative Response.* Unpublished Ph.D. Thesis, 1980.

LOCAL ARCHIVES AND PRIVATE COLLECTIONS

Northampton Public Record Office

Burke Papers
Series; AXX, AXIX contain correspondence with émigrés and matters relating to the Penn School.

Richmond Local Studies Collection

The Paton Collection

The Archives of Coutts & Co.

Client records for the years 1789–1815.

French-language newspapers published in London

L'Ambigu
Le Courrier de Londres
Le Journal de France et d'Angleterre
Le Mercure Britannique
Paris pendant l'Année

British newspapers

The Analytical Review
The Annual Register
The Anti-Jacobin Review
The British Critic
The Edinburgh Review
The English Chronicle
The Gentleman's Magazine
The London Chronicle
The Morning Chronicle
The Morning Herald
The Morning Post
The Public Advertiser
The St James Chronicle
The Times
The True Briton

ÉMIGRÉ MEMOIRS AND BRITISH DIARIES

Unless otherwise indicated, works in English are published in London and works in French in Paris.

Aspinall-O'Glander C., *Admiral's Widow, Being the Life and Letters of Mrs Edward Boscawen from 1761 to 1805*, 1942.

Auckland Lord, *The Journals and Correspondence of William Lord Auckland*, 2 vols, 1861.

Bamford, F., *Dear Miss Heber, an 18th Century Correspondence*, 1936.

Barberey, E de., ed., *Dix années d'Émigration, souvenirs et correspondance du comte de Neuilly*, 1863.

Bardoux, A., *La duchesse de Duras*, 1898.

Baston, Abbé, *Mémoires de l'abbé Baston*, 2 vols, 1977.

Bettany, L., ed., *Diaries of William Johnston Temple 1780–1796*, Oxford, 1929.

Blondin d'Abancourt, Chevalier, *Onze ans d'émigration: mémoires du chevalier Blondin d'Abancourt, 1791–1830*, 1897.

Boigne, comtesse de, *Mémoires of the Comtesse de Boigne, 1781–1814*, 3 vols, 1907–8.

Boufflers, Stanislas-Jean, *Oeuvres, suivi de pièces fugitives de Mme de Boufflers mère, née Boisgelin*, 1802.

Bouillé, marquis de, *Souvenirs et fragments pour servir aux mémoires de ma vie et de mon temps*, 1908.

Brasbridge, J., *The Fruits of Experience, or Memoir of Joseph Brasbridge, written in his 80th Year*, 1824.

Broc, H. vicomte de, *Dix ans de la vie d'une femme pendant l'émigration, Adelaide de Kerjean, Marquise de Falaiseau*, 1893.

Buckingham and Chandos, Duke of, *Memoirs of the Court and Cabinets of George the Third*, 4 vols, 1853–5.

Bibliography

Burke, E., *The Correspondance of Edmund Burke*, vols 7–9, 1968–70.
Burney, F., *The Diary and Letters of Madame d'Arblay*, edited by her niece, 7 vols, 1842.
____, *The Memoirs of Dr. Burney*, 3 vols, 1833.
Butler, C., *Historical Memoirs Respecting the English, Irish and Scottish Catholics from the Reformation to the Present Time*, 4 vols, 1819–1824.
____, *Reminiscences of Charles Butler of Lincoln's Inn*, 1822.
Castle, E., ed., *The Jerningham Letters, 1780–1843*, 2 vols, 1896.
Chateaubriand, F. R. de, *Mémoires d'Outre Tombe*, Flammarion reprint, 1982.
Corbehem, B. de, *Dix ans de ma vie ou l'histoire de mon émigration*, 1827.
Costa de Beauregard, Le Marquis de, *Souvenirs tirés des papiers du Comte A. de la Ferronnays, 1777–1814*, 1900.
Cunningham, P., ed., *The Letters of Horace Walpole, Fourth Earl of Oxford*, 9 vols, 1891.
Dampmartin, A. H., *Mémoires sur divers évènements de la Révolution et de l'émigration*, 1825.
Edgecumbe, R., ed., *Diary of Frances, Lady Shelley, 1787–1817*, 1912.
Edgeworth de Firmont, Henri Essex, *Letters from the Abbé Edgeworth to his Friends, Written between the Years 1777 and 1807*, 1818.
Esterhazy, le comte Valentin Ladislas, *Lettres de Cte Valentin Esterhazy à sa femme 1784–1792*, with an introduction and notes by E. Daudet, 1907.
____, *Nouvelles lettres du Cte Valentin Esterhazy à sa femme 1792–1795*, 1909.
Fauche-Borel, Louis de, *Mémoires dans lequels on trouvera des détails et des éclaircisssemens sur les principaux événements de la Révolution*, 1829.
Genlis, la comtesse de, *Mémoires inédites de Mme de Genlis sur le XVIIIème siècle et la Révolution française depuis 1756 jusqu'à nos jours*, 1825.
Gontaut, duchesse de, *Mémoires 1773–1836 et lettres inédites*, 1895.
Guilhermy, J. F. C., baron de, *Papiers d'un émigré, 1789–1829*, 1886.
Hare, A. J. C., *Life and Letters of Frances Baroness Bunsen*, 2 vols, 1912.
Herbert, Lord, ed., *Pembroke Papers 1780–1794*, 1950.
Hutton, J., ed., *Selections from the Letters and Correspondence of Sir James Bland Burges, Bart.*, 1885.
Kelly, M., *Reminiscences of Michael Kelly*, 2 vols, 1826.
La Ferronays, A. comte de, *Souvenirs*, 1900.
La Tour du Pin, marquise de, *Journal d'une femme de cinquante ans 1778–1815*, 2 vols, 1920.
Lescure, A. de, *Mémoires sur l'émigration*, Marquis puis Baron de Goquelat, 1881.
Lubersac de Levion, A., *Journal historique et religieux de l'émigration et déportation du clergé de France en Angleterre*, 1802.
Mallet du Pan, *Mémoires et correspondance pour servir à l'histoire de la Révolution française, recueillis et mis en ordre par A Sayous, ancien professeur à l'académie de Genève*, 1851.
____, *Correspondance inédite de Mallet du Pan avec la cour de Vienne 1794–1798* (publiée d'après les manuscrits conservés aux archives de Vienne par André Michel), 1884.
Malmesbury, Earl of, *Diaries and Correspondence of James Harris, First Earl of Malmesbury*, 4 vols, 1844.

Malouet, Pierre-Victor, *Mémoires*, 2 vols, 1868.
Marchand, J. and Roberts, S. C., eds, Rochefoucauld, F. de, *A Frenchman in England 1784*, Cambridge, 1933.
Marcillac, Olivier d'Argeos, *Louis XVIII relation d'un voyage à Bruxelles*, 1877.
Melville, L., ed., *The Huskisson Papers*, 1931.
Menerville, Elisa Fougeret, Mme de, *Souvenirs d'émigration*, 1934.
Miles, C. P., ed., *The Correspondence of William Augustus Miles on the French Revolution 1798–1817*, 2 vols, 1890.
Mitford, M. R., *Recollections of a Literary Life or Books, Places and People*, 3 vols, 1852.
Montagu, Mme de, *Mémoires of Anne-Paule-Dominique de Noailles, Marquise de Montagu*, 1870.
Montloisier, le comte de, *Souvenirs d'un émigré*, 1830.
Moody, C. L., *A Sketch of modern France in a series of letters to a Lady of fashion written in the years 1796 and 1797 during a tour through France, by a Lady*, 1798.
Moore, T., *Memoirs, Journal and Correspondance of Thomas Moore*, 1853.
Mundy, H. G., ed., *The Journal of Mary Frampton*, 1885.
Pennington, M., ed., *Letters from Mrs. Elizabeth Carter to Mrs Montagu, 1755–1800*, 3 vols, 1817.
Pinkerton, J., *Recollections of Paris in the years 1802–3–4*, 2 vols, 1806.
Portalis, R. baron de, *Henry Pierre Danloux, peintre de portraits et son journal durant l'émigration*, 1910.
Pradel de Lamase, chevalier de, *Notes intimes d'un émigré*, 1914–20.
Richmond, T., *The Local Records of Stockton and the Neighbourhood*, Stockton, 1968.
Roberts, W., *Memoirs of the Life and Correspondence of Mrs Hannah More*, 4 vols, 1843.
Romilly, Samuel, *Memoirs*, 3 vols, 1840.
Saulx Tavannes, duchesse de, *Aglaé Marie Louise de Choiseul-Gouffier, Sur les routes de l'émigration, Mémoires 1791–1806*, 1933.
Stanhope, Lady H., *Memoirs of Lady Hester Stanhope, as Related by Herself in Conversations with her physician; Comprising her Opinions and Anecdotes of Some of the Most Remarkable Persons of Her Time*, 3 vols, 1845.
Taillandier, Saint-René, *Lettres inédites de J. C. I. Sismondi, de M. de Bonstetten, de Mme de Staël et de Mme de Souza à Mme la comtesse d'Albany*, 1863.
Walsh de Serant, vicomte de, *Souvenirs de cinquante ans*, 1832.
Wickham, W., *The Correspondence*, 2 vols, 1870.
Wilberforce, W., *The Correspondence*, 2 vols, 1840.
____, *Private Papers*, 2 vols, 1940.
Williams, H. M., *Letters on the French Revolution Written in France in the Summer of 1790*, Dublin, 1892.
Wilmot, J. E., *Memoirs of the Life of the Right Honourable Sir John Eardley Wilmot*, 1811.
Windham, W., *Diary of the Right Honourable William Windham*, 1866.
Woodforde, Rev J., *Diary of a Country Parson, the Reverend James Woodforde, 1788–1792*, 5 vols, 1924–31.

PUBLISHED WORKS

Abell, F., *Prisoners of War in Britain 1756–1815*, 1914.
Adeane, J. H., *The Girlhood of Maria Josepha Holroyd, Recorded in the Letters of a Hundred Years Ago, 1776–1796*, 1896.
___, *The Early Married Life of Maria Josepha Lady Stanley, with Extracts from Sir John Stanley's 'Praeterita'*, 1899.
Alger, J. G., *Englishmen in the French Revolution*, 1889.
Amherst, W. J., *The History of the Catholic Emancipation*, 2 vols, 1886.
Anderson, W. J., *A History of the Catholic Parish of St Mary's Chelsea*, 1938.
Antoinetti, G., *Louis Philippe*, Paris, 1995.
Baines, F. E., *Records of the Manor, Parish and Borough of Hampstead*, 1890.
Baldensperger, F., *Le mouvement des idées dans l'émigration française 1789–1814*, 1924.
Balleine, George R., *The Tragedy of Phillipe d'Auvergne; le dernier duc de Bouillon*, London, 1973.
Barruel, M. l'Abbé, *Histoire du clergé pendant la révolution*, 1800.
___, *Memoirs Illustrating the History of Jacobinism*, 4 vols, 1797–98.
Bearne, Mrs., *Four Fascinating Frenchwomen: Adelaide Filleul, Comtesse de Flahaut, Marquise de Souza, Claire de Kersaint, Duchesse de Duras, Marie Caroline de Bourbon, Duchesse de Berry, Princesse Mathilde Bonaparte, Countess Demidorff*, T. Fisher Unwin, 1910.
Bellenger, Dominic Aidan, *The French Exiled Clergy*, Bath, 1986.
Berry, Mary, *A Comparative View of the Social Life of England and France from the Restoration of Charles the Second to the French Revolution*, 1828.
___, *A Comparative View of the Social Life of England and France from the French Revolution of 1789 to that of July 1830*, 1831.
Besant, W., *London in the Eighteenth Century*, 1902.
Bindman, D., *The Shadow of the Guillotine: Britain and the French Revolution*, 1989.
Bittard des Portes, René, *L'exil et la guerre, les émigrés à la cocarde noire en Angleterre, dans les provinces belges, en Hollande et à Quiberon*, 1908.
Black, J., *Natural and Necessary Enemies, Anglo-French Relations in the Eighteenth Century*, 1986.
Blanc, O., *Les Hommes de Londres*, 1989.
___, *Les éspions de la République et de l'Empire*, 1996.
Bogan, Bernard, *The Great Link: a History of St George's, Southwark*, 1948.
Bossy, J., *The English Catholic Community*, 1750–1850, 1975.
Bouchary, J., *Les faux-monnayeurs sous la Révolution française*, 1946.
Bouloiseau, M., *Etude de l'émigration et de la vente des biens des émigrés 1791–1830*, 3 vols, 1963.
Brown, P., *The French Revolution in English History*, 1918.
Burke, E., *Reflections on the Revolution in France*, 1987.
___, *The Works of the Right Honourable Edmund Burke*, 12 vols, 1899.
Burney, F., *Brief Reflections Relative to the Emigrant French Clergy*, 1793.
Callet, Auguste, *Anne Paule-Dominique de Noailles, marquise de Montagu: une chrétienne au siècle des Lumières*, 1994.
Cansick, F. T., *A Collection of Curious and Interesting Epitaphs of St Pancras*, 1869.

Carron, G. T. J., *Pensées ecclésiastiques pour tous les jours de l'année*, London, 1799.
____, *Tendres conseils de l'amitié*, London, 1801.
____, *La voix de la religion*, London, n.d.
Castries, duc de, *Les hommes de l'émigration, 1789–1814*, 1962.
____, *Le testament de la monarchie, les émigrés, 1789–1814*, 1962.
____, *La vie quotidienne des émigrés*, 1966.
Chalon, Renier, *Le Dernier Duc de Bouillon*, 1815.
Childs, F. S., *French Refugee Life in the United States, 1790–1800*, Baltimore, 1940.
Christophorov, P., *Sur les pas de Chateaubriand en exil*, 1960.
Clergy of St Anne's, Soho, *Two Centuries of Soho*, 1898.
Cléry, Jean-Baptiste, *Journal de ce qui s'est passé à la Tour du Temple pendant la captivité de Louis XVI*, London, 1798.
Clinch, George, *Marylebone and St Pancras*, 1890.
Coleridge, S. T., *Lectures 1795 on politics and religion*, Patton, ed., *Collected Works of Samuel Taylor Coleridge*, Princeton, 1971, Vols I, III, V, and IX.
Coston, H., *Antoine de Rivarol et l'émigration de Coblence*, 1996.
Crossley, Ceri and Small, Ian, *The French Revolution and British Culture*, Oxford, 1989.
Daudet, Ernest, *Histoire de l'émigration pendant la Révolution française*, 1886.
____, *Coblentz 1789–1793* (d'après docs. inédits) 1889.
Davies, William E., *The English Law Relating to Aliens*, 1931.
Deane, S., *The French Revolution and the Enlightenment in England*, 1988.
Des Essarts, Nicolas Toussaint, dit Le Moyne, *Tableau de la police de la ville de Londres*, 1801.
Devert, l'abbé Michel, *1789–1989, Aire et Dax, Deux cents ans de Souvenirs*, Mézos, 1990.
Dickinson, H. T, *British Radicalism and the French Revolution 1789–1815*, Oxford, 1985.
Diesbach, G. de, *Histoire de l'émigration*, 1975.
Disraeli, I., *Anecdotes of the French Nation during the Last Thirty Years, Indicative of the French Revolution*, 1794.
Dodwell, C. R., *The English Catholic Church and the Continent*, 1959.
Dozier, R., *For King, Constitution and Country: English Loyalists and the French Revolution*, Kentucky, 1983.
Du Beaudieu de Messières, Odette, *Le comte d'Artois, un émigré de choix*, 1996.
Duckworth, Colin, *The D'Antraigues Phenomenon*, 1986.
Elliott, M., *Partners in Revolution: The United Irishmen and France*, 1982.
Emsley, C., *British Society and the French Wars 1793–1815*, 1979.
Estourbeillon, comte R. de, *Les familles françaises à Jersey*, Nantes, 1886.
Fierro, A., *Bibliographie critique des mémoires sur la Révolution écrits ou traduits en Français*, 1988.
Forneron, H., *Histoire générale des émigrés pendant la Révolution française*, 3 vols, 1884.
Forsberg, Roberta J., *Madame de Staël and the English*, New York, 1967.
Fox, C., *London – World City 1800–1840,* 1992.

Gabory, E, *L'Angleterre et la Vendée*, 1930.
Geddes, A., *A Modest Apology for the Roman Catholics of Great Britain*, 1800.
George, M. D., *London Life in the Eighteenth Century*, 1925.
___, *English Political Caricature*, 2 vols, Oxford, 1959.
Godechot, Jacques, *Le comte d'Antraigues: un espion dans l'Europe des émigrés*, 1986.
Gontaut, duchesse de, *Louise*, 1832.
Goodwin, A., *Friends of Liberty: The English Democratic Movement in the Age of the French Revolution*, 1979.
Greer, D., *The Incidence of Emigration during the French Revolution*, Cambridge, 1951.
Griffiths, Robert Howell, *Le Centre Perdu, Malouet et les 'monarchiens' dans la Révolution française*, Grenoble, 1988.
Gwynn, Robin, *The Huguenots of London*, London, 1998.
Hampson, N., *The Perfidy of Albion: French Perceptions of England during the French Revolution*, 1998.
Horne, A. J., *For the Cause of Truth: Radicalism in London 1796–1821*, Oxford, 1982.
Huchet, Patrick, *1795, Quiberon ou le destin de la France*, Rennes, 1995.
Hutt, Maurice, *Chouannerie and Counter-Revolution, Puisaye, the Princes and the British Government in the 1790s*, Cambridge, 1983.
Jacobs, Leonard, *The Streets of Marylebone*, 1955.
Jausions, P. A., *Vie de l'abbé Carron*, 1886.
Johnson, D., Crouzet, F., and Bedorida, F., ed., *Britain and France*, 1980.
Kerbiriou, L., *Jean François de la Marche*, Quimper, 1924.
Lally Tolendal, *A Defence of the French Emigrants addressed to the people of France*, 1797.
___, *Défense des émigrés français: adressé au peuple français*, 1797.
Laprade, W., *England and the French Revolution 1789–1797*, Baltimore, 1909.
Lebon, A., *L'Angleterre et L'Émigration Française de 1794 à 1801*, 1882.
Lee, C. E., *St Pancras Church and Parish*, 1955.
Lescure, A. de, *Rivarol et la société française pendant la révolution et l'émigration, 1753–1801*, 1883.
Lockitt, C. H., *The Relations of French and English Society, 1763–1793*, 1920.
Lysons, Daniel, *The Environs of London*, 1792–6.
Mansel, P., *Louis XVIII*, 1981.
___, *The Court of France*, Cambridge, 1991. .
Maspero-Clerc, H., *Un journaliste contre-révolutionnaire: Jean-Gabriel Peltier, 1760–1825*, 1973.
Meteyard, E., *Life of Josiah Wedgwood*, 2 vols, 1885–86.
Milton G. E., *Hampstead and Marylebone*, 1902.
Newton, D., *Catholic London*, 1950.
O'Gorman, F., *The Whig Party and the French Revolution*, London, 1967; Kentucky, 1983.
Parrel, Ch. de, *Les papiers de Calonne, 1ère série: les finances des princes 1790–91–92*, 1932.
Parry, J. D., *An Historical and Descriptive Account of the Coast of Sussex*, 1833.
Paul, Anthony, *A History of Manchester Square*, 1971.
Petre, M. D., *The Ninth Lord Petre*, 1928.

Philip, M., ed., *The French Revolution and British Popular Politics*, Cambridge, 1991.
Philips, H., *Mid-Georgian London*, 1964.
Plasse, F-X., *Le clergé français réfugié en Angleterre*, 1886.
____, *Réflections sur la révolution de France*, 1889.
Prickett, S., *England and the French Revolution*, 1989.
Pugin, *Recollections of A. N. Welby Pugin*, 1861.
Reist, vicomte de, *Louise d'Esparbes Comtesse de Polastron*, 1907.
Roberts H., ed., *Survey of London*, 25 vols, 1955.
Rudé, G., *Hanoverian London 1714–1808*, 1971.
Saint Gervais, A. de., *Histoire des Émigrés Français depuis 1789 jusqu'en 1828*, 2 vols, 1828.
St George Saunders, H., *History of the Middlesex Hospital*, 1947.
Saint Victor, Jacques de, *La chute des aristocrates 1787–1792*, 1992.
Stanton, P., *Pugin*, 1791.
Summers, Judith, *Soho: a History of London's most Colourful Neighbourhood*, 1989.
Tardy, l'Abbé, *Manuel du Voyageur à Londres ou recueil de toutes les instructions nécessaires aux étrangers qui arrivent dans cette capitale*, 1800.
The Clergy of St Anne's Soho, *Two Centuries of Soho*, 1898.
Thompson, J. M., ed., *English Witnesses of the French Revolution*, Oxford, 1938.
Thrale, M., ed., *Selections from the Papers of the London Corresponding Society 1792–1799*, Cambridge, 1983.
Turquan, J., *Les femmes de l'émigration,* 1911.
Vidalenc, J-M., *Les Emigrés Français 1789–1825*, Caen, 1963.
Walpole, Horatio, Earl of Orford, *The Works of,* 9 vols, 1798.
Ward, B., *The Dawn of the Catholic Revival 1781–1803*, 1909.
____, *The Sequel to Catholic Emancipation*, 2 vols, 1915.
Weiner, M., *The French Exiles, 1789–1815*, 1960.
Welvert, E., *La princesse d'Hénin. Histoire d'une grande dame du temps-passé,* 1924.
Wheatley, H. B., *London Past and Present: Its History, Associations and Traditions*, 3 vols, 1891.
Williams, G., *Artisans and Sans-culottes: Popular Movements in France and Britain during the French Revolution*, 1968.
Wilson, E., *The History of the Middlesex Hospital*, 1845.
Wroth, Warwick W., *The London Pleasure Gardens of the 18th Century*, 1896.
Yeowell, John, *The French Chapel Royal in London*, 1958.

PAMPHLETS AND PERIODICAL ARTICLES

Adams, J., *The Death of His Most Christian Majesty Lewis XVI Considered: a Sermon*. Salisbury and London, 1793.
Anstruther, G., 'Catholic Middle Class in the London of 1800', *London Recusant*, VI (1976), 37–57.
Argenvillier, Pierre, 'Les émigrés Francais en Angleterre', *La nouvelle revue* (Paris) no. 34, 1905, 3–26.

Bibliography

Audrey, Georges, 'Mme de Staël et l'émigration essai d'inventaire des problèmes', *Le groupe de Coppet et de la Révolution Française*, 1988, 15–34.

Baldensperger, F., 'Chateaubriand et l'émigration française à Londres', *Revue d'Histoire littéraire de la France*, 14, 1907, 585–626.

Barruel, M. l'Abbé, *Trois propositions sur l'église de France, établie en vertu du Concordat*, London, 1803.

Batisse, Francois, 'Les greniers de Chateaubriand à Londres', *Société Chateaubriand*, 1974, no. 17, 57–61.

Battersby, W. J., 'The Education Work of the French Refugees', *The Dublin Review*, 223 (1949) 103–118.

Bellenger, D. T. J., 'The Hampstead Mission – Some Reflections on its Early History', *London Recusant*, IV (1974), 73–75.

____, 'The Abbé Morel', *London Recusant* V (1975), 94–101.

____, 'The Abbé Carron', *London Recusant* VI (1976), 19–36.

____, 'Voyaux de Franous', *London Recusant* VII (1977), 32–38.

____, 'The French Exiled Clergy in Kensington', *London Recusant* VIII (1978), 13–15.

____, 'Lord Petre and the French Exiled Clergy', *Essex Recusant* XXII (1980) 82–84.

____, 'The French Revolution and the Religious Orders: Three Communities 1789–1815', *Downside Review*, XCVIII (1980), 25–41.

____, 'Hampstead Catholics of the Georgian Age: the Origins of the Holly Place Chapel', *Camden History Review*, X (1982), 5–6.

____, '"Seen but not Heard": French Clergy Exiled in Kent', *Kent Recusant History*, VI/VII (1982), 152–6.

____, 'The Émigré Clergy and the English Church, 1789–1815', *Journal of Ecclesiastical History*, XXXIV, (1983), 392–410.

____, 'Dorothy Silburn (1753–1820), Mother of the French Exiled Clergy', *Northern Catholic History*, XVII, (1983), 14–16, 28 and 'Dorothy Silburn: A further note', ibid., XX, (1984), 18–20.

Bertaud, Jules, 'Les émigrés français à Londres sous la Révolution', *Le Monde Nouveau*, n. 7, 1923, 183–94.

Boisgelin, Jean de Dieu Raimond de, Archévêque d'Aix, *Discours pour la première communion à la chapelle de King Street, Portman Square*, A. Dulau, 107 Wardour St, London, 1799.

____, *Discours pour la bénédiction de la chapelle de King-street*, A. Dulau, 107 Wardour St, London, 1799.

Bradley, R. M., 'Mrs Larpent and the French Refugees', *The Nineteenth Century*, Vol. 75 (1914), 1329–40.

Burney, F., *Brief Reflections Relative to the Emigrant French Clergy Earnestly Submitted to the Humane Consideration of the Ladies of Great Britain*, London, 1793.

Calonne, de, *De l'état de la France présent et à venir*, M. de Calonne, ministre d'Etat, (J. de Boffe), London, 1790.

____, *Tableau de l'Europe en Novembre 1795*, London (J. de Boffe), 1795.

Cobb, Richard, 'Les impressions d'un prisonnier français en Angleterre aout–dec 1793', *Annales Historiques de la Révolution Française*, 1951, 176–7.

Coleridge, S. T., *Considerations Addressed to the French Bishops and Clergy now Residing in London*, 1796. Patton, ed., *Collected Works of Samuel Taylor Coleridge*, Princeton, 1971.

Des Cilleuls, Jean, *A propos de l'émigration à Londres, la misère des émigrés et l'assistance mise en oeuvre pour la soulager, Société des lettres sauvées et arts du saumurois*, no. 68, 1977, 2–15.

Evinson, D., 'The Hammersmith Charity Schools', *London Recusant*, new series I (1985), 13–15.

Filson, Judith, 'French Refugees in Richmond 1785–1815', *Richmond History*, No. 7, 1986.

Fréville, H., 'Documents inédits sur l'histoire de l'émigration française en Grande Bretagne pendant la Révolution', *Revue Enseignement Supérieure*, 1956, no. 3, 65–80.

Hutt, M. J., 'Abbé P. J. L. Desjardins and the Scheme for the Settlement of French Priests in Canada, 1792–1802', *Canadian Historical Review*, xxxix, no. 2, June 1958, 93–124.

Lacour-Gayet, Robert, 'Calonne à Saint Petersbourg et à Londres, 1794–1796', *Revue d'Histoire diplomatique*, 1962, no 76/2, 117–133.

La Marche, J. F. de, *The pastoral letter and ordinance of the Right Reverend John Francis de la Marche Bishop of Leon*, translated by J. Milner, London, 1791.

____, *Conduite à tenir par MM. les ecclésiastiques françois réfugiés en Angleterre*, London, 1792.

Lokke, C. L., 'London Merchant Interest in Saint Domingue plantations of the Emigrés, 1793–1798', *American Historical Review*, 43, 1938, pp. 795–815.

____, 'New Light on London Merchant Interest in Saint Domingue', *Hispanic American Historical Review*, 22, 1942, pp. 670–76.

Manchee, W. H., 'Marylebone and Its Huguenot Associations', in *Proceedings of the Huguenot Society of Great Britain*, 1915, Vol. 11, no. 1.

Maspero-Clerc, Hélène, 'Journaux d'émigrés à Londres 1792–1818', *Bulletin d'histoire économique et sociale de la Révolution Française*, 1972–73, 67–79.

Massé, Pierre, 'Les soucis d'une femme d'émigré', *Bulletin de la Société Antique de l'Ouest*, 1954, series IV, tome II, pp. 693–715.

Mathias, T. J., *Letter to the marquis of Buckingham chiefly on the subject of the numerous French priests and others of the Church of Rome resident and maintained in England at the public expense, and on the spirit and principle of that church, sacred and political*, London, 1796.

McGloin, James, 'Some Refugee French Clerics and Laymen in Scotland, 1789–1814', *Innes Review*, XVI, No. 1, 1965, pp. 27–55.

Milner, J., *The Funeral Oration of his Late Most Christian Majesty Louis XVI*, London, 1793.

Montlosier, Cte de, *Le Peuple anglais, bouffi d'orgueil, de bière et de thé, jugé au tribunal de la raison*, Paris, 1803.

____, *Sur la loi contre les émigrations*, London, 1796.

____, *Vues sommaires sur les moyens de paix pour la France, pour l'Europe, pour les émigrés*, London, 1796.

More, H., *Remarks on the Speech of M. Dupont*, London, 1793.

Nash, M., '*Gideon's Cake of Barley Meal*, A letter to the Rev. William Romaine on his Preaching for the Emigrant Popish Clergy with some

strictures on Mrs. Hannah More's Remarks published for their benefit', London, 1793.
Parrel, Christian de, 'Les émigrés agenais en Angleterre', *Revue des Agenais* (Agen) 1965, Vol. 3, 179–83.
Playfair, W., *A Letter to the People of England on the Revolution in France*, London, 1792.
Rendel, B., 'French Clergy in the Midland District after the French Revolution', *Worcestershire Recusant,* XXX, 1977, Pp. 17–23.
Rice, David, 'Combine against the Devil: the Anglican Church and the French Refugee Clergy in the French Revolution', *Historical Magazine of the Protestant Episcopal Church*, Vol. L, No. 3, Sept. 1981, pp. 271–83.
Senac de Meilan, *De la France de Louis XV à l'Europe des émigrés,* Paris, reprint 1984.
____, *Des principes et des causes de la Révolution*, Paris, reprint, 1987.
Sparrow, Elizabeth, 'The Alien Office, 1792–1806', in *The Historical Journal*, 33, 2 (1990), pp. 361–84.
____, 'The Swiss and Swabian Agencies, 1795–1801', *The Historical Journal*, 35,4, (1992) pp. 861–84.
Thrale, Mary, 'London Debating Societies in the 1790s', *The Historical Journal*, 32, I, pp. 57–86.
Vidalenc, Jean, 'La caisse de l'émigration 1797–1807', *Revue d'Histoire économique et sociale*, 1969, Vol. 47, no. 1, 32–63.

Index

Aiguillon, duc d', 71
Aliens Act, 35–40, 165
Aliens Office, 10
Angerstein, Lord Mayor, 45
Angoulême, duc de, 122
Antraigues, comte d', 124
Arblay, Alexandre d', 133, 163
Armée de Condé, 10
Aron, Raymond, 182
Artois, comte d', 53, 67, 108, 122
Avaray, comte d', 21
Auckland, Lord, 24
Austen, Jane, 152
Aynsley, Lady Charles, 178

Baillie, James, 45
Balbi, Mme de, 21
Balzac, Honoré de, 153
Baker, Sir George, 45
Baker, William, 45
Baston, abbé, 5, 9
Beaujolais, comte de, 83
Beaumarchais, 31
Bertin, Rose, 10
Berry, duc de, 122
Bigot de Saint Croix, Louis Charles, 88
Biron, duchesse de, 19, 76
Bishop of Saint Pol de Léon
    see La Marche, Jean François de
Blake, William, 52
Blanc, Louis, 128
Blandin, abbé, 57
Boigne, Mme de, 6, 7, 64, 85, 102, 121, 129
Boisgelin, J-de-Dieu Raymond de, 67, 129
Bordeaux, duc de, 84
Bosquanet, Samuel, 45
Botherel, comte de, 97
Boufflers, Mme de, 19, 77
Bouillé, marquise de, 31
Bouillé, marquis de, 88
Brémont, abbé, 112
Brézé, marquis de, 21

British radicalism, 23
Brocklesby, Dr Richard, 45
Broglie, Charles de, 112
Broval, Chevalier de, 83
Brunel, Isambard Kingdom, 163–5
Brunel, Marc, 164–5
Buckingham, Marchioness, 94, 104, 158
Buckingham, Marquess, 45, 68, 158
Burke, Edmund, 3, 23–4, 107–9, 158
Burney, Fanny, 8, 9, 52, 54, 85, 121, 134–6, 151, 163
Butler, Charles, 44, 45, 95

Calonne, Charles-Alexandre de, 73, 116–17
Cambis, Louisa Frances Gabriel d'Alsace
Chimay, vicomtesse de, 18, 19, 24, 75
Carr, John, 168–9
Carron, Guy Toussaint Julien, abbé, 28, 98–9, 105, 112–15, 167–8
Castries, maréchal de, 164
Catholicism in Britain, 35, 42
Chateaubriand, 7, 54, 55, 56, 77, 133, 147–50, 175
Churchill, Winston, 182
Cléry, Jean-Baptiste, 144–5
Coleridge, Samuel Taylor, 23
Combe, Alderman, 45
Committee, English, 45
Committee, French, 60
Committee, Lay, 45
Committee, Mansion House, 44
Committee, Wilmot, 44–7
    membership, 45–8, 57–8, 69, 93, 97
Committee, Ladies', 81, 95
Conan Doyle, Arthur, 151
Condé, prince de, 178
Constitution of Year III, xviii–xx
Cooke, Dr, 45
Courrier de Londres, 37, 41, 72
Coutances, Bishop of, 88
Coutts Bank, 19
Crewe, Mrs Francis, 81

256

Index

Danloux, Henry Pierre, 52
Danloux, Mme, 64
De Boffe (bookshop), 54
Deffand, Mme du, 19
Devonshire, Duke and Duchess of, 77
Delille, Jacques, 13, 77, 99, 145–7
Desorgues, Théodore, 145
Dickens, Charles, 151
Doublet, abbé, 112
Douglass, John, Vicar Apostolic of the London District, 42–3, 56, 95, 114
Duclos, abbé, 112
Dulau (bookshop), 45
Duport, Adrien, 26
Dundas, Henry, 38, 48
Duras, duchesse de, 23, 64
Dutreuil, Jean-Léonard, 166

Ely, Bishop of, 93
Emigration
  historiography, 10
  demography, 39–44
  legislation, (French), 11, 20, 25, 27
Erard, Sebastian, 73
Esterhazy, comte d', 21

Falaiseau, Adèle de Kerjean, marquise de, 14
Flahaut, comtesse de, 55, 56, 103, 136, 140–3
Flahaut or Flahault [de la Billarderie], Charles, 166
Fitzjames, duc de, 31
Fitzwilliam, Earl, 45
Forster, Edward, 45
Fox, Charles James, 36
French Catholic Chapels:
  Chapel of the Annunciation, 65, 68, 175
  Chapel of La Sainte Croix, 56
  Chapel of Notre Dame, Saint George's in the Fields, 89
  Saint Mary's, Chelsea, 79
  Saint Mary's, Church Row, Holly Place, 81
French newspapers:
  l'Ambigu, 124, 127, 145
  Courrier d'Angleterre, 124
  Courrier de Londres (see *Courrier*), 124

Le journal de France et Angleterre, 124
Mercure Britannique, 124
Fructidor, coup d'état, 126, 129

Gaulle, Général de, 182
Glyn, Sir Richard Carr, 45
Gontaut, duchesse de, 3–4, 8, 63, 68, 70, 88
Gordon Riots, 155
Goudemetz, abbé, 51
Greer, Donald, 175
Grenville, !st baron, William Wyndham, 37, 65, 128, 165
Guéry, Mme de, 74

Harcourt, duc d', 98
Hawkins Browne, Isaac, 45
Henin, princesse d', 53, 76
Hogarth, William, 52
Holyrood Palace, 53
Hopkins, Lord Mayor, 45
Huguenots, 51, 66

Indemnity Bill, 153

Jaucourt, comte de, 133
Jemappes, 63
Jenkinson, Robert Banks, 45
Jersey (émigrés), 96–7, 98
Joucelles, baronne de, 56
Juniper Hall, 12, 77, 133–5, 144

Kelly, Michael, 71
King, Dr Lawrence, 109
King's House Winchester, 56, 158
Kingdom, Sophia, 163

La Châtre, Mme de, 12, 133
La Marche, Jean-François de, Bishop of Saint Pol de Léon, 27–8, 33–5, 60–1, 88, 97, 108–9
La Nougarède, Marie-Gabriel-Noël Raymond de, 166
La Riandrie, marquis de, 166
La Tour du Pin, Mme de, 9, 14, 62, 63, 85
La Suze, Mme de, 53
Lafayette, Général, 122
Lally Tolendal, 75, 119–21, 125, 131, 148
Lamartine, Alphonse de, 128

Index

Lameth, brothers, Charles and Alexander, 26
Laurance, Dr French, 45
Legislation, Catholic, Britain, 155–6
see Emigration
Lille, comtesse de, (wife of Louis XVIII), 67
Liscoët, marquis de, 109
London Corresponding Society, 36
Lonjac, Brillaud de, 72
Loughborough, Lord, 33
Louis XVIII, 43, 114–15, 117–18, 122, 129, 176, 178
Louis Philippe, 83, 122
see also duc d'Orléans
Luxembourg, duc de, 18

MacGeoghegan, Mary Ann, 166
Macnamara, marquise de, 104
Mallet du Pan, 64, 73, 77, 119, 124
Malouet, Pierre Victor, 26
Maraine, abbé, 109–11
Marat, Jean Paul, 49
Masson, Soeur, 57–8
Maury abbé, 124
Ménerville, Mme de, 68, 70, 92, 101
Mercer, Margaret, 166
Mérelle Mlle, 72
Metcalfe, Philip, 45
Michelet, 128
Middlesex Hospital, 57–8
Mirabeau, Honoré-Gabriel Riquetti, comte de, 20
Mitford, Mary Russel, 14, 75, 166
Montboissier, comte de, 88
Montesquieu, Charles de, 166
Montmorency, Mathieu de, 133
Montlosier, François-Dominique de Reynaud, chevalier de, 6, 73, 119, 125, 131, 148
Montpensier, duc de, 83
More, Hannah, 14, 33
Morel, abbé, 81, 165
Mounier, Jean Joseph, 119
Moustiers, comte de, 106

Narbonne, Louis de, 133, 135
Nédonchel, Mlle de, 53
Nef, John, 100

Noailles, Mme de, 31
Norbury Park, 139
Noyon, Bishop of, 88

O'Leary, Arthur, 56
Orléans, duc de
see Louis Philippe

Paine, Tom, *Rights of Man*, 36
Peltier, Jean-Gabriel, 7, 26, 119, 148
Penn School, 108–11
Pepperell, Sir William, 45
Philips, Mrs Susanna, 134
Phipps, Dr, 58
Pitt, William Moreton, 45
Pitt, William the Younger, 48
Polastron, Louise de, 58, 88
Polignac, Marquis de, 53
Portland, Duke of, 45, 109
Prince of Wales, Frederick, 31
Provence, comte de
see Louis XVIII
Pugin, Augustus, 163–4
Pugin, Augustus Northmore Welby, 163–4

Queen Charlotte, 54
Quiberon, 90–3, 94–5, 108

Radnor, Earl of, 45
Ranalagh, 13
Reform Bill, 22
Relief:
amounts, 46
British donors, 159–61
monies requested, 60–1
origins, 32, 43
records, 10
totals, 47–8
Rémusat, Charles de, 155
Reynolds, Sir Joshua, 52
Rivarol, Antoine de, 53
Rugby (school), 103

Saint Quentin, Dominique de, 106, 166
Saulx-Tavannes, duchesse de, 80
Sanderson, Sir James, 45
Saumerez, Dr, 58
Scott, Sir William, 45

Selwyn, George, 19, 20, 21
Senac de Meilhan, 101, 144
September Massacres, 29
Sheffield, Lord, 30, 33, 45
Sheffield, Lady Abigail, 157
Silburn, Dorothy, 28, 57, 58
Skinner, Alderman, 45
Smith, Culling, 45
Southey, Robert, 183
Souza Botelho, José Maria Marquis de, 141
Staël, Mme de, 6, 53, 119, 133–40
Staël, Auguste de, 2

Talleyrand-Périgord, Charles-Maurice de, 31
Tardy, abbé, 4, 13, 49
Teachers (*émigrés*) at the Somerstown school, 113
Thiers, Adolphe, 128
Thomas, Sir George, MP for Arundel, 45
Thorton, Henry, 45
Tourzel, Louis, 67
Trayecourt, marquise de, 56
Tréguier, Bishop of, 88
Tuvache, abbé, 112

Vallon, Annette, 170
Valmy, 63
Varennes, 21–2
Vauxhall, 13, 14
Vendémiaire 13
Vigée Le Brun, Elizabeth, 10
Villedeuil, Laurent de, 18

Walford, Sir Henry, 58
Walpole, Horace, 21, 75, 76
Walsh de Serant, vicomte, 87, 103
Watson, Brook, 45
Wedgwood, Josiah, 33
Welby, Catherine, 163
Wilberforce, William, 45
Willes, Dr, 45
Williams, Helen Maria, 15
Wilmot, John, 33, 167
Wilmot Committee
  see Committee
Wordsworth, William, 170
Wyndham, William
  see Grenville

Young, Arthur, 8, 131
York, duchess of, 93–4

DATE DUE

SSCCA 942
.0044
1
C295

CARPENTER, KRISTY
  REFUGEES OF THE
FRENCH REVOLUTION :
EMIGRES IN LONDON

SSCCA 942
.0044
1
C295

HOUSTON PUBLIC LIBRARY
CENTRAL LIBRARY

2/12